The Old Testament Story

The Old Testament of the Bible was written over many centuries. It contains fascinating characters—from royal statesmen to nomadic prophets, poetry, epic stories, philosophy . . . It has great depth and richness; it tells of the ways of God with mankind.

The sheer variety of the Old Testament can make it bewildering for the new reader. This book is designed to act as a guide. It will help to make sense of the many different writings, to set them against their background, to show how they came to be written, in order to bring out their meaning.

John Drane has already covered the whole of the New Testament in three books: *Jesus and the Four Gospels, Paul,* and *The Life of the Early Church.* The books have been well received and published in several editions. *The Times Educational Supplement* called *Paul* 'an extremely valuable illustrated documentary,' and *Catholic Herald* described *The Life of the Early Church* as 'scholarly and open, lively and clear, lavishly and imaginatively illustrated.'

This book is to be accompanied by a companion volume, *The Old Testament Faith,* in which the author examines in more detail the religion of the Old Testament, its faith, its worship and moral teaching.

These 'illustrated documentaries,' while fully aware of modern scholarship, are not over-technical. Points of detail are covered in separate 'information boxes'. Maps, time-charts and diagrams show the historical and geographical background. With the many photographs, the presentation is equally suitable for individual use and for schools and colleges.

John Drane is a Lecturer in Religious Studies at Stirling University.

For Mark

THE OLD TESTAMENT STORY

John W. Drane

A LION BOOK

Copyright © 1983 Lion Publishing

Published by
Lion Publishing plc
Icknield Way, Tring, Herts, England
ISBN 0 85648 431 8
Albatross Books
PO Box 320, Sutherland, NSW 2232,
Australia
ISBN 0 86760 315 1

First edition 1983
All rights reserved

Typesetting by
First Page Ltd, Watford, England

Printed in Italy by
International Publishing Enterprises,
Rome

Design and graphics by Tony Cantale

Contents

Continued over

Chapter 5. The two kingdoms

Chapter 6. Judah and Jerusalem

Chapter 7. Dashed hopes and new horizons

Chapter 8. The challenge of a new age

Sources of quotations

Chapter Two

John Bright, *A History of Israel*, pp. 91 & 94.

John Van Seters, *Abraham in History and Tradition*, p. 309.

Chapter Five

Albrech Alt, *Essays on Old Testament History and Religion*, Blackwell, 1966/ Doubleday, 1967, p. 246.

Chapter Seven

G.W. Anderson, *A Critical Introduction to the Old Testament*, Duckworth, 1959, p. 118.

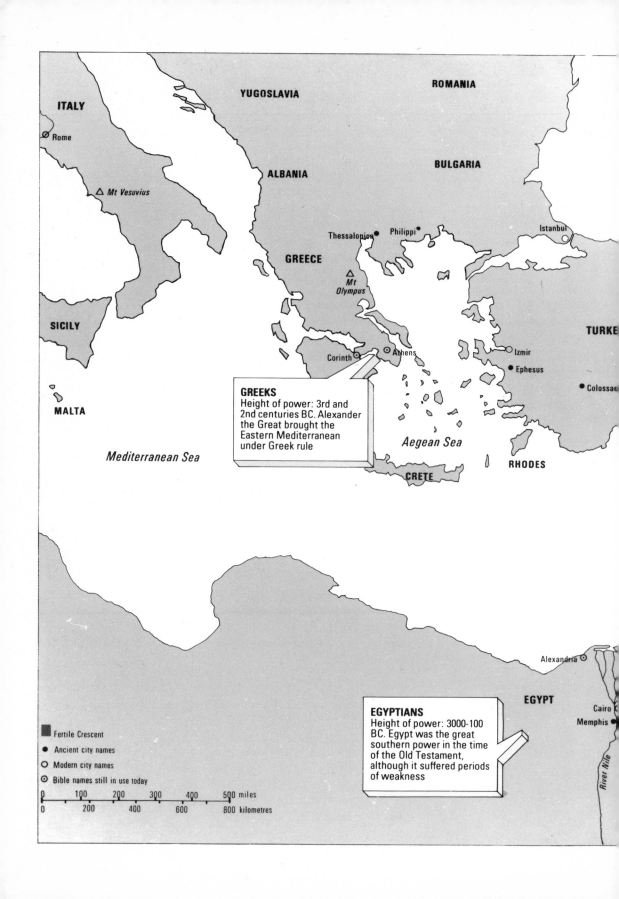

ITALY

Ø Rome

△ Mt Vesuvius

YUGOSLAVIA

ROMANIA

ALBANIA

BULGARIA

Istanbul

Thessalonica ● ● Philippi ●

GREECE

△
Mt
Olympus

TURKEY

SICILY

Corinth ⊙ ⊙ Athens

Izmir ○
● Ephesus

● Colossae

MALTA

Aegean Sea

Mediterranean Sea

GREEKS
Height of power: 3rd and
2nd centuries BC. Alexander
the Great brought the
Eastern Mediterranean
under Greek rule

RHODES

CRETE

Fertile Crescent

● Ancient city names

○ Modern city names

⊙ Bible names still in use today

Alexandria ⊙

EGYPT

Cairo ⊙

Memphis ●

EGYPTIANS
Height of power: 3000-100
BC. Egypt was the great
southern power in the time
of the Old Testament,
although it suffered periods
of weakness

River Nile

0	100	200	300	400	500 miles
0	200	400	600	800 kilometres	

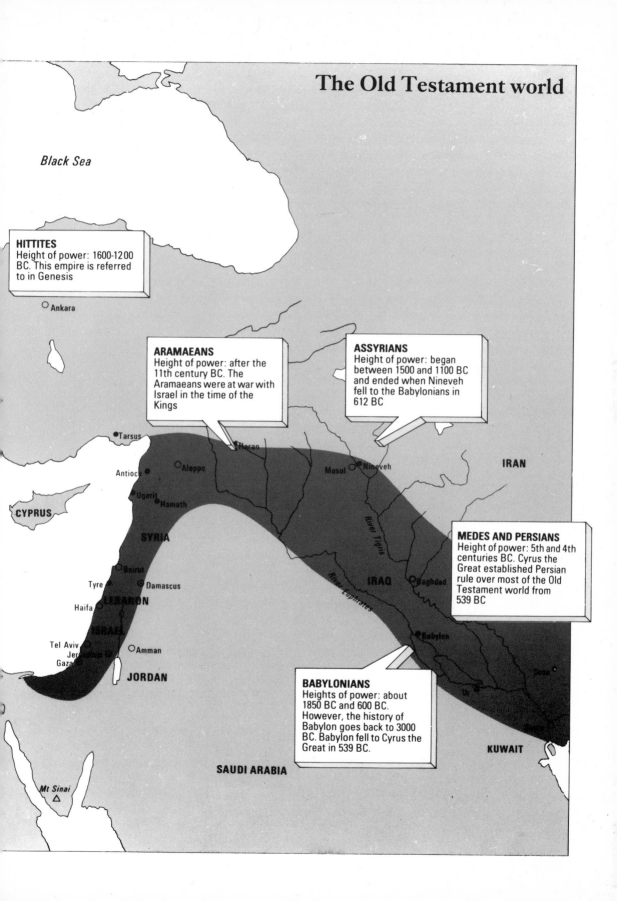

The Old Testament world

Black Sea

HITTITES
Height of power: 1600-1200 BC. This empire is referred to in Genesis

○ Ankara

ARAMAEANS
Height of power: after the 11th century BC. The Aramaeans were at war with Israel in the time of the Kings

ASSYRIANS
Height of power: began between 1500 and 1100 BC and ended when Nineveh fell to the Babylonians in 612 BC

MEDES AND PERSIANS
Height of power: 5th and 4th centuries BC. Cyrus the Great established Persian rule over most of the Old Testament world from 539 BC

BABYLONIANS
Heights of power: about 1850 BC and 600 BC. However, the history of Babylon goes back to 3000 BC. Babylon fell to Cyrus the Great in 539 BC.

● Tarsus

● Haran

○ Aleppo

Antioch ●

● Ugarit
● Hamath

Mosul ● ○ Nineveh

IRAN

CYPRUS

SYRIA

River Tigris

● Beirut

Tyre ● ● Damascus

Haifa ● LEBANON

IRAQ ○ Baghdad

River Euphrates

Tel Aviv ●
Jerusalem ● ○ Amman
Gaza ●

● Babylon

ISRAEL

JORDAN

Ur

KUWAIT

SAUDI ARABIA

Mt Sinai
△

1 Introducing the Old Testament

THE OLD Testament is one of the great classics of world literature. There can be few other books that are so old and yet still read by so many people. Though its stories happened long ago and in unfamiliar places, we are still fascinated by them today. For in its pages we have the rich literary treasures of a whole nation: the ancient people of Israel. Its story begins in the Stone Age and ends in the world of the first Christians. The most recent parts are over 2,000 years old, while the origins of its earliest works are lost forever in the mists of antiquity. But its unique combination of epic stories, history, reflective philosophy, poetry, and political commentary is held together with all the elements of adventure, excitement and suspense that we might expect from a modern thriller. The Old Testament has survived the ravages of time to become in our day the raw material for Hollywood movies on the grand scale, as well as a book to which many people still turn for personal inspiration.

Over and above all this, it has one great theme. For its writers were convinced that both their books and their nation came into being not just through social, economic, or political pressures, but because of God and his activity. Beyond all the interest of its individual stories, the Old Testament is a deeply religious book. It asserts that this world and all its affairs are not just a haphazard sequence of coincidences: they are in the control of a supreme God. Not a God who is a remote, unknowable divine force, but one with whom men and women can – and do – have personal dealings. This message is set out in the first few pages of the book of Genesis, and it is explained and emphasized many times in what follows.

The story

Genesis 1:1—2:4
Isaiah 44:1—50:11

Genesis 11:31—12:5
Deuteronomy 6:3

Genesis 21—27
Genesis 25—35
Genesis 37—50

The framework of the Old Testament as we know it today makes it clear that this God is the God of the whole world. But as the story unfolds, it also narrows down to tell us how he became a living reality in the life of a particular group of people. What God did for them was conceived on a grand, international scale. In its earliest episodes, it is a story that spans most of the ancient world, beginning with a childless couple – Abraham and Sarah – in the Mesopotamian city of Ur and leading on to a nation in a 'land flowing with milk and honey'.

In between, we have the immortal stories of Isaac, the son of Abraham and Sarah, of Jacob, and of how his family unwittingly ended up as slaves in Egypt. This was one of the great low points of Israel's early history. But under Moses, a dynamic leader trained in the court of the Egyptian kings, it was to become the central focus of Israel's national consciousness. Generations of later Old Testament writers had no doubt that even this was a part of God's plan for his people. With great insight and sensitivity the prophet Hosea pictures God as a loving father, and Israel as his child: 'When Israel was a child, I loved him and called him out of Egypt as my son . . . I was the one who taught Israel to walk. I took my

Hosea 11:1–4

people up in my arms . . . I drew them to me with affection and love. I picked them up and held them to my cheek; I bent down to them and fed them.' Almost 200 years later, and after many calamities, this conviction was still of central importance: 'When I chose Israel, I made them a promise. I revealed myself to them in Egypt and told them: I am the Lord your God. It was then that I promised to take them out of Egypt and . . . lead them to a land I had chosen for them, a rich and fertile land, the finest land of all.'

Ezekiel 20:5–6

Escape from Egypt

With their dramatic escape from slavery in Egypt – the event we call the 'exodus' – Israel's destiny began to take shape. But between the exodus and their entry to the land of Canaan, we find the story of God's Law given to Moses at Mt Sinai. As the Old Testament writers thought out the meaning of their nation's experience of God, they always gave his Law a central place. The occasion when the Law was given was a fearful and serious moment: 'the whole of Mount Sinai was covered with smoke, because the Lord had come down on it in fire. The smoke went up like the smoke of a furnace, and all the people trembled

The Old Testament is an exciting book, full of battle and adventure. But it is more than just a story-book. Through it all builds the great theme of the relationship between a people and their God.

Exodus 19:18–19

violently . . . Moses spoke, and God answered him with thunder.'

As we read the laws of the Old Testament today (contained mostly in the books of Exodus, Leviticus and Numbers), we can easily identify with the fear of ancient Israel. What we find more difficult to understand is the great joy that went with it. For when we read these laws from our own modern perspective, they may seem harsh and unreasonable. But the people of the Old Testament never thought like that. They never regarded the Law as a heavy burden, for they looked back beyond the smoke and fire of Sinai to the events that went before it – and they knew that God's law was very firmly based on his love. Their obedience was the free and loving obedience of those who are grateful for undeserved benefits. It is no coincidence that the Ten Commandments begin not with an instruction, but with a reminder of God's love and goodness: 'I am the Lord your God who brought you out of Egypt, where you were slaves . . . '

Exodus 20:2

In due course, the nomadic way of life that went right back to Abraham himself was replaced by a settled farming life in a new

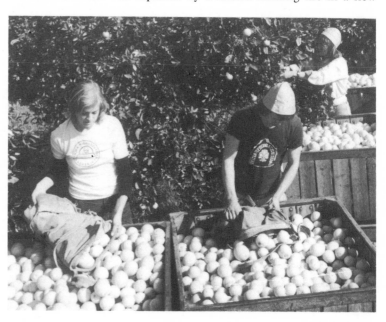

When they settled in the 'promised land', the Israelites moved from a nomadic life to a settled, agricultural existence.

land. Here, Israel began to ask new questions about their faith in God. So far, they had known the God Yahweh ('the Lord') whom Moses served as a God of the desert. But new questions began to bother them. Did he know how to grow crops? What was his experience in rearing sheep to have many lambs? These may seem rather naive questions, but for these people they were the most important questions of all. Life itself depended on the answers, and the struggle to find those answers dominates the rest of the Old Testament story in one way or another.

For when Israel settled in her new land, other gods and goddesses were already worshipped there – and they had long and apparently successful experience in agricultural matters. So there began a long battle of loyalties between Yahweh, the God of the desert, and the new gods and goddesses of the land of Canaan: Baal, Asherah, Anat, and their accomplices. Israel was tempted to forsake her own God in preference for these others. From the earliest times, there were local heroes like the so-called 'judges' who were prepared to resist such spiritual treason. But as time passed, things went from bad to worse, and the great prophets of the Old Testament protested over and over again that the people of Israel had left their own true God for the worship of false gods.

Decline of the nation

Isaiah 49:6

This figure is a Canaanite Baal, or storm god. The struggle against idolatry recurs throughout the Old Testament. Was Israel's Lord just one god among many, or was he the only God?

Isaiah 49:7; 41:4

Israel's national fortunes reached their high point in the days of David and Solomon (about 1010-930 BC). But then they began to decline. The great kingdom was partitioned. Then first the northern part collapsed, to be followed in due course by the southern part. Prophets, from the courageous Elijah to the introspective Jeremiah, spoke out in both north and south against the social and political corruption which signalled the decline of the entire nation. Though they spoke in different circumstances, to the people of their own time, they were united in their belief that the people of Israel had come to ruination because of their increasing neglect of the Law of God, and their increasing fondness for the false gods and goddesses of Palestine.

Israel's demise was complete by the year 586 BC, when the capital city of Jerusalem, together with its magnificent buildings, was captured and partly destroyed by the Babylonian king Nebuchadnezzar II. This was a disaster of immense proportions. But once more, out of the ashes of defeat there arose new life. The new leaders of Israel had an even greater vision than their predecessors. For they were convinced that even this new disaster was all a part of God's plan for his people. They set out to re-assess the lessons of the past, and they were quite sure that God would not forget his earlier promises. There would be a new creation and a new exodus on an even greater scale than before. For the whole world would now be the scene of God's renewed activity. Israel would be 'a light to the nations – so that all the world may be saved'.

With this, the story has come full circle. It began with Abraham and the promise that through him God would bless many nations – a promise that was challenged from many different directions. Politically and economically, it was always under threat – whether from the Egyptians, the Canaanites, the Assyrians, or the Babylonians. Religiously, it was undermined from within as the people of Israel were tempted to forget the God of their ancestors and turn to the worship of other, more convenient religions – religions which allowed their moral and spiritual responsibility to be left behind in the shrine instead of forming the basis of everyday life in home and market place. But God's intention for his world never failed: 'the holy God of Israel keeps his promises . . . I, the Lord, was there at the beginning, and I, the Lord, will be there at the end.'

Understanding the story

It is easy to get a general impression of the Old Testament story. But for many people, this most fascinating of books is also the most puzzling. So how can we make sense of it for ourselves? That is a big question. But for the moment, let us just make a few comments on some of the most distinctive features of the Old Testament and its contents. By doing so, we can suggest a few general principles, which we can then apply in later chapters to the understanding of specific problems.

● Most of us are familiar with the Old Testament as the first half of the Christian Bible. The fact that we call it 'the Old Testament' only serves to emphasize that. For it is 'old' not because it is ancient, but by contrast to the records of the early church which we call 'the New Testament'. Christians believe that these two quite separate writings properly belong together. They have always felt that the events surrounding the origins of the Christian faith were part and parcel of God's dealings with men and women through the ancient nation of Israel, recorded in the Old Testament. This is right: but we must never assume that the Old Testament was actually written by Christians, nor that its message is primarily a Christian message. Christians are not the only people who have a special interest in the Old Testament. These books are the sacred writings of the Jewish faith (Judaism), and if we are to make sense of them then we must read them in their own terms. Though Christians may feel that the Old Testament is incomplete without its Christian sequel, we shall never fully understand it if we look at it through exclusively Christian spectacles. This is why many people today prefer not to speak of 'the Old Testament' at all, but rather of 'the Hebrew scriptures' or 'the Hebrew Bible'.

● We must also bear in mind that the Old Testament is quite different in character from a modern book. It is even different from the books that make up the New Testament. All the New Testament books had their origin in the same social and religious context, and on the whole we can be tolerably sure of the identity of their authors, and of the reasons why they wrote. But in the case of the Old Testament, there are very few books for which we can positively identify a particular author or date. The Old Testament is essentially an edited anthology – a collection of writings by different people, and from different ages. Nobody ever sat down to gather the New Testament into one unified collection: it just arose spontaneously from the reading habits of the early church. But somebody did set out to edit and organize the books of the Old Testament, to form a coherent account of the life of the nation of Israel. In fact, more than one person did so. The earliest editions of Old Testament materials were probably gathered together during the reigns of David and Solomon. Like any other prosperous nation, Israel began at this time to take a keen interest in her past. By now she had a settled way of life in her own land – a stark contrast with the experiences of her earliest ancestors. They no doubt had their own tribal histories which they preserved and handed on by word of mouth from one generation to another. But they had not written them down. They were more concerned with the problems of daily survival than with creating literary masterpieces. That was left to scribes working in the more leisurely atmosphere of the later royal courts of Israel.

Of course, they could only bring the story up to their own time. What comes later was the work of yet further writers. Much of the Old Testament is associated with the names of the prophets, and many of its books contain their sermons and speeches dealing with various aspects of national life and policy. Parts of the Old

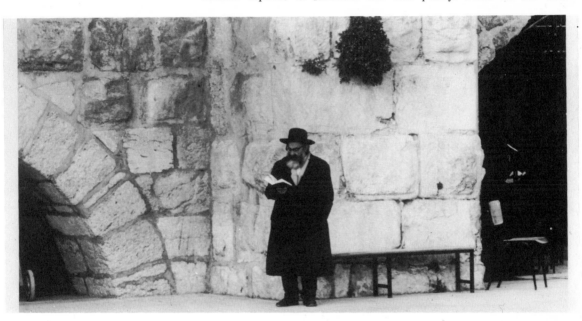

The Old Testament is the Bible of the Jew as well as the Christian. In it he sees the growth of his nation, and all the promises God made to Israel. The difference lies in the two understandings of how these promises are being fulfilled.

Testament story were doubtless written by those whose outlook was deeply influenced by these prophets. But the final stage in the Old Testament story was reached only after the destruction of the state, which the prophets had so clearly foreseen. As Israel's new leaders began to pick up the scattered pieces of a great legacy, they consciously set out to apply the lessons of the past to their own hopes for the future. And to help do that, they began to collect the whole of Israel's national literature, as well as writing their own assessment of the nation's achievements.

● A further distinguishing mark of the Old Testament is the enormous time span that it covers. Whereas the whole of the New Testament was written in the space of something like sixty or seventy years, the Old Testament story covers many centuries. Even if the story proper only begins with the exodus, that still takes us back 1,200 years before the Christian era – and the Old Testament also contains accounts of things that pre-date even that. .

The very earliest parts of the Old Testament take us to a world very different from our own – a world where civilization itself was a relatively recent arrival. Its story begins in modern Iraq, in what the ancients called 'the Fertile Crescent'. This part of the world had witnessed many remarkable developments long before the story of

Facing page: The Old Testament is a structure, put together by a people as its life developed. Our understanding of it is helped enormously if we know how it is made: what the different materials are in which it is built, and what the foundations are.

Israel's history began. Great empires had come and gone, and as early as 3000 BC the Sumerian people living in ancient Mesopotamia had written down their traditional stories and beliefs for the generations that would follow them. One of their great successors was the Babylonian king Hammurabi, whose law code written on clay tablets some 1,700 years BC still survives as a lasting monument to the culture of those ancient times. Many other texts from this ancient world have come to light in recent years – from Nuzi in Iraq, from Ebla in northern Syria, and from Ras Shamra further south. Then there are the many records and monuments of that other great and ancient civilization centred on the River Nile in Egypt.

By comparison with these empires, the people who wrote the Old Testament were latecomers. The shape of their world was already formed by other nations – and to understand their story fully we need to know something of the story of these other peoples too. For the fortunes of Israel were always inextricably bound up with the manoeuverings of the two super-powers of the day: the one based on the Nile, and the other based on the rivers Tigris and Euphrates. But then the Old Testament takes us beyond even the last of these great empires, for Israel survived longer than them all, and her national literature also documents the period that prepared for the

The nation of Israel came into being in a world where other civilizations were already old. The culture and literature of Babylon, on the River Euphrates, has some points of contact with the Old Testament.

arrival of the next great super-power of world history: the Roman Empire.

It is hardly surprising if we find the Old Testament slightly confusing at times. For its pages cover almost half the history of civilization. The circumstances of the early parts of the story are quite different from the situation we meet in the later parts – and neither bears too much resemblance to the world we know today.

● We can also appreciate something of the Old Testament's distinctive character when we look at its books purely as literature. As we have already seen, it is above all a religious book. It does not set out to give what we might regard as an impartial, independent account of the events it describes. The Old Testament story has

been written for a purpose, and its different parts were used by men and women living at different times to speak to the people of their own generation.

Some have taken this to mean that the Old Testament story is essentially fictional: a kind of moralizing tale that is valuable for whatever lessons it teaches, but which is out of touch with what actually happened. But this attitude is unrealistic. It takes no account of the fact that many events and people mentioned in the Old Testament are also mentioned in the records of other nations of the time. It is also based on a false confidence in our ability to gain access to the 'bare facts' of history. Even today, our knowledge of an event which we did not witness depends very heavily on the perspective of those who did. When we watch a news report on television, the impression we receive depends entirely on the perspective of the camera and the reporter. If the camera had taken its pictures from a different angle, or if the reporter had interviewed different people – still more if we had been there ourselves – our overall assessment of what was taking place may well have been significantly different. Even a documentary programme which tries to see all sides of an issue must eventually reflect the perspective of its writer.

We do not normally regard this as a barrier to understanding. We may wish to make a different judgement ourselves on this or that matter, but we simply take it for granted that to understand any situation fully we need to take account not only of the facts but of

The scrolls of the Law in an Israel synagogue remind us of the high place the Old Testament writings have always held in Judaism. For Jews and Christians see these books as the record of how God revealed himself to humanity.

the outlook of our sources of information. It is the same with the Old Testament. The more clearly we can understand the intentions of those who wrote and handed on these books, the more likely are we to arrive at a useful appreciation of their significance and meaning.

We must remember that these writings are not just one person's assessment of the history of a nation: they are a national archive. The people who wrote and edited these books were themselves a part of that nation and its history. It is not easy for the detached observer to grasp exactly what this means. But we can find a useful analogy in the pictures that medieval artists painted of the life and times of Jesus. The crucifixion was a favourite theme, and there are many great works showing Jesus hanging on a cross between two thieves. But when we look more closely, the people around the crosses often seem somewhat out of place. Instead of Roman soldiers, we see soldiers of the sixteenth century. The people too belong to that age – and the city where the scene takes place is not Jerusalem in AD 33, but Venice or Rome in AD 1500.

When we look at such a picture we do not usually feel that it casts doubt on the reality of the crucifixion of Jesus. Indeed, we may unconsciously follow the artist's example, and pencil in an image of ourselves and our own society. In a way, this is what the writers of the Old Testament story were doing as they depicted their national past. From generation to generation, they knew that the story of Abraham, Moses, and the rest was their own story. They were a

The Old Testament world was different from ours in many ways, and we need to be aware of the differences. But this does not prevent us from applying its teachings to the world of today. We share a common humanity with the people of whom we read.

The library of Old Testament books

The Pentateuch
Genesis
Exodus
Leviticus
Numbers
Deuteronomy

History
Joshua   Ezra
Judges   Nehemiah
Ruth   Esther
1 and 2 Samuel
1 and 2 Kings
1 and 2 Chronicles

Poetry and Wisdom
Job
Psalms
Proverbs
Ecclesiastes
Song of Solomon

The Prophets
Isaiah   Joel   Habakkuk
Jeremiah   Amos   Zephaniah
Lamentations Obadiah Haggai
Ezekiel   Jonah   Zechariah
Daniel   Micah   Malachi
Hosea   Nahum

History and Law

History

Drama, Poetry, Proverbs

Prophecy, Poetry, History

part of it, because they saw in it the continuing story of God and his dealings with their nation. As a result, they could recognize in the failures and triumphs of the past the realities and the potential of their own age.

Organizing the Old Testament

The Old Testament is a complete library of literature, containing books of many different types. If we were to take them all separately to a modern library, it is certain that they would not all be placed on the same shelf. Some books we instantly recognize as history: Genesis, Joshua, Judges, 1-2 Samuel, 1-2 Kings, 1-2 Chronicles, Ezra and Nehemiah. Others, like Exodus, Leviticus, Numbers and Deuteronomy, are law books, though not the kind a modern lawyer would use. For they contain a mixture of civil and religious laws, as well as some stories that we might more reasonably regard as history. Then there are books of poetry: religious poetry in Psalms and Lamentations, and love poetry in the Song of Solomon. Other Old Testament books contain what we might regard as philosophy. Job, Ecclesiastes and Proverbs deal with some of life's deepest questions – the existence of God or the problem of unjust suffering – as well as offering guidelines for contented living. On top of this there is a wide range of what seem like social and political pamphlets – the books of the prophets – though even these are always written from a religious standpoint. And finally there are a number of books which appeal to different readers in different ways. For some, Ruth, Esther and Jonah look like novels, presenting a distinctive message by means of a fictional story. Others would rather classify them as history – though nevertheless, history with a meaning.

But this is not how the Jews arranged these books. They looked at them in a different way. The order of the books in the Christian Old Testament comes not from the manuscripts of the Hebrew Bible, but from the Greek translation that was made in Egypt sometime before the beginning of the Christian era (the Septuagint). A Hebrew Bible is usually arranged in three separate sections:

● **The Law** This consists of the first five books, from Genesis to Deuteronomy. Genesis, of course, contains nothing at all that we would recognize as 'law'. It is a collection of stories, and at first sight we would expect it to be regarded as some sort of history. But the Old Testament notion of 'law' was much more comprehensive and far-ranging than ours. For us, 'the law' is a set of rules and regulations – a legal code that can be interpreted by lawyers with special training, and applied in a court of law by a judge. It would certainly be unusual for a modern person to agree with one of the poets of ancient Israel who wrote, 'your law is my delight'. But the Hebrew word for 'law' *(Torah)* had a much broader reference than just rules and regulations. It really meant 'guidance' or 'instruction', and in the Old Testament the Law was the place to discover what men and women should believe about God, and what duties he required of them in return. This is why the Torah is closely bound up with the stories of Israel's early history. For it is a basic assumption in the Old Testament that knowing and obeying God is not just a matter of blind obedience to a few religious and moral rules: it is rather a question of experiencing God's concern and love in a personal and social context.

Psalm 119:77

● **The Prophets** The Jews included here books that we would be more likely to call history: Joshua, Judges, 1-2 Samuel, and 1-2 Kings. These they called 'the former prophets', while the rest ('the latter prophets') consisted of those books associated with the names of Isaiah, Jeremiah and Ezekiel ('the major prophets') together with the writings of the twelve other so-called 'minor prophets', Hosea to Malachi. We might find this combination of history and sermons rather unusual. But by calling the history writers 'prophets', the Jews drew attention to the fact that these books were not just simple records of fact. They were interpretations and applications of the meaning of history. All the prophetic works – former and latter – are accounts of how God had spoken to his people Israel. Sometimes he spoke through the events of history. At other times through the words of people. But it was the same God and the same message.

● **The Writings** This is where we find the remaining books. These include the poetry of Psalms, Proverbs and Job, as well as 'the five scrolls' (the Megilloth): Ruth, Song of Solomon, Ecclesiastes, Lamentations, and Esther. These five are different from one another in a literary sense. But they were grouped together because each of them was used at one or other of the Jewish religious festivals: Ruth at Pentecost, Song of Solomon at Passover, Ecclesiastes at Tabernacles, Lamentations to celebrate the destruction of Jerusalem, and Esther at Purim. Finally, the Hebrew Old Testament is completed by the books of Daniel, Ezra, Nehemiah, and Chronicles.

The reason for this unusual arrangement of the books was historical. For the three sections roughly represent the three stages in which the Old Testament was put together. The first part of it to be permanently recorded was the Law, followed by the prophets,

There is more than just history in the books of the Old Testament. They also bear record to a people of creativity, who expressed their joy and their worship in songs and poems of great beauty.

and then much later by the Writings. This is why the books of Ezra, Nehemiah, and Chronicles were included in the final section. We would tend to think of them as history books, and list them alongside the 'former prophets'. But they were written later than that, from the perspective of the age that survived the destruction of Jerusalem in the sixth century BC. The books of Chronicles contain many of the same stories as the books of Samuel and Kings. But they are an analysis of the meaning of those stories, and an application of their lessons to the people of a later generation. By then, both the Law and the Prophets were widely accepted as sacred and important books, and it would not have been possible to make any further additions to their number.

Archaeology and the Old Testament

If we compare a book on the Old Testament written 100 years ago with one written today, the thing that is most obvious is the radical change that has taken place in our knowledge of the world of the Old Testament. Last century, study of the Old Testament was largely a literary affair: the text itself was studied in minute detail, and dissected in much the same way as an anatomist might deal with a corpse. But today, Old Testament study is vibrant and living, and is dominated by social and cultural considerations that would have been quite foreign to earlier generations of scholars. One of our major concerns is to see how the Old Testament fits into the world of its day – to analyse its contents not just ideologically, but historically and sociologically. This has all been made possible by the recent explosion of our knowledge of the ancient world. Thanks to the consistent efforts of archaeologists, we now have a better idea than ever before of what it was actually like to live in the world of the Old Testament. We can appreciate the social and political realities of life in ancient Israel in a new way that has shed untold light on many difficult passages of the Old Testament.

Explorers have always had an interest in the materials left over from earlier civilizations. In the seventeenth century many ancient objects of interest and beauty were taken by such people to their wealthy patrons all over Europe. But it was not until the eighteenth century that anyone took a scientific interest in the subject. The archaeological exploration of Bible lands began when Napoleon's armies invaded Egypt in 1798, taking with them a team of scholars to study the ancient monuments. They made many significant discoveries – not least the Rosetta Stone. This had an inscription in both Greek and Egyptian hieroglyphs, and it enabled scholars to decipher ancient Egyptian for the first time. But it was only at the end of the nineteenth century that truly scientific procedures began to be applied to sites in the Middle East on a widespread scale.

A typical site in Palestine will take the form of a large mound, or *tell*. Many of these sites look just like large hills. perhaps as high as thirty or forty metres, and covered with trees or grass. But under the surface is to be found the ruin of an ancient city. Sometimes cities were built on a natural hill, for that was an easy site to defend. But many of these tells began at ground level, and have been raised to their present height by the normal processes of building over many years. For in the ancient world most buildings were made of mud and wood. When a settlement was either destroyed by an enemy, or just fell into decay, the inhabitants would gather together any available materials that could be re-used, and set to work to build their own town on the ruins of the old. The new level could be as much as two or three metres higher than the one that preceded it. So over many years, the ground level was gradually raised, and the whole mound took on the appearance of a giant cake with many different layers superimposed one on top of the other.

Archaeologists have used a number of basic rules to guide their investigations at sites like this:

● Digging must be done in such a way as to keep separate and distinct the successive strata, or layers, of occupation. The ideal way to do this, of course, would be to start at the top and slice off each layer in turn. But this

The Rosetta Stone, found by scholars who accompanied Napoleon's army when he occupied Egypt, is in Greek, in demotic and in ancient Egyptian hieroglyphics. It provided the first clues for understanding ancient Egyptian; the first hieroglyphs were deciphered through distinguishing the name 'Ptolemy' in all three scripts.

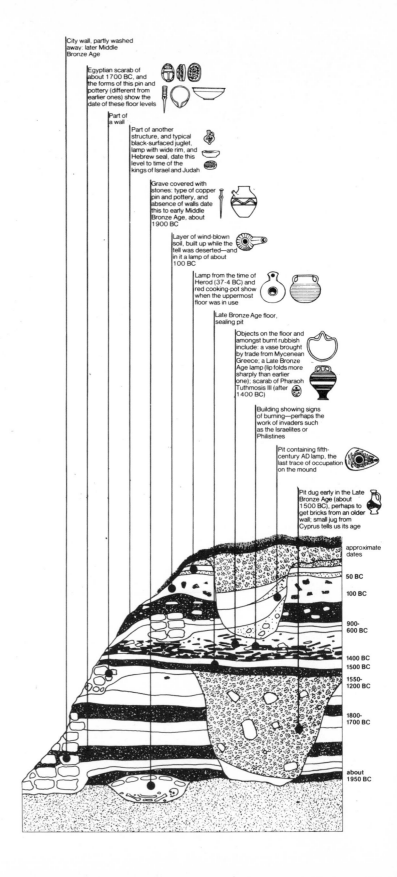

City wall, partly washed away: later Middle Bronze Age

Egyptian scarab of about 1700 BC, and the forms of this pin and pottery (different from earlier ones) show the date of these floor levels

Part of a wall

Part of another structure, and typical black-surfaced juglet, lamp with wide rim, and Hebrew seal, date this level to time of the kings of Israel and Judah

Grave covered with stones: type of copper pin and pottery, and absence of walls date this to early Middle Bronze Age, about 1900 BC

Layer of wind-blown soil, built up while the tell was deserted—and in it a lamp of about 100 BC

Lamp from the time of Herod (37-4 BC) and red cooking-pot show when the uppermost floor was in use

Late Bronze Age floor, sealing pit

Objects on the floor and amongst burnt rubbish include: a vase brought by trade from Mycenean Greece; a Late Bronze Age lamp (lip folds more sharply than earlier one); scarab of Pharaoh Tuthmosis III (after 1400 BC)

Building showing signs of burning—perhaps the work of invaders such as the Israelites or Philistines

Pit containing fifth-century AD lamp, the last trace of occupation on the mound

Pit dug early in the Late Bronze Age (about 1500 BC), perhaps to get bricks from an older wall; small jug from Cyprus tells us its age

approximate dates

50 BC

100 BC

900-600 BC

1400 BC
1500 BC

1550-1200 BC

1800-1700 BC

about 1950 BC

Excavation of a tell

The mound seen here is a 'tell' – the site of ancient Lachish. As archaeologists excavate a section of the tell, they find evidence of the different stages of the town's history.

Great care is required as an archaeological dig progresses. Each fragment of pottery or other artefact has to be catalogued and the level at which it is found must be carefully noted.

would be impractical. It would be too time-consuming, and impossibly expensive. Instead, the archaeologist usually cuts into the mound as we would cut a slice from a cake. This gives access to a cross-section of the mound's contents, and the whole process is called 'stratigraphic excavation'. Its one disadvantage is that the archaeologist may cut his slice at the wrong place in the mound. For instance, the site of the city of Hazor in northern Israel was excavated in 1928 by the famous archaeologist John Garstang. He

concluded that the city was deserted between 1400 and 1200 BC. But thirty years later, the Israeli archaeologist Yigael Yadin dug a trench at a different point on the same mound, and found extensive evidence of people living there at just that period!

● It is vital to have an accurate recording of every level that is excavated, and of every object that is found. Plans must be drawn and photographs taken, because once a layer of the mound is removed, no one can put it back together again. If objects are taken away indiscriminately it is impossible to assess their significance. They must be studied in relation to the precise spot where they are uncovered, and in relation to other things that are found with them.

● Archaeologists must also compare what they find with what others have found in other places. Pottery provides a good example of the importance of this. For every bucketful of significant objects, dozens of bucketsful of pottery are discovered. This is because pottery was always in common use, and it was very easily broken – but it was virtually impossible to destroy completely. Fashions in pottery changed in the ancient world. The size, shape, texture, and decoration varied from time to time, and though some styles were in use for a

A pottery jar, found at the Qumran monastery by the Dead Sea, shows how the pieces were reassembled after excavation.

long time, others were limited to a specific period. So when the archaeologist finds the same types at several different situations he may reasonably conclude that the layers in which they are found were occupied at about the same time. In fact, pottery is one of the most important clues to the dating of a particular find. It was Sir Flinders Petrie who, at the beginning of the twentieth century, first realized this. By comparing pottery from different sites, and noting its various styles, he evolved what he called a 'Ceramic Index' – a collection of pottery types which could be accurately dated, and which proved an invaluable aid to the work of all subsequent excavators.

But what use is all this to students of the Old Testament?

● It is not very often that archaeologists discover things that have a direct reference to events and people mentioned in the Bible – though there are many examples of this, especially in the records of the Assyrian and Babylonian kings, where we find accounts of many of the events recorded in the Old Testament.

● More often, archaeology helps us to set the Old Testament story in its true context. It is, for example, highly unlikely that any archaeologist will ever find a reference to the story of Abraham. But archaeology has shown that migrations like that of Abraham were taking place all over the Fertile Crescent during the second millenium BC, and that some of the customs mentioned in Genesis were practised at the time.

● Sometimes, the findings of archaeologists can illuminate specific passages in the Old Testament. In I Samuel 4, we have the story of how the Philistines captured the ark of the Covenant from Israel in a fierce battle near the town of Shiloh, where the ark was kept. Readers of the Bible had often surmised that Shiloh itself must have been destroyed at the same time, for when Israel recovered the ark it was not returned there. Now, excavation has shown that Shiloh was indeed destroyed at the time of this incident in the eleventh century BC.

● Archaeology is also often a help in interpreting difficult parts of the Old Testament. For example, Ezekiel mentions three people as examples of great goodness: Daniel, Noah, and Job (Ezekiel 14:14). But it is curious that the prophet should place Daniel, believed to be one of his own contemporaries, in the same class as two ancient figures. Archaeology has shown that he was probably not talking of the hero of the Old Testament book of Daniel at all, but of an ancient king renowned for his religion and justice, who is mentioned in religious poems from Assyria to Canaan, some of which are nearly 1,000 years older than Ezekiel.

● Sometimes the findings of archaeology seem as if they cannot be reconciled with what we read in the Old Testament. For example, according to Joshua 7:1 — 8:29 a great battle was fought at a place called Ai during the conquest of Canaan. But according to the archaeologists, the town was destroyed about 2400 BC. It was not rebuilt, and so there was no town there in the days of Joshua. Of course, there could be many reasons for this apparent discrepancy. It may be that archaeologists have wrongly identified the site. It would not be the first time such a mistake had been made, but it seems unlikely in this instance. It is also possible that other discoveries could be made in the future which would resolve the problem. Or it could be, as many think, that we should look for the meaning of the Old Testament story elsewhere – perhaps in the fact that the word Ai in Hebrew means just 'the ruin'. Whatever the full explanation may be, we must take seriously both the Old Testament picture and the evidence of archaeology.

2 The founding of the nation

Genesis 11:27—50:26
Exodus 1:1—20:21

As FAR back as we can see, the people of ancient Israel had a well developed sense of their own history. They were especially conscious of the fact that their own way of life and religion was different from that of their neighbours. The main concern of the average Canaanite farmer was with agriculture. His religious worship was designed to ensure that nothing would interrupt the cycle of the seasons from one year to another. But for Israel the key to understanding life's mysteries was not to be found in the world of nature, but in the unique and unrepeatable facts of history.

Like other farmers, the people of ancient Israel celebrated the annual gathering of the harvest in a religious ceremony. But as they

The annual harvest celebration was a time when the Israelites remembered their indebtedness to God. They gave the 'firstfruits' of the harvest as an offering to maintain the worship of the Lord.

Israel's agricultural year

did so, their thoughts centred not on ploughing, sowing, and reaping, but on the history of their nation. When they presented a part of the harvest to God, they affirmed their deepest convictions about life in words that are still recited daily by pious Jews in the twentieth century:

> 'My ancestor was a wandering Aramean . . . who took his family to Egypt to live. They were few in number when they went there, but they became a large and powerful nation. The Egyptians treated us harshly and forced us to work as slaves. Then we cried out for help to the Lord, the God of our ancestors. He heard us and saw our suffering, hardship, and misery. By his great power and strength he rescued us from Egypt. He worked miracles and wonders, and caused terrifying things to happen. He brought us here and gave us this rich and fertile land. So now I bring to the Lord the first part of the harvest that he has given me.'

Deuteronomy 26:5–10

No other statement sums up so eloquently what the Old Testament is all about. In just a few words, this ancient creed (the *Shema*) recalls the most important elements in the Old Testament story. It tells how God had rescued a disorganized group of slaves from Egypt and made them a nation in their own right; and how in response to his undeserved goodness, the people had given him their worship and obedience.

The early Old Testament stories are of people on the move, owning no land, taking with them their flocks and all they possessed.

Beginnings

Genesis 32:28

Facing page: Haran, in modern
Syria. From here Abraham, the
'wandering Aramean', moved south
into Canaan.

The 'wandering Aramean' is occasionally given the name 'Israel', but he is more often referred to in the Old Testament as Jacob. It is not clear why he should have been referred to as an Aramean. The Arameans became prominent in the Old Testament world only after about the eleventh century BC, when they established a small empire based in Syria. But like the Israelites, who also emerged as a nation at about the same time, their origins must go further back than that. Throughout the third millenium BC (3000-2000 BC) large numbers of wandering nomads were constantly moving from the deserts of Arabia into the territories controlled by the great civilization centred on Mesopotamia. The reasons for these movements are complex and uncertain. In about 2000 BC, groups of people whom the Babylonians called 'Ammuru' ('westerners'), and who are perhaps to be associated with the Amorites of the Old Testament, moved in and established their own culture in Babylon itself, at Mari, and elsewhere. Many scholars believe that some of these people were the ancestors not only of the Arameans and the Canaanites, but also of Israel herself. The Old Testament certainly suggests there was some close ethnic connection between all these groups, and its earliest stories of Jacob's ancestors are set in this kind of context.

The first patriarchs

Genesis 11:27–30

Joshua 24:2

Genesis 15:7;
Isaiah 29:22

Exodus 20:2;
Deuteronomy 5:6

Genesis 24:4

The story begins with Abraham – or, rather, with his father Terah – in the city of Ur, at the very heart of the ancient Mesopotamian civilization. For some undisclosed reason, they left their home city and the whole family moved some 560 miles/900km north-west to the city of Haran. Both these towns had important shrines for the worship of the moon god Sin, and some Old Testament scholars have supposed that this could explain their move. There is certainly plenty of evidence to suggest that Abraham and his family were originally pagans. In a later account of the same events, a much later leader of Israel began his story of Israel's history with the words, 'Long ago your ancestors lived on the other side of the River Euphrates and worshipped other gods.' Some have discerned traces of some sort of religious argument, which involved Abraham's family in physical danger. For in a rather obscure passage, Abraham is said to have been 'rescued' from Ur in just the same way as the escaping slaves were later 'rescued' (the same Hebrew word) from Egypt.

On the other hand, it is only in the Hebrew manuscripts of Genesis 11 that the city of Ur is mentioned at all. The Greek (Septuagint) version places Abraham's original home 'in the land of the Chaldeans', and this could have been a place much nearer to Haran in North Syria than to Ur near the Persian Gulf. Other stories certainly suggest that Abraham's roots were much stronger in Haran than in Ur, for when he later sent for a wife for his son Isaac, he told his servant to go to 'the country where I was born', and this turns out to be not Ur, but the area around Haran.

Despite this close connection with the town of Haran and its

The nomadic existence described in Genesis fits in well with the picture archaeologists have built up of the life of the region in the early part of the second millennium BC.

surrounding countryside, Abraham did not make his permanent home there. The book of Genesis tells how he moved on to a different part of the Fertile Crescent – this time travelling another 450 miles/700km south-west, into the land of Palestine. There he lived a wandering life, moving about from place to place to find enough grazing for his flocks and food for his family. This was the only way newcomers could settle, for the best parts of the land were already occupied by both farmers and city dwellers. This explains why Abraham moved mostly in the south of the country, just to the north and west of the Dead Sea. This was not the best land, but it had many areas suitable for grazing, and only a small resident population. When the grass was exhausted there, nomadic tribes could move either to an oasis like Beersheba or into the fields adjoining towns like Shechem and Hebron. No doubt this land was farmed by the Canaanites, but they probably allowed nomads like Abraham to put their animals onto it after the crops had been gathered. But even this source of supply was uncertain, and like many other nomadic peoples of the period, Abraham was forced to

Genesis 12:10–20 move as far afield as Egypt at a time of severe famine.

The patriarchs and history

One of the major preoccupations of Old Testament scholars for the greater part of the twentieth century has been the question of how the patriarchs Abraham, Isaac, and Jacob can be related to the history of Old Testament times. A hundred years ago, the stories were commonly regarded either as fiction, or as the vaguely remembered exploits of tribes – even at times of ancient gods or goddesses – personified to become the story of just a few individuals. On this view, the patriarchs could not be regarded as real people, but as representations of various social

and religious movements in the millennium before Israel became a nation in the true sense.

As the twentieth century has progressed, however, there has been a marked change of opinion on the subject, largely due to the discoveries of archaeologists. In particular, ancient documents found at the sites of Mari and Nuzi had a far-reaching impact on the study of these stories, and in recent times it has been taken for granted that the stories of the Hebrew patriarchs not only reflect the existence of real individuals, but that their exploits and

These Bedouin, bargaining for sheep, have plenty in common with Abraham and Lot, whose shepherds are described as quarrelling over pasture nearly 4,000 years earlier.

way of life accurately reflect the conditions of the Middle Bronze Age period (2000–1500 BC). Professor John Bright's judgement is typical: 'We can assert with full confidence that Abraham, Isaac, and Jacob were actual historical individuals . . . a part of that migration of seminomadic clans which brought a new population to Palestine in the early centuries of the second millennium BC.' A number of pieces of evidence seem to support this claim:

● **The patriarchal names**
Names like Abraham, Isaac, and Jacob have been found in many ancient documents. They seem to have been especially popular among the Amorite peoples living in various parts of northern Mesopotamia about 2000 BC. Other names familiar from Genesis – Terah, Nahor, Serug, Benjamin, Levi, Ishmael – were also widely used, though not always relating to people.

Sometimes they appear as the names of places. Of course none of the occurrences of these names outside the Bible actually refers to the people mentioned in the Old Testament. But they do show that names of this type were commonly used during the second millennium BC.

● **The patriarchal life-style**
The Tale of Sinuhe shows a nomad chief living in much the same way as Abraham in about 1900 BC. Like Abraham, this chieftain also took part in a war with some kings (Genesis 14). But it is impossible to identify the kings mentioned in the Old Testament with any known rulers, though their names are typical of the time. There is, however, plenty of evidence to show that the general wandering existence portrayed in Genesis reflects many aspects of what is known of life in the early part of the second millenium BC. Evidence from both Mari and Egypt shows that many tribes were moving about freely at this time, and the excavation of Canaanite cities has suggested that the details of the patriarchs' journeyings could be authentic. They roam about in the places which would have been available to them at this period – and these were generally not the places where nomads could have found a temporary home in later times.

● **The patriarchal customs**
The social and legal customs of the patriarchs are often different from those of later Israel. For example, in Leviticus 18:18 a man is forbidden to be married to two sisters at once – but Jacob was (Genesis 29:15–30). Abraham himself married his half-sister Sarah (Genesis

20:12), though this was also prohibited later (Leviticus 18:9, 11; 20:17; Deuteronomy 27:22). The fact that these anomalies have been preserved in the stories of the patriarchs suggests that the people who wrote them down did not try to assimilate them to the practices of their own day, but handed on authentic traditions as they had received them.

This impression may be confirmed by certain legal documents discoverd at Nuzi. For some of the customs described here seem to explain and illuminate otherwise obscure parts of the Old Testament stories. For instance, there is the story of how Abraham's childless wife Sarah presented him with a slave girl by whom to have a child (Genesis 16:1–14). A text from Nuzi explains how in certain marriage contracts a childless wife could be required to provide her husband with just such a substitute. Furthermore, if a child was subsequently born to the slave, Nuzi law forbade the expulsion of the slave wife – and perhaps this could explain why Abraham was so reluctant to send away Hagar and Ishmael (Genesis 21:9–13). Another way in which childless couples at Nuzi could ensure the continuation of their family line was by adopting a slave who would take the place of a son. He would then inherit their property – though if a natural son was eventually born, the slave-son would lose his rights. When Abraham expressed a fear that his slave Eliezer could succeed him (Genesis 15:1–4), some such custom could have been in his mind. Other customs associated with the stories of Jacob have also been documented at Nuzi.

Until recently, these have been considered compelling arguments for placing the stories of the patriarchs in the early part of the second millenium BC. There have always been elements of the stories that are difficult to fit into such a context – things like the mention of Philistines (Genesis 21:34; 26:6–22), Chaldeans (Genesis 11:31; 15:7), and camels (Genesis 12:16; 24:35; 30:43; 32:7,15), which were apparently not in widespread use before the twelfth century BC. Scholars like Bright have explained these references as incidental anachronisms introduced unconsciously when the stories were first written down. But this view is now being challenged. It is argued by some that the alleged anachronisms are more basic to the stories than was once thought, and also that the relevance of the 'parallels' from Mari and Nuzi has

been greatly exaggerated. Writing of the story of Abraham, John Van Seters says: 'one cannot use any part of it in an attempt to reconstruct the primitive period of Israelite history'. Instead, he traces the origin of these stories to the time when they were written down, and concludes that they must be essentially a work of fiction. There is much of importance in what he claims, but these two issues are not of equal weight.

The nature of tradition

If a story about events taking place sometime between 2000 and 1200 BC was written down between 1000 and 900 BC, that does not necessarily mean that it is going to be worthless as history. This is especially the case with stories that have been handed on by word of mouth for many generations before being committed to writing. There are many examples of this in more recent times. For instance, when the American Alex Haley set out to trace his ancestors who had been seized from Africa by slave traders, his only sources of information were oral family history. But in the course of his search, not only did he find that this was confirmed again and again by written records: he also discovered that at the appropriate points the oral history of his family in America – and even written documents, where they existed – corresponded in a remarkable way with tribal histories going back for many generations in Africa itself. The existence of so-called anachronisms in the Old Testament does not undermine this general consideration. We have already compared the early Old Testament histories to classical medieval paintings which depict contemporary Europeans in scenes from the Bible, and the fact that a story has been recorded for the benefit of a later age does not make it historically worthless.

The use of parallels

The strongest positive support for the essentially historical character of these stories has been the evidence of Nuzi and Mari. This too has been challenged at a number of points:

● It is rightly pointed out that for such parallels to mean anything, they must come from a time and place with which the Hebrew patriarchs could reasonably be associated. The place is no problem: both Mari and Nuzi are located in areas that play an important part in the Genesis stories. But the date is another question. For it has usually been claimed that these parallels date the patriarchs somewhere between 2000 and 1800 BC. But the Nuzi texts only go back to about 1500–1400 BC. Against this, it has been argued that customs of the sort described do not come from nowhere, and they must have existed long before they were written down. That is probably true, but it does not really take us very far. For they were also in existence long after they were written down, and most of the practices to which attention has been drawn were probably carried on throughout the whole period from 2000 to 1200 BC.

● Then there is the fact that the Nuzi materials have often been used very selectively. For example, the childless wife who gave her husband a slave girl was not typical of Nuzi practice in general. The more normal rule would have been to allow the man to find another wife. Some of the other parallels cited by Bright are not entirely representative: indeed, out of more than 300 Nuzi texts dealing with family affairs, less than a half dozen are regularly used to reconstruct a background for the Genesis stories!

● Some Nuzi texts have actually been misinterpreted in the enthusiastic rush to find parallels to the Old Testament. It was at one time claimed that a Nuzi text could explain Rachel's theft of Laban's household gods (Genesis 31:17–21). It

was supposed that the possession of them would give her certain rights of inheritance. But it is now clear that the Nuzi 'parallel' does not suggest this at all. Of course, one mistaken parallel does not discount the others, but it does remind us of the difficulties involved in making such comparisons accurately. Part of the difficulty is that the Nuzi texts are legal documents, whereas in Genesis social and legal practices are described only incidentally. In such circumstances, it is all too easy to try to fill in what we perceive as gaps by stretching the external evidence to fit – even when it could be quite irrelevant.

It is clear from all this that some scholars have in the past tried to claim too much, in particular on the question of precise dates for the patriarchs. But it is equally clear that the way of life depicted in these stories in Genesis is quite different from the practices of later Israel, and has some significant similarities to what we know of life in the second millenium BC. Any understanding of the historical setting of Abraham, Isaac and Jacob must account for these features, and for that reason many continue to believe that they preserve for us a broadly accurate account of the activities of those characters whom they describe.

Abraham's journeys

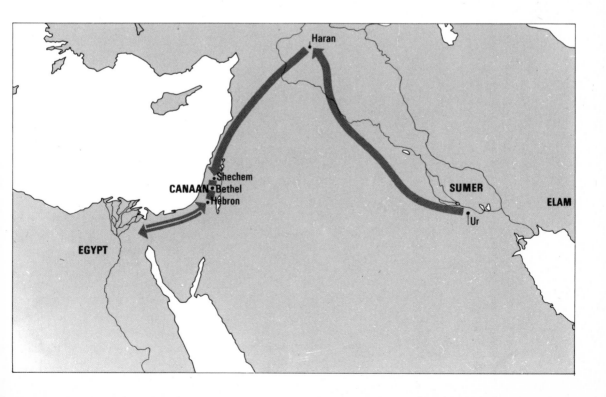

Perhaps the most we can certainly say about the stories of Abraham is that his journeys correspond to population movements that were taking place in the Fertile Crescent throughout the Middle and Late Bronze Ages (roughly 2000–1200 BC). Desert tribes were constantly moving into the Fertile Crescent from outside, and within this green belt individual tribes were always moving from one place to another in search of food and water for themselves and their flocks.

The patriarchs and their God

Genesis 12:1–2

Genesis 26:24; 31:5,29,42,53; 32:9; 46:1,3; 48:15; 49:25; 50:17

To us, it seems natural to want to relate Abraham to the social world of his day. But the central interest in the book of Genesis is not in the movements of nomads and refugees in the ancient world: it is in Abraham's experience of God. His move from Haran was not determined by political and social issues; it was the result of a challenge and a promise made to him by God. Nor was this an experience unique to Abraham. It was also the common experience of his successors, Isaac and Jacob – not to mention the conviction of the rest of the Old Testament, that a personal experience of God was vital for the very survival of the whole nation of Israel. One of the reasons for our difficulty in placing the patriarchs historically is just the fact that the stories told about them are of a personal nature, telling how they met God in every circumstance of life.

For them, God was not a remote, impersonal force. Nor was he someone who must be approached only through the complex paraphernalia of religious rituals carried out in especially holy places. He was with them in the problems of everyday life, helping them to find wives and to have children, as well as meeting their deepest personal and emotional needs. It is no coincidence that for these people, the most natural way to describe God was to call him 'the God of my father'. For he was as close to them as their own family. Indeed, in an important sense, he was a part of their family: he was their leader, and they were his children. Unlike those who had a more settled existence, these wandering tribes were never tempted to think of their faith in God as something that was to be locked up in a temple or some other sacred place. It was something that went with them, and affected their everyday life wherever they happened to be.

This is why many later writers came to regard Abraham as supremely 'a man of faith'. This was the great legacy of the patriarchal generation to the history of Israel. They were deeply committed to the belief that religion was of no value if it could do no more than produce a theology. It must be relevant and meaningful in the normal experiences of human life. In later ages, Israel was often tempted to forget this ideal, and to suppose that her God, like the gods of other nations, would be satisfied with the perfunctory performance of religious rituals. But there were always those who were ready to call her back to the ideals that had been held by her earliest ancestors, as they embarked on a new life and a new destiny with only God's promise to guide them.

Down into Egypt

This same theme found its greatest expression in the one event in their early history that Israel was to remember most fondly: the deliverance of a group of their ancestors from slavery in Egypt.

We have now moved beyond the story of Abraham's visit to Egypt, and into the family life of Jacob. As a result of feuding and jealousy among Jacob's family, one of his sons found himself being carted off to Egypt as a slave. But after many hardships and misadventures, the unfortunate Joseph was unexpectedly elevated to an important position in Egyptian society. In the face of a great famine, the Egyptian king appointed this foreigner to supervise the rationing of food, and especially to control its distribution to those wandering tribesmen who would inevitably make their way over the Sinai peninsula to the more prosperous land of Egypt. It was while engaged in this work that, unknown to them, Joseph's brothers (who had sold him into slavery years before) came before him to ask for food. After much suspense and heart-searching, Joseph revealed his true identity, and the brothers, along with their aged father, were reunited and went to live in Egypt.

Their new-found prosperity was, however, only temporary. Jacob, Joseph, and the rest all died in old age, but their descendants were not to have a happy life. A new Egyptian ruler came to power, and he did not like what he saw: 'These Israelites are so numerous and strong that they are a threat to us'. And so the family of Jacob was gradually reduced to slavery, poverty and despair.

It is tempting to set the story of Joseph in the times of the Hyksos Empire in Egypt. These rulers were themselves non-Egyptians, and

Genesis 37

Genesis 39—41

Genesis 42

Genesis 43—47

Exodus 1:9

Brick-making in Egypt has not changed all that much from the days of Israel's slavery. But they were reduced to making bricks without straw.

for that reason they would be more likely to appoint an outsider like Joseph to a position of some authority. Much of the detail of the Old Testament story seems to reflect what we know of the life of Egypt at this time – and the 'new king, who knew nothing about Joseph' would perhaps be an appropriate way to describe a native Egyptian king who came to power after the Hyksos had been driven out.

Exodus 1:8

The Old Testament is not concerned with such details, however. For though this period of slavery was a real evil, it was also the source of great triumph. As the oppression of the slaves grew worse, so the need for deliverance grew stronger – deliverance that was an impossible dream, but that finally became a reality through the dynamic leadership of a man called Moses. Though he had an Egyptian name, and was brought up as an Egyptian, Moses had been born into an Israelite family.

Exodus 2:1–10

No doubt he was familiar with Egyptian life and culture. Some have suggested that he was also deeply influenced by the religion of Egypt. For the Pharaoh Akhen-aten had been a fanatical worshipper of just one god – the sun god (Aten). Moses too was devoted to the service of just one God. Certainly there are resemblances between Atenism and the religion of Moses. Like the God of Moses, Aten was described as 'the god beside whom there is none other'. The worshippers of Aten also laid heavy emphasis on their god's teaching, just as Moses later emphasized the importance of the Torah. Then again, parts of an ancient hymn in praise of the wonders of creation use similar language to an Egyptian hymn to the sun which was attributed to Akhen-aten. But this use of similar language and imagery in worship is a common thing throughout the ancient world, and in any case many scholars think that the hymn of Akhen-aten was itself based on another piece of religious poetry that originated in Canaan.

Psalm 104

What Moses taught the slaves from Egypt had many distinctive features that are not found in Egyptian religion. Like the patriarchs, Moses knew a God who was not just a manifestation of the world of nature, but the God who controlled the world and who could be known in a personal way. The origin of Moses' faith was found not in Egypt, but in the deserts of the Sinai Peninsula. After dropping out of Egyptian society, Moses had come to this region where he met the leader of a nomadic tribe, a man called Jethro. He married Jethro's daughter, and looked after his sheep. And it was while doing so that he met God. Standing by a bush that was on fire yet seemed as if it would not burn away, Moses was commissioned by 'the God of Abraham, Isaac, and Jacob' to rescue the slaves from Egypt. Moses wanted to see neither the Egyptians nor the slaves. Finally, he agreed to return to Egypt to try to persuade the king to release the slaves. But he also had a message for the slaves themselves. In their affliction, they had not always remembered God. But now they would experience him for themselves in a new and dynamic way. For Moses took with him a fresh and deeper understanding of the nature of God. He was to tell the slaves in

Exodus 3:1–10

Moses married into a nomadic tribe from the Sinai peninsula. In Sinai Moses met the Lord at the 'burning bush', and there he brought the Israelites after the exodus.

Exodus 3:14   Egypt: 'The one who is called I AM has sent me to you'.

The Hebrew word for 'I am' is connected to the name which Israel came to use for God: 'Yahweh'. Hebrew has no vowels, and so this name was written down as YHWH. Vowel sounds are needed to pronounce it, of course, but we do not know precisely which sounds were used at this early period of Israel's history. When the Old Testament was written down in its present form, Jewish religious teachers regarded the personal name of God as too sacred to say. So whenever they found it they would substitute the Hebrew word *Adonai* , which means 'my lord'. In this way, the vowels of *Adonai* came to be pronounced with the consonants of God's name YHWH, and this is the source of the familiar English term 'Jehovah'.

There are many things we do not understand about the name 'Yahweh'. But its general significance is clear: it is a declaration that God is the Lord of the whole world and its history. What he had done in the past, he was doing in the present – and would continue to do in the future.

The exodus

What God did for Israel's ancestors enslaved in Egypt was never in any doubt. It is a central part of Judaism even today. At the annual Passover festival, the Jewish child asks about its meaning, and is given the answer:

'We were Pharaoh's slaves in Egypt, and the Lord our God brought us forth with a mighty hand and an outstretched arm. And if the Holy One, Blessed be He, had not brought our forefathers forth from Egypt, then we, our children, and our children's children would still be slaves in Egypt. So, even though all of us were wise, all of us full of understanding . . . we should still be under the commandment to tell the story of the departure from Egypt. And the more one tells the story of the departure from Egypt, the more praiseworthy he is.'

As far back as we can see, we find the deeply held conviction that in these events God himself had been at work on his people's behalf. They had not escaped by their own effort – nor even because they had a specially deserving cause – but simply because the God of whom Moses spoke had, for some inexplicable reason, chosen to deliver them.

The account of that momentous deliverance has all the ingredients of a great epic story. The slaves leave secretly in the middle of the night, only to be pursued by the Egyptian armies. Just as they are about to be caught, trapped by a stretch of water, a way miraculously opens before them and the slaves get to the other side,

The exodus

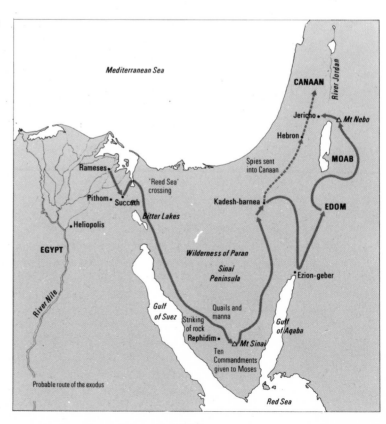

Probable route of the exodus

Exodus 12;13:17–22;14—15

Exodus 16—18

while the pursuing army perishes beneath the waves. Guided by Moses, they head out into the Sinai desert, and their first and greatest destination: Mt Sinai.

It is difficult to be clear about the actual location of these events. For example, the crossing of the water has traditionally been located at some point on the Red Sea. But the Old Testament does not make this identification. The Hebrew words speak of a 'sea of reeds', which would be an unlikely name for the Red Sea. In any case, the area of Goshen where the slaves had lived was much further north than the Red Sea, probably near the city of Avaris. It is therefore likely that the water that divided to allow them to cross was somewhere in the region of what is now the Suez Canal.

The location of Mt Sinai is also questionable. Traditionally, it has been located in the south of the Sinai Peninsula, at the site now called Jebel Musa. But since Moses' father-in-law Jethro, who was

Exodus 3:1;18:1–12

a Midianite, is clearly associated with this mountain, some have suggested that it should be located much further east, across the Gulf of Aqaba, which was the land of the Midianites. Others have suggested that Sinai should be located at Jebel Hilal, just to the south of Palestine itself, since the escaping slaves had an encounter

Exodus 17:8–16

with Amalekites, and they lived much further north than the traditional site. But it is difficult to locate the mountain by this means. For both these other tribes were nomads themselves, and could have been found almost anywhere. It is certainly not unlikely that a group such as the Old Testament describes would have headed south on their escape from Egypt, rather than going directly east. For the main roads between Egypt and Canaan were patrolled by many Egyptian garrisons, whereas the only activity in the south centred around a number of isolated copper mines.

There need be no reasonable doubt about the facts of the story. The conviction that in this event Israel had her true beginning is deeply embedded in the very oldest parts of the Old Testament – and it is hardly the sort of story that a proud nation would invent to explain their origin, if it had no basis in fact. Like most other nations, Israel later assimilated and accepted people from other racial and cultural backgrounds. But it was to this event, and this group of her ancestors, that Israel traced her unique relationship with God.

The covenant

The exodus was just the beginning of the story. For it was not until the escaping slaves reached Mt Sinai that the full impact and meaning of all this became clear to them. Just as the escape from Egypt formed the core of later Israel's national consciousness, so the events at Mt Sinai became the crucial factor in her religious outlook. For here in a solemn convocation, the escaping slaves recognized their debt to Yahweh and to his servant Moses, and

Exodus 19—24

pledged themselves to serve and worship him. The reality of the experience is not to be found in the dramatic descriptions of the presence of God on the holy mountain. The central feature of this awesome occasion was the commitment that God made to Israel, and the obligations that Israel accepted in return.

God's care and concern for his enslaved people had been active even before they were aware of it. The escape from Egypt was the culmination of God's purposes for them. And from this point onwards, the memory of that momentous event and the people's response to it was to dominate the national life of Israel.

This is what the Old Testament means by 'the covenant': an agreement in which the freed slaves were reminded of what God had done for them, and they were called in return to promise to fulfil his commands and to be loyal to him. These commands were essentially moral requirements. Honesty, truth and justice were far more important to Yahweh than the mechanical performance of religious rites. They are summarized in the Ten Commandments, and formed the basic foundation for the whole of later Israelite society.

Exodus 20:1–17

How old is the covenant?

Readers of the Old Testament have often supposed that the high moral ideals recorded in the book of Exodus and elsewhere are too sophisticated to have originated in the primitive age of Moses. The great German Old Testament scholar of the nineteenth century, Julius Wellhausen, argued that the whole idea of the covenant as it is portrayed here was a reading-back into Israelite history of the circumstances and beliefs of a much later age – the age of the great prophets.

Some still approach the Old Testament with this assumption, but it has been seriously challenged in a number of ways, especially through the findings of archaeology. Wellhausen was studying the Old Testament at a time when archaeology scarcely existed as a scientific enterprise, and it was all too easy for him to regard the history of ideas as an evolutionary progression from very primitive notions to very sophisticated ones. Since he saw the pinnacle of Old Testament thinking in the later prophets, it was taken for granted

An Egyptian frieze depicts ploughing and sowing. The Israelites were leaving the cultivated regions round the Nile for a wilderness where water was scarce and crops non-existent.

This figure of a goat was excavated from the Royal Graves at the site of Ur. It has been dated to approximately 2500 BC. The site of this ancient city, associated with Abraham, gives evidence of a civilization that reached back to the fifth millennium BC.

that the earlier generations had a much cruder outlook. But more recent discoveries have demonstrated quite categorically that this was not the case. The ancient civilizations of the Akkadians, the Sumerians, the Egyptians and others were of a high order, and much of the civil (case) law of the Old Testament bears a close resemblance to concepts of justice going back at least as far as the law code of King Hammurabi of Babylon (about 1700 BC).

The researches of others into the religious life of later Israel have also suggested that the distinctively religious and moral requirements of the Old Testament law (the apodictic law) can be traced to a very early period. Following the findings of the Scandinavian scholar Sigmund Mowinckel and the German Albrecht Alt, many scholars believe that an important aspect of the religious life of Israel was a festival held every autumn, in which the covenant between God and his people was both commemorated and renewed. On this occasion, the people were reminded of what God had done for them, and of his requirements of them – to which they in turn reaffirmed their allegiance. It is argued that the Ten Commandments, and other laws associated with them in the book of Exodus, were recited on such occasions. And since our evidence for such a covenant renewal ceremony comes very early in Israel's history, there is every reason to suppose that the high ideals found there, and the covenant basis on which they exist, go back to the earliest period of Israel's experience of God.

Joshua 24

The ark of the covenant

According to the Old Testament, the spiritual realities of this covenant relationship were expressed in Israel's worship of God, even in the desert. Worship was conducted in a special tent-shrine, often called the 'tabernacle'. But the central focus was a wooden box called 'the ark of the

This carrying chest belonged to Egyptian Pharaoh Tutankhamun. The ark of the covenant may have been made along similar lines.

covenant'. Like similar 'holy boxes' in Egypt, it was decorated with religious symbols, and overlaid with gold. Naturally, it needed to be portable, and was equipped with rings so it could be carried shoulder-high on poles.

According to one of the most ancient pieces of poetry in the Old Testament, this portable ark represented in symbol the fact that God was with the escaping slaves (Numbers 10:35-36). Yahweh was not a God who could be depicted as an idol. But the ark was a kind of visible throne for the invisible Yahweh. It was a symbolic reminder of the central events of Mt Sinai: God was with his people, and he alone was to be their guide. Indeed, the connection with the covenant-making events may have been quite a literal one, for according to some Old Testament passages, the ark itself contained the actual tablets on which the covenant agreement had been set out (1 Kings 8:21).

As time passed, the ark assumed even greater importance in the life of the people. The fates of Israel's earliest kings – Saul and David – hinged on their treatment of the ark. Saul despised it – and was rejected. David respected it – and was politically successful. It also came to play an important part in the worship of the temple at Jerusalem. The religious poetry of Psalm 132 suggests that in a covenant renewal ceremony the ark would be paraded through the streets of the city, returning to the temple as a sign of God's renewed and lasting presence with his people. Other psalms also reflect its important position in the ritual of worship at the temple, though they do not always mention it by name. Many scholars believe that when the Old Testament uses the title 'the Lord of hosts', this is really a reference to God's presence as symbolized in the ark. Other terms, such as 'glory' also seem to be used regularly in reference to it (e.g. 1 Samuel 4:21–22).

The Old Testament gives no hint of the ark's ultimate fate. No doubt it was one of the religious objects that later kings of Judah moved in and out of the temple as their religious allegiances changed (see chapter six). But all trace of it disappears after the invasion of Nebuchadnezzar in 586 BC.

The form of the covenant

The general idea of a 'covenant' was not unique to ancient Israel. Covenants regulated all sorts of behaviour in the ancient world, notably international relations. When we look closely at the legal framework of the covenant drawn up between Israel and her God at Mt Sinai, we can see a number of similarites with other legal documents from the late Bronze Age period (1400–1200 BC). One of the clearest examples of this legal form is to be found in a series of treaties relating to the Hittite Empire. These treaties clearly define the duties of smaller states which had been annexed by the more powerful Hittites. Naturally, the subject matter of such treaties was generally of a political nature. These legal forms were also used by other nations than the Hittites. But the interesting thing about them for us is their similarity to the Old Testament arrangement. The secular covenant agreements usually have a number of elements, many of which are also found in the Old Testament:

● **Introduction of the Speaker** In a political treaty, the king would introduce himself by name, just as God does in the introduction to the Ten Commandments (Exodus 20:1).

● **Historical Background** The king then reminded the other party of what he had done on their behalf – usually military intervention of some kind. In the Old Testament, God reminds his people of their deliverance from Egypt (Exodus 20:2).

● **Requirements** Then follow the obligations which are placed by the king on the other party. In a political treaty these would normally be military obligations; in the Old Testament, the requirements of the Torah.

● **The Document** Arrangements were then made for the treaty to be written down, and deposited in a suitable place to be read at specified times. There is no such provision closely linked with the Ten Commandments in the book of Exodus, but there are similar instructions in Deuteronomy 27:1–8.

● **Witnesses** were called to seal the covenant – usually, the gods of both states. In the Old Testament we find a number of examples of witnesses to the covenant. In Exodus 24, twelve pillars were set up, probably for this purpose – and in the covenant ceremony recorded in Joshua 24, a large stone was erected to be a witness (Joshua 24:25–28).

● **Curses and Blessings** were then invoked for those who broke or kept the treaty. In the Old Testament, there is a long series of such curses and blessings in the book of Deuteronomy (Deuteronomy 27:11 — 28:68).

It is not suggested that Moses actually used a legal document of this kind – still less that he got it from the Hittites, though Israel did later make such a treaty with the Gibeonites (Joshua 9). There are many problems involved in tracing the exact relationship between the covenant made at Mt Sinai and these covenant forms used in the political sphere. It is not at all difficult to locate all the elements of the secular treaty form somewhere in the Old Testament, but there is no one single context which contains them all. We must also remember that Israel was in covenant with her God, not with a military ruler, and this must have added a distinctive element to her understanding of the covenant. Nevertheless, the fact that the events at Mt Sinai were articulated and preserved in a form of words that had such a widespread use in the time of Moses gives us no reason to look to a much later date for the origin of Israel's distinctive faith.

To the promised land

Mt Sinai was not the final destination of the escaping slaves. But it was an essential first step, for in this encounter at the holy mountain, we can see how this motley collection of refugees was beginning to be moulded into the nucleus of a nation. Informed by a new understanding of God, and fired with a new consciousness of their own part in his plans, they pressed on eastwards to the borders of Canaan, the land which eventually would see their embryonic faith achieve its full maturity. Many years were to pass before that would happen. For the land was no more theirs than it had been Abraham's, or Isaac's, or Jacob's. It belonged to other people – people with long experience of living in sophisticated urban communities, and with far greater material resources at their disposal.

Even the journey through the desert was to prove hazardous. For the refugees had to work out for themselves the full implications that the events of Mt Sinai should have in their everyday living. In addition to that, they came into conflict with many other groups of wandering nomads who, like them, were wanting to establish a

The mountains of Sinai, where Israel's covenant relationship with the Lord was formed.

permanent homeland for themselves. But Moses' faith and determination never wavered. Though he himself did not live to set foot in the land that was to become his people's national home, he had no doubt of the final outcome of their struggle. For like Abraham before him, he was convinced that the direction of his own life, and the future of the escaped slaves and their descendants, was not at the mercy of impersonal social and political forces. It was in the control of a loving and all-powerful God: 'People of Israel, no god is like your God ... There is no one like you, a nation saved by the Lord. The Lord himself is your shield and your sword, to defend you and give you victory.'

Deuteronomy 33:26,29

Dating the exodus and conquest of Canaan

Twenty years ago it would have been difficult to find any reputable scholar who would not have dated the exodus and Israel's entry into Canaan somewhere between about 1280 and 1240 BC. But today an increasing number are inclined to give more weight to an older view that dated these events about 1440 BC. Many of the arguments are complex, and much of the so-called evidence is uncertain. All we shall try to do here is to indicate the issues that are involved, and take note of some of the problems to be faced in finding an answer to this question.

Old Testament chronology

According to 1 Kings 6:1, Solomon began to build the temple in Jerusalem in the fourth year of his reign, which is said to be 'Four hundred and eighty years after the people of Israel left Egypt'. Working back from Solomon's time, that brings us to a date of almost exactly 1440 BC for the exodus. At first, this may seem to be clear-cut and decisive. But other facts need to be taken into consideration:

● If we add together the successive periods of rule of the various judges, the time between the exodus and Solomon works out at a minimum of 554 years. Of course, we do not know for certain that the judges followed one another in chronological succession. Since they were mainly local leaders, there was probably a good deal of overlap between them, in which case this period of time could in reality be much less than it first seems to be. In addition, the period of forty years often figures in these stories, and that span of time was used conventionally in the Old Testament to indicate one generation. So perhaps it was never intended to be a very precise measurement of time.

● At the end of the book of Ruth, the genealogy of Solomon separates him from Nahshon, his ancestor who lived at the time of the exodus (Numbers 1:7) by only six generations. That would normally be about 200 years – though here, as in other biblical ancestor lists, some generations may have been left out.

● According to Exodus 12:40, the Israelite tribes left Egypt after they had lived there for 430 years. If we assume that the exodus took place in about 1250 BC, that would mean that Joseph went to Egypt in the time of the Hyksos rulers. They were themselves not Egyptians, and would therefore have been more likely than native rulers to favour a

person like Joseph. But if we date the exodus in 1440 BC, and then add 430 years to that for Israel's stay in Egypt, we would arrive at a date for Joseph much earlier than most scholars would assign to Abraham! But here again there is an element of doubt. For the Septuagint makes the 430 years include both the time the Israelites were in Egypt, and the time they were in Canaan before this.

So the most we can conclude on the basis of the dates in the Old Testament is that it is very difficult to take the statement of 1 Kings 6:1 at its face value. Indeed it may well be that it was never intended to be taken as a strict chronological statement. For 480 years is twelve times forty, which could therefore indicate a dozen generations, or simply a very long time. If we understand this figure in this way, then most of the other Biblical dates seem to favour an exodus sometime in the thirteenth, and not the fifteenth century.

The Tell-el-Amarna Letters

We have already mentioned these documents briefly. They consist of a series of pillar-shaped tablets written in cuneiform script, mostly in a form of Akkadian, which was the diplomatic language of the time. They date from the early fourteenth century, and were written by various rulers in Canaan and Syria to Pharaoh Akhen-aten (1369–1353 BC) and his predecessor Amenhotep III (1398–1361 BC). In particular, they complain of the activities of groups of people called 'Aperru', whose warlike activities were creating tensions and disturbance throughout the area. At one time scholars were inclined to identify the Aperru with the Old Testament Hebrews, and the invasions into southern Canaan mentioned in the Amarna Letters were thereby identified with the invasion of Joshua. If this could be shown to be true, it would of course suggest that the exodus from Egypt had taken place earlier than the date of these letters – which in turn could plausibly take us back to 1440 BC again. But we now know that it is simplistic and improbable simply to identify Aperru and Hebrews. And in any case, the stories of the book of Joshua concern armed infiltration into Canaan from the east rather than from the south. But it is possible that the general movements of which these texts speak may be reflected in other parts of the Old Testament story.

The Amarna Letters, tablets written in cuneiform script, give evidence of a period of instability in the relationships between Egypt and her neighbours in the years before Israel setted in Egypt.

Pithom and Rameses

We are on much safer ground with a statement in Exodus 1:11, that 'The Israelites built the cities of Pithom and Rameses to serve as supply centres for the king of Egypt'. Pithom was actually an old town, but the finest structure in it was a temple built by Rameses II (1290–1224 BC), and there is no evidence for any earlier pharaoh building there. Rameses is certainly to be identified with the capital city of Rameses II, built by him on the site of the ancient capital Tanis,. This had been the capital of the Hyksos kings in the century preceding their expulsion in 1540 BC, but the pharaohs of the succeeding dynasty had their capital at Thebes (except for Akhen-aten, who moved even further from Tanis). All this would appear to date the exodus sometime after 1290 BC. And evidence from the reign of a later pharaoh, Merneptah, suggests that it could not have been later than about 1240 BC. For in about 1220 BC, he recorded an attack on various peoples in Canaan, in the course of which he mentions 'Israel' as part of the settled population of the land.

Archaeology in Canaan

The storm centre of this whole debate is found in the evidence for destruction at various sites in Canaan itself.

● At one time, the strongest argument for dating the exodus towards the end of the fifteenth century BC was the conclusion of the English archaeologist John Garstang that Jericho had been taken by Joshua not later than 1400 BC. Indeed, he excavated the remains of walls and other buildings which he believed proved the historical truth of the Old Testament story even down to its details. But his interpretation of the evidence does not square with the facts (see chapter 3).

● The same is true for most other sites that have been excavated. For while there is much evidence of destruction throughout Canaan in the thirteenth century BC, there is very little that can positively be connected with the Old Testament story. Many sites do provide evidence of a destruction in which the sophisticated culture of the Canaanite city-states was replaced by a much more primitive life-style, and some scholars have taken this as evidence of the Israelite invasion. But in reality, it is not quite so simple. For we have no real evidence to inform us of the nature of a typically Israelite culture at this period, other than by the circular assumption that this less sophisticated style was Israelite! In any case, with only a few exceptions the cities that have yielded most evidence for such a thirteenth century destruction are not those that feature most prominently in the Old Testament record.

● Those who favour a fifteenth-century date for the exodus have recently argued that the evidence of decay and collapse in thirteenth century Canaanite society had nothing to do with the Israelite conquest. Instead, they argue, it reflects the events depicted in the book of Judges. But this view is itself problematical, for there is no absolutely clear-cut archaeological evidence to support a fifteenth – century invasion either, unless we are prepared to indulge in a wholesale modification of the dating that archaeologists have given to events throughout this entire period.

If we restrict our attention to these detailed points, there is no doubt that the argument is very finely balanced, and probably the only safe conclusion to draw is that we cannot certainly date the exodus and conquest. But the very un-certainty of this evidence has led a number of scholars to wonder whether we are asking the right question here. Instead of searching for evidence of a once-for-all conquest of Canaan by the Israelite tribes, perhaps we should understand their arrival in the land from a different perspective – either by supposing that only one particular group was involved in the exodus events, or by seeing the emergence of Israel as a nation more in terms of the internal development and change of Canaanite society. These alternatives are considered in the next chapter.

The 'round tower', excavated at Jericho, dated to the Neolithic period (7000 BC). The archaeological remains show that Jericho had many different periods of occupation. So to extract from the archaeological evidence a definite date for Israel's 'conquest' is virtually impossible.

3 A land flowing with milk and honey

Joshua
Judges

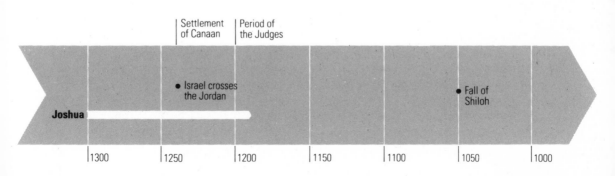

Settlement of Canaan | Period of the Judges

• Israel crosses the Jordan

• Fall of Shiloh

Joshua

1300 | 1250 | 1200 | 1150 | 1100 | 1050 | 1000

Canaan before Israel

THE LAND of Canaan had a long and illustrious history of its own. Documents discovered at Ebla in north Syria testify to the existence of many important towns there as early as 2300 BC, and the city of Jericho is believed to be the oldest city in the world, going back perhaps as far as 9000 BC.

So the land to which Moses led his people was a well organized country. Throughout most of the second millennium BC it was controlled by the Egyptians. But they worked through local rulers, of whom there were a great many. Egyptian records and archaeological findings paint a picture of intensely populated city-states, especially in the central, most fertile parts of the country. Each city was independent, with its own land – just enough to provide for its needs – and its own rulers. The next city might be as little as 3 miles/5km away, but every local king considered himself directly responsible to Egypt, rather than to his neighbours. This was an important part of Egyptian strategy. For the land of Canaan was of strategic importance to Egypt's own political security. The great trade routes linking Egypt with the other power centres in the ancient world ran through Canaan, and it is no coincidence that the greatest concentration of small city-states was to be found along the road from Egypt to Syria and Mesopotamia. In the hill country, things were not so well organized. Fewer people wanted to live there anyway, and in addition, a city in the hills needed much more land to be self-sufficient. For this reason, it had always been easier for nomadic peoples to move about in these more remote areas of the country.

By the end of the Late Bronze Age, however, Egypt's power was diminishing and at about this time (1220 BC) we find the first

The Philistines occupied a coastal strip; this picture is of one of their warships. In the time of the judges and the early kings they were a highly aggressive enemy.

This stone monument (or 'stele') was erected by King Merneptah of Egypt after a military expedition into Canaan. Its text includes the earliest known reference to 'Israel' outside the Bible.

reference outside the Bible to 'Israel' as the name of a nation. After a military expedition into Canaan, King Merneptah of Egypt erected a stone monument as a record of his exploits. In its inscription, he triumphantly declared that 'Israel is laid waste'. Subsequent events showed this optimism to be unjustified. For Egypt's power in the area soon collapsed, and the strong alliance of Egyptian-backed Canaanite city-states began to lose its grip. Within a short time, the whole land had fallen into the hands of only four or five separate rulers, all of whom were newcomers. Israel was certainly one such group. The Philistines were another. They had originally come from Crete, and they settled mainly along the sea coast. Here, they adopted the political organization of their predecessors, and established five city-states of their own: Gaza, Ashkelon, Ashdod, Ekron, and Gath. They also eventually gave their name to the whole country (Palestine).

Israel's new state was quite different. Under the old regime in Canaan, political power went hand in hand with possession of a city. This meant that real power must always be kept in the hands of just a few privileged people. But the covenant at Mt Sinai had given Israel a different understanding of human society, in which class

Facing page: Settling Canaan.

structure had no part to play. No one had any right to claim a position of superiority, for they had all been slaves together, and the only thing that made them a nation was the undeserved generosity of God himself. Israel's national identity was always firmly based on her understanding of the nature of God, and this was to have far-reaching consequences not only during the early period of her history, but throughout her entire existence as a nation. It meant that all elements of her populaton (the tribes) were of equal importance, and their ultimate responsibility was not to some centralized power structure, but to God alone.

Israel moves in

These changes in Canaanite political life are all well documented from Egyptian records, as well as from archaeological evidence at various sites throughout the land. Between about 1400 and 1200 BC radical changes came about. The power of Egypt declined, and the relatively advanced culture of the Canaanite city-states was replaced by a less sophisticated way of life – and at the end of it, Israel had emerged as a force to be reckoned with. So much is clear. But when we try to discover exactly how these changes took place, we are soon involved in one of the most complex issues in the study of the Old Testament. For there is no generally agreed understanding of the course of Israel's development at this period. Different scholars have formed their own theories. All of them can claim some support in the Old Testament itself, but none of them is free from problems. At least three main explanations have been proposed in recent years:

● **Armed struggle** A quick reading of the stories in the Old Testament book of Joshua can give the impression that the land of Canaan became the land of Israel almost overnight, as a result of a series of spectacular battles and conquests. But in fact Joshua records the capture of only a few Canaanite city-states, and makes it clear that even at the end of Joshua's successful military exploits Joshua 13:1–7 much of the land remained unconquered. Nevertheless, the successes of Joshua's armies form the core of the Old Testament story, and many scholars believe that the successful settlement of the Israelite tribes in Canaan owed more to this than to any other cause.

The evidence of archaeology has often been claimed to support this belief. In the 1930s, the English archaeologist John Garstang carried out extensive excavations at the site of Jericho, and he discovered what he took to be incontrovertible evidence of Joshua's capture of the city: walls that had literally fallen flat, and much Joshua 6 evidence of destruction by fire. According to Professor Garstang, this had happened not long after 1400 BC, and on his reckoning this was almost exactly the time when the Israelite armies were invading the land. Investigations by later archaeologists, however, have shown this picture to be totally false. Following the usual procedure, Garstang dated his finds by reference to the layer of the mound at Jericho in which he found them. But what he did not

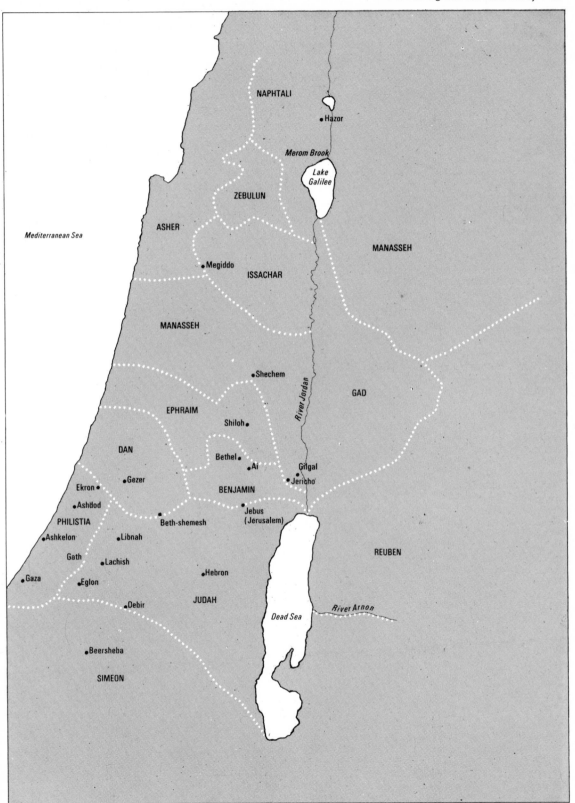

NAPHTALI

•Hazor

Merom Brook

Lake Galilee

ZEBULUN

ASHER

Mediterranean Sea

MANASSEH

•Megiddo

ISSACHAR

MANASSEH

•Shechem

River Jordan

GAD

EPHRAIM

Shiloh•

DAN

Bethel•

•Ai   Gilgal
                •Jericho

•Gezer

BENJAMIN

Ekron •

•Ashdod

PHILISTIA

•Jebus
(Jerusalem)

Beth-shemesh

•Ashkelon   •Libnah

Gath   REUBEN

•Lachish

•Gaza   •Eglon   •Hebron

•Debir   JUDAH

River Arnon

Dead Sea

•Beersheba

SIMEON

know was that over the centuries much of the top of the mound had been worn away at this point – and for that reason, the remains he found were actually from a much lower level than they appeared to be. In fact, they were from a city that had existed on the site a full thousand years earlier than the time of Joshua. Unless other finds come to light (and archaeologists have not yet worked over the whole mound of Jericho), it seems that nothing substantial is left of the city that stood there at the end of the Late Bronze Age.

Evidence from other sites is more specific, and shows that there was a violent and widespread destruction of Canaanite cities during the thirteenth century BC. The fact that this destruction was followed by a much more primitive culture than the one it replaced

The time of Joshua and the judges is often called the period of 'the conquest'. Certainly many battles were involved, not only as Israel moved in to Canaan but also as they struggled to take full possession. In a sense, these conflicts still continue.

has been taken to prove that it was the work of the Israelite tribes: coming in from the desert, their way of life would be much less sophisticated than that of the Canaanite cities. That is no doubt true, but it does not in itself prove that the destruction uncovered by archaeologists was the work of Israel's armies. Others have argued that this collapse of Canaanite culture came about because of internal feuding among the city-states, which in turn was encouraged by the decline of the Egyptian power that had so successfully united the land. In addition, some also argue that the exodus and conquest of Canaan took place earlier than this, perhaps in the fifteenth century BC. If that is true, then the thirteenth-century evidence would be irrelevant anyway, though it could be related to the general social unrest that seems to be depicted in the Old Testament book of Judges. In any case, we need to remember that the Israelites were not the only ones who were staking their claim at this time. Philistines, Ammonites, and others were all pressing in from various quarters, and much of this destruction could be their work.

In the present state of our knowledge, archaeology has little truly useful information to give us about the Israelite conquest of the land. This has led some to doubt whether there ever was a 'conquest' in any real sense. They point out that the military strength of the Canaanite city-states would easily have repelled wandering tribes with no real experience of warfare – especially since the Canaanites possessed relatively sophisticated equipment, such as chariots. But this argument carries little weight. For one thing, Canaanite culture was declining anyway. And in addition, the history of guerilla warfare readily demonstrates how minority groups inspired by a vision of what they believe to be right can often

Although the book of Joshua suggests that the Canaanites were easily defeated by Israel, this may only have been because the separate city-states failed to unite. Their weaponry, from war chariots down to such swords and daggers as these, was fairly sophisticated.

overthrow highly organized and well-equipped armies that in theory should have quelled their opposition effortlessly. The whole picture of Israel's early history is so dominated by the stories of military success that to ignore it would require a wholesale rejection of the Old Testament account – and there is no reason why we should do that. But equally, the Old Testament gives us no reason to include only this one element in our portrayal of Israel's life in these early days. According to the book of Joshua, the military campaigns secured for Israel a foothold in the central hill country, which was to be the heart of her territory. But the flatter and more fertile areas like the Plain of Jezreel were not taken over at this time – and in addition, many fortified towns such as Jerusalem and Gezer also stayed firmly in Canaanite hands.

● **Infiltration** The apparently incomplete nature of the initial conquest of the country has led other scholars to suggest that much – or even all – of the land was taken over in a different way, as the Israelite tribes gradually infiltrated Canaanite society until eventually they became the dominant group. This understanding of the situation has been especially articulated by the German scholar Albrecht Alt.

He began by analysing the social structure of the land both before and after the period when Israel was emerging as a nation.

He noted that the structure of Israelite society was quite different from the closely controlled hierarchy that had been established by the Canaanite city-states. But he also drew attention to the fact that those invaders like the Philistines, who settled where the city-states had been strongest, were forced by social and economic pressures to take over this form of government themselves. Since this did not happen in Israel, he argued that the Israelites must have established their rule first in those parts of the land where the power of the city-states was minimal. That is, in the hill country. Instead of a violent conquest, Alt believed that the Israelite tribes had settled in a gradual way. Instead of wandering about as nomads with their flocks from season to season, they began to stay for longer periods in particular places. Then they eventually penetrated the structure of the few power centres that were to be found in the hill country, until they became a significant element of the settled population.

This is an unconvincing view of the matter if we take it to be the only way in which Israel settled her land. The kind of patient, self-conscious process of infiltration that Alt described is more plausible to modern theorists than it would be to homeless refugees, especially those who were convinced that their destiny was not a matter of chance but was all part of the design of their loving and powerful God. In addition, the political system developed by Israel at this early stage had nothing to do with the kind of social tensions that Alt described: instead, it was a conscious projection into the political sphere of the religious experience of the slaves from Egypt. It is also doubtful whether Israel's earliest nomadic life followed the kind of pattern that Alt suggested. For these and other reasons, only a minority of others have accepted his interpretation of Israel's settlement in her land.

But despite this, the theory in a broader sense does seem to explain some of the facts that emerge from the Old Testament story. For it seems likely that some cities came into Israelite hands by other means than conquest. Shechem is a good example of this. There is no record of a military conquest here by Joshua, and yet even before his death it was a major centre of Israelite activity, and seems to have served as a sort of capital town. The evidence of archaeology is consistent with this, for Shechem did not share in the general wave of destruction and decline that was going on elsewhere in the thirteenth century BC. Of course, it is possible to explain the archaeological evidence differently in order to support an earlier date for the conquest of Canaan. We know that the Egyptians destroyed the city sometime between 1545 and 1525 BC, and if the Israelite tribes arrived shortly after that, they would have found Shechem unoccupied, and so they could have settled the area without the need for conquest. On the other hand, there are many difficulties involved in dating the exodus and conquest quite so early. Others have pointed out that an earlier story tells how Shechem was conquered by Jacob and his sons, and they suggest that when the invading tribes arrived several centuries later they found the city was occupied by people who were, literally, their

Joshua 24

Genesis 34;48:22

Joshua 6:22–25
Judges 1:22–26

A figurine of a Canaanite goddess, found at Ugarit. Much of the religious mythology of the Canaanites was concerned with sex and fertility.

relatives – and this is why they did not need to overthrow it. It is not possible to be certain how and why Shechem came to be so important to Israel, but it does seem to be an example of a city that was taken over in a more or less peaceful way.

● **Conversion and revolution**   Another interesting possibility is that some inhabitants of Canaan could have been won over to Israel's side by a process of religious conversion. The family of the prostitute Rahab at Jericho may be an example of this, as also may be another group associated with the city of Bethel. Then there is the rather odd position of the Gibeonites, who came and asked to be incorporated into the nation of Israel, and who were accepted by Joshua on the basis of a covenant treaty.

Incidents like these have been taken as evidence that Israel's 'conquest' of Canaan was far more dependent on moral victories than on military might. Indeed some have asserted that there was no 'conquest' in any physical sense at all, but that what changed the population from 'Canaanites' into 'Israelites' was the result of some sort of social revolution, a 'peasant's revolt', led not by political considerations but by moral and religious convictions. They point out that the new understanding of God's character derived from the covenant at Mt Sinai was quite different from the religion of Canaan. Moses had declared that God was interested in people on a personal level, and that he was active in the events of everyday life for their benefit. This was in stark contrast to Canaanite religion, where the gods existed to preserve the existing order both in the world of nature and in the world of politics. They were powerful supporters of the ruling classes, whereas the God of Israel was committed to support the oppressed and downtrodden – and he had proved it in the events of the exodus. It is therefore not surprising that many Canaanite peasants should have been attracted by this new assessment of the human situation. As a result, they overthrew their local city rulers and allied themselves with Israel's dynamic concept of God as the true ruler and guide of his people. And in the process, 'Canaan' became 'Israel'.

This view has not found a great deal of favour among Old Testament scholars. Some have argued that it owes more to the modern Marxist view of history than it does to the Old Testament. No doubt it has been influenced by modern concerns, but that in itself does not make it untrue, for one of the most fruitful ways of understanding the past can often be by use of a theoretical model of this kind to provide a framework within which to assess the event. A much stronger argument against this view is that there is no positive Old Testament evidence in its favour. Indeed, the opposite is true. For on this view, the term 'Israel' does not denote a racial or national entity. Instead, it becomes a descriptive term for people sharing the same ideology. 'Israel' becomes not so much a nation as a kind of political party. But of course the Old Testament accounts of the conquest of Canaan are united in portraying Israel as a national group that is quite separate from the Canaanites.

To be sure, others could be accepted as a part of the nation of

Joshua 24

Israel. Indeed, the solemn assembly at Shechem was almost certainly an important occasion when such converts to faith in the God of Israel were formally incorporated into the nation. But there is no support in the Old Testament for the view that such racial outsiders comprised the majority of the nation. If this had been the case, we would surely have expected to find some trace of it, however slight, in the relevant Old Testament passages.

The story of how Israel settled in her land is obviously very complex. Great political and social movements leading to the formation of a new nation can hardly be simple and straightforward. Modern thinkers are often tempted to try to understand the past from just one perspective, and Old Testament scholars are no exception. They have tried to depict the early history of Israel in black and white terms, usually rejecting the diversity of the Old Testament story in favour of just one of its strands. But history seldom develops in such a simple way, and it is not at all unlikely that Israel became a nation in her own land by adopting different tactics at different times and places.

Israel settles down

Judges 1:27–36

In some ways, the real struggle for the land only began after Joshua was dead. Israel was fortunate in that she did not need to contend with any of the great world powers of the time. The Egyptians and the Hittites were both in decline, while the new power of Assyria was not yet ready to expand into Canaan. The real challenge was in Canaan itself, where the Israelite tribes held control of only a few areas of the country. To make matters worse, the Israelite settlements were isolated from each other by two powerful groups of Canaanite city-states: one group just to the north of Shechem, centred on towns like Megiddo, Dothan, and Beth-Shan; and another to the south of Shechem, extended westwards from the northern end of the Dead Sea right across to the Mediterranean coast. On top of that, the Israelite tribes were not always able to subdue the Canaanite population even in those areas where they had achieved some sort of dominance. The tribes of Manasseh, Ephraim, Zebulon, Asher and Naphtali were all forced to come to some mutual agreement with the native population of the land. When we add to this the fact that other invaders were also trying to carve out their own territories, it is hardly surprising that the situation was so volatile.

All this is described in the Old Testament book of Judges. The book takes its name from the fact that its heroes are called 'judges'. To us, this suggests they were concerned with the administration of law, and the Hebrew word for 'judge' is in fact very similar to titles given to government officials elsewhere in the ancient world – at Mari, Ebla, and Ugarit. Some of the people mentioned in Judges may well have had some administrative function. But it can be misleading to compare the 'judges' of early Israel with figures in other cultures. For without exception, they all had a monarchy, and a much more sophisticated political apparatus than Israel had at this time. The great judges of the Old Testament stories were not anonymous officials. Nor did they owe their position to a bureaucratic or hereditary appointment. It was something that stemmed naturally from their remarkable gifts of great wisdom, bravery, and leadership – qualities that were demonstrated not in legal arguments about justice, but in the actual work of getting justice for their people. They were men and women of great political vision and religious devotion. They were determined that the promises of God and the commitment of his people, expressed in the covenant made at Mt Sinai, should be enshrined in the very fabric of their new society.

The Old Testament names twelve judges, but records details about only six of them. Of these, only one, Othniel, is linked with the tribes that settled in the south. All the others are associated with northern tribes. This perhaps reflects the relative strength of Israel in different parts of the country at the time. But it could also suggest that the stories themselves were first handed down, and later written down, in the northern part of the country. The meaning that the editor of the book of Judges found in these stories is certainly similar to the message of the prophets who later flourished in that part of the country. Like many other Old Testament writers, he suggests that the true meaning of Israel's experience can only be understood from a religious viewpoint. He tells us plainly at the beginning of the book that all the stories follow the same pattern, and teach the same lesson:

- When Israel was faithful to God, she prospered.
- When she deserted her God, Yahweh, for other gods, she was unable to resist her enemies.
- Finding herself in great distress, Israel turned again to God, and he provided a deliverer (the judges).
- After the death of a judge, the same pattern of events was repeated again.

Every one of the stories about the judges is used to illustrate and give substance to this theological understanding of Israel's fortunes. For this reason, it has often been suggested that the narrative is less than accurate as history. Given the personal nature of much of the story, it is obviously impossible either to prove or disprove that. But the overall picture that emerges appears to be true to life.

Deborah and Barak fight with the Canaanites, the native inhabitants of the land, while the others deal with various groups who, like Israel, were trying to gain access to the land for themselves: the Moabites (Ehud); the Midianites (Gideon); the Ammonites (Jephthah); and the Philistines (Samson). Most of these people were local heroes, fighting local battles. The story of Samson is almost a personal crusade against the Philistines. The fact that he was able to marry a Philistine woman suggests that, though the Philistines soon became Israel's greatest enemy, relationships with them at this stage were still more or less friendly.

The story of Deborah and Barak gives us more insight into the

Judges 1:11–15; 3:7–11; Joshua 15:13–19

Judges 2:11–23

Judges 4—5

Judges 3:12–30
Judges 6:1—8:35
Judges 10:6—12:7
Judges 13:1—16:31

Judges 5

Judges 4:23–24

After the dreariness of the barren wilderness, the country into which the Israelites were moving must have seemed startlingly beautiful and fertile. They described it as 'a land flowing with milk and honey'.

nature of Israelite society at this period. Their exploits against the Canaanites, led by Sisera, the army commander of Jabin, king of the city of Hazor, are vividly described. This great poem (or song) was almost certainly written by an eye witness of the events which it describes. It was certainly written sometime in the twelfth century BC, and that takes us right back to the time of the judges themselves. Deborah and Barak were probably trying to break through the line of Canaanite city-states that isolated the northern area of Galilee from the Israelite settlements around Shechem. For though Jabin's city, Hazor, lay to the north of Galilee, the battle itself took place just to the south-west of the Plain of Jezreel, and involved a coalition of Canaanite city-states. Possession of this great plain was of vital importance. All of the trade routes had to go this way, and whoever controlled this area effectively controlled most of the land. The outcome of the battle was victory for Israel. The Canaanite kings were not entirely routed, but their power was broken, and it was only a matter of time before Israel was able to overthrow Jabin and his influence.

The Canaanite kings had many sophisticated weapons, including chariots, and it was only because they were able to form an effective alliance that the Israelites were successful. Deborah managed to unite six of the Israelite tribes – Zebulun, Naphtali, Ephraim, Benjamin, Manasseh, and Issachar – and the one thing that brought them together was their common faith in God. The editor of the book of Judges was not exaggerating when he claimed that obedience to God led to success, while disobedience led to failure. When the tribes were united by their common heritage derived from the covenant at Mt Sinai, they were an effective coalition. But when they began to drift away from the worship of the God of whom Moses had spoken, purely sectional and selfish interests came to be all-important, and they were powerless against their enemies.

Life in the days of the judges

What was life really like in those early years when the character and identity of the nation of Israel were being established? Like any other emerging nation, Israel certainly had her troubles. Looking back from his own more settled times, the editor of the book of Judges felt that at times it verged on anarchy: 'Every man did what was right in his own eyes' (Judges 21:25).

It is not hard to see why he felt like that. The gruesome story of how a woman traveller was sexually assaulted and murdered in the town of Gibeah is no doubt a typical example (Judges 19). But what happened as a result of this incident is of great significance in understanding the nature of Israelite society at this time. For the woman's male companion sent a message to all the other tribes, telling them what had happened. They were all outraged, and formed a large army to punish the tribe of Benjamin for allowing such a thing to happen in their territory. In the struggle that followed, the tribe of Benjamin was all but exterminated (Judges 20). Under normal conditions, the different tribes of Israel were primarily concerned with their own affairs. But when the need arose, they obviously had a strong sense of national solidarity, and could unite to confront a common threat – whether it came from outside enemies, or from internal subversion. But what was it that held them together like this? We may find a clue in the deep remorse that was felt after the Benjaminites had been subdued. For there was great concern that Benjamin should not be wiped out altogether: 'Israel must not lose one of its twelve tribes. We must find a way for the tribe of Benjamin to survive . . .' (Judges 21:17). The alliance of twelve tribes – and no less – was clearly of some importance to them.

As long ago as the middle of the nineteenth century, German scholars were suggesting that this incident gives us an important insight into the social and political organization of early Israel. But it was not until the 1930s, with the work of Martin Noth, that the full implications of this became clear. He observed that many ancient communities were divided into a regular number of groups, or tribes. In the Old Testament itself we find twelve Ishmaelite tribes (Genesis 25:13–16) and twelve Edomite tribes (Genesis 36:10–14). Unfortunately, nothing else is known about these near-neighbours of Israel. But we do have more specific information about associations of tribes in ancient Greece and Italy, especially a group that was associated with the shrine of the god Apollo at Delphi. These groups came to be known as 'amphictyonies', from two Greek words which mean 'to live around'. In this case, they lived around a particular religious centre, and their common allegiance to the worship of their god was the thing that bound them together and gave them mutual obligations to one another.

Professor Noth identified a number of distinctive features of the life of such an amphictyony, which he believed can also be found in the Old Testament:

● **A fixed membership** The Greek amphictyonies always had either six or twelve members. The reason for this was perhaps a practical one, for with twelve months in a year it meant that each tribe could take it in turn to look after the central sanctuary. Whatever the origin of Israel's twelve tribes, it is certainly interesting that, though the actual names given to the tribes could vary, the number twelve is always preserved in the Old Testament.

● **A central shrine** The main focus of the Greek amphictyonies was the

Israel and the judges

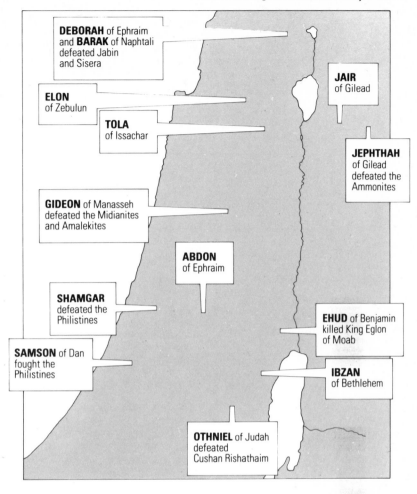

DEBORAH of Ephraim
and BARAK of Naphtali
defeated Jabin
and Sisera

JAIR
of Gilead

ELON
of Zebulun

TOLA
of Issachar

JEPHTHAH
of Gilead
defeated the
Ammonites

GIDEON of Manasseh
defeated the Midianites
and Amalekites

ABDON
of Ephraim

SHAMGAR
defeated the
Philistines

EHUD of Benjamin
killed King Eglon
of Moab

SAMSON of Dan
fought the
Philistines

IBZAN
of Bethlehem

OTHNIEL of Judah
defeated
Cushan Rishathaim

shrine of their god, and this also became a centre for the administration of laws that were common to all the member states. By definition, an amphictyony must have such a central place of worship. But was there such a place in ancient Israel? The story in Joshua 24 seems to suggest that Shechem could have been a kind of central sanctuary. But later, when the tribes united against Benjamin, they went not to Shechem, but to Bethel (Judges 20:18) – and not long after, in the time of Samuel, Shiloh appears as the most important place of worship (1 Samuel 1–4). The apparent absence of just one shrine could be due to the fact that, unlike other gods, the God of Israel could not be contained in just one place. He was present with his people everywhere, and this presence was symbolized by the portable ark of the covenant. Perhaps therefore this sign of God's presence that could be moved about from place to place was itself the central focus for all the tribes.

But if so, could it also have been a kind of administrative centre, served by its own officials? Martin Noth believed that it could, and he argued that the officials of the Israelite amphictyony were to be identified with the so-called 'minor judges' – that is, those of whom we know nothing more than their names (Judges 10:1–5, 12:8–15). He further suggested that the law which they administered is found in Exodus 21-23, the 'Book of the Covenant'.

● **An annual festival** In the Greek amphictyonies, each member state sent official delegates to an annual convention, which took place at the central shrine. This was partly a religious occasion, and partly a kind of administrative council. The evidence for such an annual pilgrimage in the Old Testament is limited. But there is the story of how Joshua gathered the tribes together at Shechem, to remind them of their obligations under the covenant (Joshua 24), and the later story of

Samuel's parents tells how they went to the sanctuary in Shiloh once a year – though there is nothing to suggest they were any sort of official delegates (1 Samuel 1:1–8). It is in fact very difficult to find evidence of the existence of such delegates in early Israel, though Noth believed that passages like Numbers 1:1–15 could have been lists of such people. But this is very uncertain.

● **A common purpose** The job of an alliance like this was to defend the central shrine and to uphold the common interests and laws of the constituent states. There are two striking illustrations of this kind of common concern in the book of Judges. On the one hand, we have the story of how six tribes united under Deborah to oppose a common threat from the Canaanites (Judges 4—5). And on the other, we have the story of how eleven tribes acted against a gross violation of covenant law by the tribe of Benjamin (Judges 19—20). According to Noth, these two incidents document the development of the amphictyony, with an alliance of twelve tribes arising out of the six-tribe group headed by Deborah. But other interpretations are possible, especially if one is prepared to imagine that the stories have been rewritten in the light of social conditions in later Israel.

Martin Noth's reconstruction of life in the time of the judges has been very influential in Old Testament study for the past fifty years. It has always been difficult to match every detail of the Old Testament with the evidence from Greece and Italy, and for that reason some have not accepted it. They point out that the Greek amphictyonies flourished in a time and place far removed from Israel in the period of the judges – and in any case, they suggest, the Greek evidence is not as clear-cut as Noth liked to think.

Certainly, his idea must always remain just a theory. But it does shed light on some aspects of Israel's national consciousness. It is certain that a shared faith in God was the main strength of the alliance between the Israelite tribes. Though that faith may not have been expressed in just one central place, its power was none the less real for that. Though the tribes had their own leaders from time to time – the judges – they realized that God himself was the real 'judge' of his people (Judges 11:27), and their devotion was to be given not to human leaders, but to him alone (Judges 8:23; 9:1–57). It would be surprising if such a devotion did not have a tangible form in the social and political institutions of Israel's national life.

Israel and the religion of Canaan

A clay tablet, one of many found at Ugarit (Ras esh-Shamra) with 'cuneiform' writing.

Politically, the Canaanite city-states were eventually displaced by the Israelite tribes. But ideologically, the Canaanites exerted an enormous influence on Israel for many centuries. The editor of the book of Judges makes it quite plain that the religion of Canaan was a more formidable force than its armies, and when Israel was tempted to adopt it, disaster was the inevitable outcome: 'Then the people of Israel sinned against the Lord and began to serve the Baals. They stopped worshipping the Lord, the God of their ancestors, the God who had brought them out of Egypt, and they . . . served the Baals and the Astartes. And so the Lord became furious with Israel and let raiders attack them and rob them . . . and the Israelites could no longer protect themselves . . . They were in great distress' (Judges 2:11–15).

This message was never irrelevant to the life of Israel. Centuries later, the great Old Testament prophets, from Elijah to Jeremiah, were saying the same thing: that the people of Israel were going to ruin because of their love for

the gods and goddesses of Palestine.

So who were these gods and goddesses – 'the Baals and the Astartes'? Some of the answers to that question have been unearthed by archaeologists at the tell of Ras esh-Shamra, on the coast of modern Syria, just opposite Cyprus. This was the site of the ancient Canaanite citadel of Ugarit. Its heyday was in the fifteenth and fourteenth centuries BC, something like 200 years before the time of the exodus. But we have every reason to believe that the religion practised in southern Palestine at the time of the Israelite conquest was very similar to the religion of these people who lived further north. In an annexe to the temple at Ugarit, archaeologists have made one of the most exciting discoveries of all time. For in a large collection of clay tablets, we find the story of Baal and the other Canaanite gods and goddesses who are mentioned in the Old Testament. These tablets date from about the thirteenth century BC, and are written in a language that has come to be known as Ugaritic. It is

On the coast of modern Syria, at the tell of Ras esh-Shamra, was once the Canaanite city of Ugarit. This picture is of an entrance to the great palace there. Archaeologists have unearthed at Ugarit a great deal of evidence about Canaanite religion and civilization in the centuries leading up to the exodus.

An altar to the god Moloch (or Molech), with a receptacle for collecting the blood. Moloch was the god of the Ammonites, and was associated with child sacrifice. Some of the religious practices of the region were cruel and depraved, which helps to explain why the Israelites were warned off them so strongly. But later in the Old Testament child sacrifice appeared in Israel too.

similar to Hebrew, and is one of the earliest known scripts to use an alphabet. The tablets contain much valuable and important information not only about the gods of ancient Ugarit, but also about religious practices. And the many religious objects also found here – altars, statues, etc. – help us to understand how these gods were worshipped.

A number of gods and goddesses play a part in these stories. There is El, the chief of the gods, and his female companion Asherah. But they take a back seat to Baal, the weather god, and his lover Anat, the goddess of love and war. One story tells how Baal was attacked by Mut, the god of barrenness and sterility. As in many ancient fertility myths, he overcomes Baal and his powers of life and fertility, and scatters his body to the four corners of the earth. While El, the father-god, leads the heavenly mourning for his lost son, Anat, the goddess of fertility, goes out to take her revenge:

She seizes Mut, the son of El,
with the knife she cuts him,
with the shovel she winnows him,
with fire she burns him,
with millstones she grinds him,
on the field she throws him.
The birds eat his remains,
the feathered ones make an end to
    what is left over.

Baal's power is brought back as he renews his sexual relationship with Anat – and that in turn ensures the fertility of the earth and its inhabitants for another season. This was the main point of Canaanite religion. Without the rains that fall from October to April, agriculture would have been impossible. And so when the rains stopped in May, it seemed as if Baal was dead, and needed to be revived. Many experts believe that the story of Baal's revival by Anat was the central feature of an annual New Year Festival in ancient Canaan. On this occasion, held every autumn, the king and a temple prostitute would act out the story of Baal and Anat, to make sure that all would be well for another year. No doubt the same kind of rites went on in every local shrine throughout the land. Temple prostitutes feature prominently in the Old Testament descriptions of Canaanite worship, and sexual intercourse with them was considered to be as much a part of the job of a farmer as were the actual operations of agriculture.

This is why the challenge of Canaanite religion often proved irresistable to the Israelites. For though they knew their God Yahweh was all-powerful in the desert, and in war, they doubted his ability to control the weather and the fertility of fields and flocks. This led to all sorts of compromises. Some gave up the worship of Yahweh altogether, and

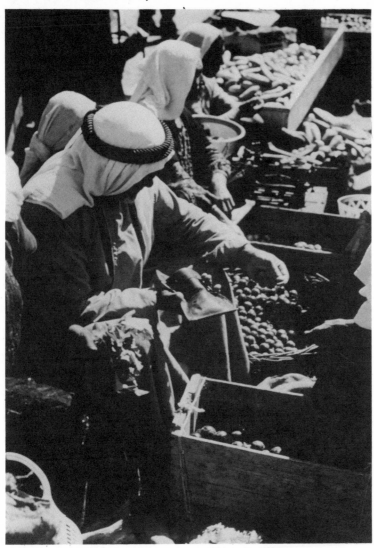

In occupying Canaan, the Israelites were moving from a nomadic to a more settled existence. The life of agriculture and of towns would have required them to develop laws and traditions not needed in the nomadic life.

of belief and worship. After all, the Canaanite city-states were successful in getting the best from the land, and if they claimed this was due to their religion, then at least it would seem to be worth consideration. But in reality, the worship of Yahweh and the worship of Baal could not be mixed, for there were fundamental differences between the two ways:

● Yahweh, the God of Israel, was a God who acted in history. He was not a god of nature who was revealed only in the yearly cycles of summer and winter. He was a personal God, who had disclosed his character in personal ways, through his encounters with Abraham and Moses.

● The Canaanite rituals were first and foremost magical rites. They were designed to bully the gods into making the earth fertile year by year. This was the whole reasoning behind the sexual intercourse which a farmer would have with a temple prostitute. For it was hoped that the farmer's activities would induce the gods to do the same, and thus produce more fruitful crops. By contrast, the God of Israel could not be bullied by magic. He had not been forced to call Abraham, or to deliver the slaves from Egypt: all that he did arose from his own spontaneous love and care for his people.

● The Canaanite view encouraged the assumption that religion had nothing to do with behaviour in normal life, but only with the special ritual that was performed in the shrines. This notion is still widely held today. But it runs completely contrary to the Old Testament's understanding of God. The God of Israel was not most concerned with the empty performance of hollow rituals, but with the way people behave in everyday life. This lesson was hammered home over and over again by the prophets, as they declared that Israel's religious duty was not something that took place in a shrine, but in the market-place: 'to do what is just, to show constant love, and to live in humble fellowship with our God' (Micah 6:8).

● In view of this, it is not surprising that Israel's God demanded exclusive worship. The gods and goddesses of Canaan were always tolerant of other gods – they were, in a sense, their own relatives! But the God of Israel had demanded the exclusive obedience of his people (Exodus 20:1–3). And now that we can understand the nature of Baal worship, it is not difficult to see why the writers of the Old Testament were so adamant in emphasizing this.

worshipped the Canaanite deities instead. Others tried to amalgamate the two, while yet others worshipped mainly Yahweh, but felt obliged to use Canaanite shrines and Canaanite rituals in doing so. The texts from Ugarit have shown that the denunciations of Israel by the great prophets were far from exaggerated. But the extent of the compromise that was made is clear from the Old Testament itself. Even the leading Israelite families could give their children Canaanite names. One of the sons of Saul was Jonathan ('Gift of Yahweh'), but another was Ish-Baal ('Man of Baal') – while the names of Baal and Anat were attached to many Israelite towns and villages.

It is not surprising that the Israelites were tempted to adopt Canaanite ways

4 A king like the other nations

1 and 2 Samuel　　**Proverbs**
1 Kings 1:1—12:20　**Ecclesiastes**
Psalms　　　　　　**Job**
Song of Solomon

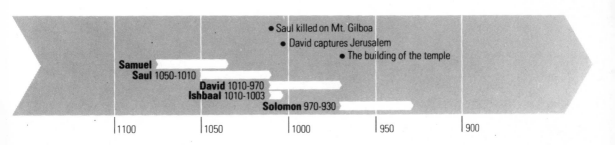

Saul killed on Mt. Gilboa
David captures Jerusalem
The building of the temple

Samuel
Saul 1050-1010
David 1010-970
Ishbaal 1010-1003
Solomon 970-930

1100　　1050　　1000　　950　　900

Psalm 74:12

'YOU HAVE been our king from the beginning, O God; you have saved us many times.' The words were written centuries later, but they sum up well enough the ideals of the early days of Israel's history. Though the tribes may from time to time have their human leaders, in the end God himself was their only true sovereign. Even the great judges were not important in themselves. They were just men and women whom God had inspired to lead their people in times of special need.

The judges themselves recognized this. When some of the tribes suggested to Gideon that his bravery and courage deserved the reward of a permanent position of power, he would have nothing to do with it. It was, he declared, impossible for his people to be ruled both by God himself and by a human king. His son Abimelech did not have the same scruples, and he managed to persuade the people of the city of Shechem to make him their king. But his success was short-lived. The tribes were determined that the monarchies of the Canaanite city-states would not form a model for Israelite society. The belief that God was their ruler was not just a pious fiction, but something that would be applied in everyday life.

Judges 8:22–23

Judges 9

The histories of the kings often concentrate on warfare, on great events, the life of the towns. But Israelite society was still mainly rural, and normal life was lived in the village and the countryside.

The tribes were held together not by the institutions of a shared government, but by the experiences of a shared faith, symbolized by the ark of the covenant. But it was perhaps inevitable that eventually the symbol should be mistaken for the reality. The priests concerned with the common worship of the tribes now saw the opportunity to carve out a comfortable niche for themselves. They began to think of their own position and their ritual operations as the true focus of Israel's faith.

Samuel and the ark

1 Samuel 1—3

We can see from the stories about Samuel's early life that the ordinary people did not go along with this. But life at the time was so insecure that they could do little about it. For an apparently greater threat was looming: the Philistines.

While the Philistines had been establishing their position, they were held in check by neighbouring tribes or local heroes like Samson. But now they were out for the total domination of the country. They were a strong and powerful force. They had adapted the government of the Canaanite city-states to their own advantage. But they had one thing their Canaanite predecessors never had: a strong sense of national unity. Though they were independent, the Philistine cities could act in a concerted and unified way. This made them a formidable enemy. For they were also technically more advanced than Israel, and knew how to use chariots and iron weapons in war.

1 Samuel 4:1—11
1 Samuel 5:1—7:1

Both politically and militarily, Israel was less well organized than the Philistines, and could offer no effective resistance to the advancing armies. After a devastating defeat near Aphek, the leaders of the Israelite tribes realized that they were powerless. Where were the inspiring leaders and the brave exploits of previous generations? Why was their God no longer with them, as he had been with the great judges? They decided they must make certain that God went with them into battle: 'Let's go and bring the Lord's Covenant Box from Shiloh, so that he will go with us and save us from our enemies.' Unfortunately, their plan did not work out. The ark of the covenant was captured, its shrine at Shiloh destroyed, and the Israelite army was decimated.

Their religious mistake was clear enough. Following the lead of the sons of Eli the priest (who were themselves killed in the battle), they had forgotten the close personal nature of Israel's relationship to God – preferring instead to suppose that he could be contained in a box. But now the box was gone, and they were effectively the vassals of the Philistines. It seems unlikely that the Philistines wanted the whole land for themselves. They were trying to take over the position once occupied by the Egyptians: they would be the rulers, and the Israelites and Canaanites would be their subjects. That did not make it any less painful for Israel. But what could they do to get rid of them? Samuel seemed powerless, yet he was the only surviving representative of the old order. And though the ark of the covenant took its own revenge on the Philistines and was eventually returned to Israel, the old fervour and enthusiasm did not return with it. It seemed as if the old tribal alliance and its simple trust in God had failed.

Saul

Moreover, the Philistines were not the only challenge that the Israelite tribes had to face. Other groups, many of them racially related to Israel, were pressing in from the east side of the River Jordan. Among them were the Ammonites. They attacked the people of Jabesh Gilead, and made it a condition of peace that the right eye of every citizen should be put out. It was not long before this news had travelled far and wide – and a powerful army was raised from among the tribes of Israel to deal with this new threat.

The man who put new life into the Israelites was Saul. He was on his way home from the fields when he heard what was happening in Jabesh Gilead. Like the judges before him, he was moved to fury by 'the spirit of God'. He cut up the oxen he was driving, and sent the pieces throughout the whole district, with the gruesome message: 'Whoever does not follow Saul and Samuel into battle will have this done to his oxen!' So Saul rallied his army, and Jabesh Gilead was set free.

1 Samuel 11:6

1 Samuel 11:7

Up to this point, the story is quite similar to the tales told about the judges. But a new departure was made after Saul's great victory, for the people gathered at the shrine in Gilgal, and acclaimed him as their king. According to the stories in 1 Samuel, this was not a spontaneous action but the culmination of much debate among the Israelite leaders. For the appointment of a king was not something to be taken lightly. After all, if it was wrong for Gideon to be king, how could it now be right for Saul? The Old Testament reports this argument in some detail. Indeed, the two sides were put with such vigour that scholars commonly reckon they can trace two distinctive accounts of Samuel and his role in the affair:

1 Samuel 11:13–15

● In one Samuel seems to be a relatively unknown local figure, who appoints Saul as king under God's direct guidance. The monarchy will save Israel from her enemies, and for this reason is generally looked on with favour in these sections of the story.

1 Samuel 9:1—10:16; 11:1–15

● In another account Samuel seems to be a national figure, and a man who disapproves of the appointment of a king, because this would mean a rejection of God himself as the true king of Israel

1 Samuel 8:1–22; 10:17–27

We need not doubt that the editors of the book of Samuel have taken material from many different sources and incorporated it into their own story. Nor need we be surprised that they should have included what some modern readers might regard as contradictory stories. They are only contradictory if we look at them from a purely literary viewpoint. But they represent a tension that must have existed at the time, and which was never really satisfactorily resolved. On the one hand, a strong leader was needed to unite the tribes into an alliance powerful enough to fight the Philistines; but on the other, the existence of such a leader would inevitably weaken the conviction that God was Israel's only true king. This tension is clearly reflected in the stories about Saul.

In some respects, he was not so much a king as a kind of perpetual judge. It was certainly important that he should be seen to have the kind of popular appeal and military prowess that the judges had possessed. But in practical terms, Saul had his difficulties. Up

For his campaigns against the Philistines, Saul did not conscript a people's army for particular battles. Rather he recruited a fairly small professional army, paid for by taxation.

to this point, the main military force in Israel had been the large army of volunteers from the tribes. It was with such a spontaneously recruited force that Saul had been able to avenge the people of Jabesh Gilead. But this kind of arrangement was only for great emergencies. It was not the way for a king to operate. Nor was it altogether practical to get rid of the Philistines in this way. Guerilla warfare would be far more effective than large pitched battles – and for that, a small body of professional soldiers would be much more suitable than a large force of untrained volunteers. So, like the the Philistine and Canaanite kings, Saul formed his own personal army.

1 Samuel 13:2;14:52

By all accounts it was a successful move, for he was able to drive the Philistines at least from the hill country, which gave him greater

1 Samuel 13—14

freedom of movement. But this military efficiency was bought at a price. For though Saul lacked most of the trappings of the oriental monarch, and even his headquarters at Gibeah was by no means a palace, he was separating himself from his people. His professional army owed its allegiance not to the tribes in general, but to Saul himself as its commander in chief. Since Saul appears to have had no resources of his own, he must have needed someone else to pay for the army – and that meant the tribes. Though there is no direct evidence for it in the Old Testament, he was probably forced to raise some kind of taxation from his people. It could well have been financial stringency that forced Saul to disregard Samuel's instructions about the goods of the defeated Amalekites. But as a result of this, Saul came to be regarded as a headstrong, selfish man who put his own will and wisdom before the will of God, and who was too ready to jettison the old religious ideals when they interfered with his own military strategy.

1 Samuel 15:1–35

If Saul's army had been successful against the Philistines, his life might well have turned out differently. But he made very little headway against the well-organized Philistine armies, and in terms

Right: The kingdom of Saul

Far right: The kingdom of David

Trade in Solomon's time

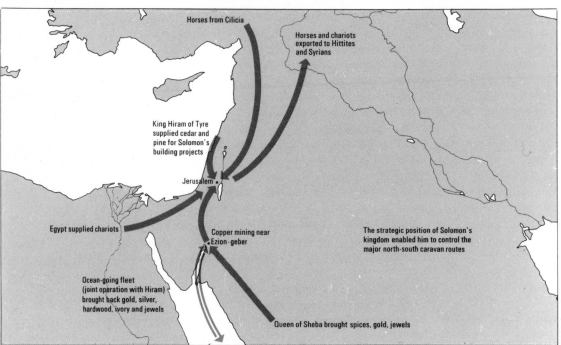

of territory, Saul was very much a king without a kingdom. The three Canaanite cities of Jerusalem, Aijalon and Gezer still separated the centre of the country from the south, and to the north the strategic Plain of Jezreel was still controlled by the Philistines.

In order to survive, Saul needed to be a king over people rather than territory. But he had lost much of his popular support by choosing to enlist his own personal army. No doubt he could have regained his initial popularity if he had not been overtaken by jealousy and suspicion of one of his young subjects, a shepherd called David. The deep depression to which this led suggests that by the end of his life Saul was mentally deranged. He died a lonely and forlorn figure by his own sword after a crushing defeat at the hands of the Philistines on Mt Gilboa. The complexity of Saul's personality eludes us, but he emerges as a tragic figure. He had great potential as the recognized successor to the judges, but the nature of the conflict in which he was involved more or less forced him to go against the old tribal ideals of his people – and led to his downfall.

'Has even Saul become a prophet?'

The question arises out of an incident recorded in 1 Samuel 10:5–13. After being anointed by Samuel, Saul went up to worship at the sanctuary of Gibeah, and as he was on his way he encountered a group of prophets who were shouting and dancing to frenzied music, in some sort of religious ecstasy. Quite unexpectedly, Saul himself was caught up in the same excitement, and he too joined in their dancing and singing. This was such an unexpected turn of events that bystanders spoke of Saul becoming 'a different person' under the influence of this religious enthusiasm, and many expressed their surprise that a reputable person like him should become mixed up with it all.

The fact that this could happen to Saul will probably surprise no one today. We all know of religious groups whose fervour and excitement leads them into wild and uncontrollable behaviour of this sort – often stimulated by music, as was the case here.

Many readers of the Old Testament, however, are surprised to see people like this described as 'prophets'. For the typical prophet of the Old Testament is not a person who indulges in religious excitement: he is a person with a message from God to his people, who expresses that message in clear language, appealing not to the emotions of his hearers but to their reason and sense of religious commitment.

A number of observations can be made on this issue:

● Some have drawn attention to the statement in 1 Samuel 9:9, that 'At that time a prophet was called a seer . . . ' A seer would be someone who tried to discover God's will by semi-magical means – much like a modern fortune-teller. Perhaps then, it is argued, the confusion is just a matter of terminology, and the great classical prophets with their incisive comments on social and political affairs simply evolved over a period of time out of such unsophisticated practitioners. There are certainly some statements in the Old Testament that could be taken to support this view. Amos, for example, seems to distinguish himself from a 'prophet' who would give messages for money (Amos 7:14), while Micah 3:6–7 seems to refer to the same sort of people.

● At the same time, some passages do seem to refer to ecstatic experiences in the lives of the great prophets. Even Jeremiah was described as a 'madman' (admittedly, by his enemies, Jeremiah 29:26–27.) Hosea was accused in much the same way (Hosea 9:7) – and some of the experiences of these later prophets (especially people like Ezekiel) were certainly most unusual. We also know of at least one occasion when the prophet Elisha gave his message to the accompaniment of music (2 Kings 3:15–19), while the behaviour of one of his fellow prophets provoked a king of Israel to call him 'that crazy fellow' (2 Kings 9:11).

● There are parallels to all this in other cultures of the time. From the Old Testament itself we have a description of the behaviour of the prophets of Baal, who sought to invoke the power of their god by a self-induced religious ecstasy (1 Kings 18:20–29). Unfortunately we know very little about such people in Canaan itself. But we do have some evidence from Mari in the form of a series of letters dating from the eighteenth century BC. They concern a wide variety of prophetic functions, one of the most important of which was the encouragement of a king in times of particular difficulty – especially the giving of advice in times of war. It is perhaps significant here that we find mention of prophets advising kings elsewhere in the Old Testament, though their advice (as at Mari) was not always what their masters wanted (2 Samuel 12:1–15; 1 Kings 22:1–28).

What then are we to make of all this? One possibility is that these bands of ecstatic enthusiasts arose spontaneously as a means of inspiring the people of Israel in times of great difficulty. And no time was more difficult for them than the time of Saul, with the threat of the Philistines hanging over them. This function of these ecstatics may later have been continued and refined in those prophets who were attached to the royal courts of Israel and Judah. Their precise relationship with the great preaching prophets of the Old Testament is still uncertain. But both types of prophet obviously thought of themselves as the communicators of a message from God to his people.

David

David was made of different stuff from Saul. He was a charismatic figure in every sense of the word, and would overcome tribal suspicions and resistance to the idea of a king, to unite the whole of Israel into a remarkably powerful alliance.

When the Old Testament stories were first written down, David was already Israel's greatest national hero. He was the traditional composer of Israel's best-loved songs (the Psalms), and the man about whom many of the most popular stories were told. We can see this in the way the writer of the book of Samuel introduces him to his narrative. In contrast to the stories of Saul, the accounts of David's life have been composed with great artistry and literary skill. The stories of his friendship with Saul's son Jonathan, and of his unexpected defeat of the Philistine giant Goliath have become favourites even with modern readers.

1 Samuel 19—20
1 Samuel 17

David's rise to power

David was obviously a striking character. Not many shepherds become kings, and he must have had some extraordinary talent to rise so quickly to a position of such eminence in Saul's court. The features that impressed Saul also impressed his people, and it was not long before they were singing David's praises in the streets: 'Saul has killed thousands, but David tens of thousands'. This kind of popularity aroused Saul to intense jealousy, and so he dismissed David from the court, giving him instead the command of a thousand soldiers in his private army. But David could not be held back. His military exploits were amazing, and 'everyone in Israel and Judah loved David because he was such a successful leader'. His admirers even included Saul's daughter Michal, who fell in love with David and married him. But Saul became more and more envious, and set out deliberately to kill him. As a result, David was forced to go into exile, in the south of the country.

There he was secure from Saul, for between them lay a number of fortified Canaanite city-states, including Jerusalem. In the south, David probably forged some sort of alliance with the Philistines, for he was able to organize a kind of court at Adullam and to protect

1 Samuel 18:7

1 Samuel 18:16

1 Samuel 18:17–27

1 Samuel 19—22

1 Samuel 22:1–2

At Ein Gedi by the Dead Sea, a stream flows down a gorge to the shore. The whole area abounds in caves, and this is the region where David hid from Saul and his soldiers during the years of his exile from court.

1 Samuel 25

1 Samuel 27

himself and his troops by running a protection racket. He also strengthened his position here by marriage alliances, and obviously became closely involved with Achish, the Philistine king of Gath. Achish wanted to take David with him to the battle of Gilboa, where Saul met his death. But he was left behind when his loyalty was questioned by the other Philistine chiefs. They were right to do

1 Samuel 29

so, for David had been playing a double game with Achish. But it turned out to David's advantage. For while the Philistines had been arguing about David, Amalekite raiders had attacked the town of Ziklag. On his return, David went out to avenge his people. He took back all that the Amalekites had taken, and more besides – and then tactfully distributed it among the people of the towns where he

1 Samuel 30

was best known.

1 Samuel 31

Saul was finished. He died in disgrace, and for all practical purposes, his kingdom fell into the hands of the Philistines. But David's position was assured. He had already established himself among the southern tribes, and he was now recognized as their leader – the king of Judah, reigning at Hebron. The southern tribes of Judah had always been isolated from the northern tribes, and they had probably never been a full part of Saul's kingdom. So they had no qualms about accepting David. He had already shown his prowess in battle, and he continued to protect the people for a further seven-and-a-half years.

2 Samuel 2:10–11

But David was not satisfied with this. He knew that Israel would never be truly great until northern and southern tribes were fully united. In the north, Saul's son Ishbaal (Ishbosheth) had taken his father's place. But he had no popular support. In his fury against David, Saul had gone so far as to kill the priests who looked after the tribal sanctuary at Nob. That in itself was enough to ensure that no son of his would ever be acclaimed by the tribes. Ishbaal's only real supporter was Abner, the commander of Saul's personal army. And when even he defected to David's side, Ishbaal was finished. David agreed to become king of all the Israelite tribes, and the northern group gave their allegiance to him. The Philistines could see what was coming. They did not like the idea of a united kingdom of Israel, and they moved in to try to cut the links between north and south. But they were defeated many times, and from then onwards the kingdom of David was the dominant political force in Palestine.

1 Samuel 22

2 Samuel 2:8 — 4:12

2 Samuel 5:1–5

2 Samuel 5:17–25

A new king and new ways

Jerusalem was captured by David, who moved his capital there from Hebron. Known ever since as 'the city of David', Jerusalem became and has remained the focus of devotion for the people of Israel.

A new kingdom needed a new capital. Hebron was too far in the south, and the north had no organization to speak of since the defeat at Gilboa and the murder of Ishbaal. So David found a new capital in Jerusalem. It was a masterly stroke. This city had belonged to neither northern nor southern tribes, and so it would not engender new jealousies. It had been one of the last remaining bastions of Canaanite sovereignty that had effectively isolated north from south during the time of Saul. So its brilliant capture by David's troops, climbing up a water shaft into the city, also removed one of the last physical barriers to the unity of the new kingdom.

2 Samuel 5:6–10

It was therefore 'the city of David' in a distinctive way. He built new fortifications, and a palace for himself. He employed foreign craftsmen for the work, and established a relationship with the Phoenicians that was to last for some considerable time. Unfortunately, very little remains now of the Jerusalem of David's time. But there can be no doubt that he and his successor Solomon transformed it into a major administrative centre, probably aided by the considerable bureaucratic expertise of its original Jebusite inhabitants, who were now incorporated into the kingdom of Israel. This was just a small section of a fairly large foreign population that became a part of David's kingdom. For as he extended his influence in all directions, he defeated Edomites, Moabites, Ammonites, and Syrians, as well as Philistines – and their towns and people gave their allegiance to David.

2 Samuel 5:11–12

The spoils captured in these military expeditions, and the taxes paid to him by conquered peoples, financed the erection of many fine buildings in Jerusalem. It also enabled David to increase the number of mercenaries in his personal army, and to establish a full royal court at his new palace. But he was always careful to preserve those all-important links with his people's past. One of his earliest acts was to bring the ark of the covenant to Jerusalem. To the tribes, this had always been the central symbol of their whole existence. It reminded them of their escape from Egypt, of their covenant with God at Mt Sinai, and of the common worship of Yahweh their God that held them together.

2 Samuel 6

We need not doubt that David's religious commitment played an important part in all this. But the arrival of the ark of the covenant in Jerusalem also had social consequences. It gave David's own position a special seal of approval. More than that, for in a sense, the ark installed in David's city now became David's personal possession. It certainly removed the power centre from the tribes themselves, and vested it in a state authority that was separate from the old tribal loyalties. In other words, David achieved what Saul had failed to do: he established his own position independently of the continued acclamation of the people. The nation was controlled by his own army, with his own city – even, perhaps, his own national shrine at the centre of things.

David was undoubtedly a great leader: a military strategist who overcame Israel's enemies, and a politician who brought the people of the whole of Palestine to a unity never known before – and certainly never since – under a ruler of their own race. Admittedly, this was made easier by the relative weakness of Egypt and Assyria at the time. But David's achievement was still remarkable.

The old ways and new ideas

2 Samuel 11

David was, however, vulnerable. One of the most significant stories told about him in the Old Testament is of his adultery with Bathsheba and the murder of her husband Uriah. It was not unusual for an oriental king to behave like this. But it is surprising to find the bold denunciation of David's behaviour by the prophet Nathan, and the deep sincerity of David's subsequent repentance. Even David was to be subject to a greater power than himself. But his position itself was not threatened. For on a previous occasion, Nathan had declared that God would make a specially close personal relationship with David's family. Not only would David's son succeed him, but God himself would be 'his father, and he will be my son'. And David was assured that God would 'make your kingdom last for ever. Your dynasty will never end'.

2 Samuel 12:1–15

2 Samuel 7:1–17

2 Samuel 7:14

2 Samuel 7:16

Many kings in the ancient world, especially in Mesopotamia, thought of themselves as sons of the gods. But whereas for them, this idea often became a crude legitimation of everything they did, in the Old Testament it established a moral framework within which the kings were to operate. The king in Jersualem was now firmly linked to the covenant relationship between God and his people established at Mt Sinai. The king was incorporated into that, and this gave him special privileges. But he was also faced with the moral requirements of the Sinai covenant, and his position as God's 'son' meant he could be punished by God, just as any other parent would punish his children for wrongdoing.

2 Samuel 7:14

Inevitably, the kings of David's dynasty did not live up to these high aspirations. They were, after all, only human – and the tragedy, as Samuel had foreseen, was that the kings of Israel were to become like the kings of other nations, more often concerned for themselves than for their covenant obligations to God and to their people. But this promise to David and his family was to assume great importance at a later stage in Israel's history, as frustrated political ambitions came to be transferred to a future hope for an ideal descendant of David, the Messiah.

1 Samuel 8:10–18

Solomon

2 Samuel 13—19

2 Samuel 20:1–22

1 Kings 1:5–10

1 Kings 1:11—2:46

Towards the end of David's reign, the prospective heirs began to jockey for position. Revolts led by David's son Absalom and by Sheba, a man from the tribe of Benjamin, were crushed, and by the time of David's death his son Adonijah was the most obvious successor. He had the support of Abiathar the priest and Joab, who was commander of the popular army drawn from the Israelite tribes. But another son, Solomon, had more powerful friends. His mother Bathsheba had been David's favourite wife, and she was supported by Nathan, the priest Zadok, and Benaiah, the commander of David's personal army. In the end, Solomon won. With the exception of Abiathar the priest, who was sent off into exile, Adonijah and all his supporters were killed. Right from the start, Solomon's position as king was founded on court intrigues and military strength. Unlike his father David, and Saul before him, he did not seek popular acceptance by the tribes, and in Solomon Israel certainly got a king like the kings of the other nations around them. Unlike Saul and the Judges (and, to a lesser extent, David), Solomon was not a leader among equals, but the figurehead of a new ruling class that was determined to maintain its position of superiority by whatever means were necessary. For the first time, Israel was a state, rather than a nation, and this led to far-reaching changes in Israelite society.

The empire

1 Kings 11:14–25

1 Kings 4:26; 10:26

Solomon did not continue the military conquests of David. Indeed, there is evidence to suggest that both the Edomites and the Syrians recovered some territory from Israel during Solomon's reign. Solomon was more concerned with the defence of his own position than the defence of his people. So he poured vast resources into the development of the private army that his father had left to him. What had probably been in David's day little more than a personal bodyguard for the king now developed into a sophisticated fighting force, with 1,400 chariots and 12,000 men and horses. Chariots had once been the monopoly of the Canaanite city-states, and it was this more than anything else that had prevented the tribes in the days of the Judges from penetrating to the plains in the centre of the country. Solomon probably utilized Canaanite expertise in such weapons, for his own chariots were stationed exclusively in the Old Canaanite cities.

Alliances

1 Kings 9:16–17

1 Kings 9:26–28; 10:22

1 Kings 10:28–29

This perhaps opened the door for Canaanite influences in Israel. But foreign influence was to be felt more particularly in Solomon's trading activities. He traded with Phoenicia, with Arabia, with Syria and Cilicia, and probably with north and east Africa too. He allied himself with Egypt by marrying an Egyptian princess. This must have been an important alliance, for he had a special palace built for his Egyptian wife. The pharaoh of the time also took it seriously, for he captured the city of Gezer and gave it to Solomon as a wedding gift. This is the latest occasion we know of when Israel acquired a Canaanite city, and the archaeological evidence from Gezer shows clearly enough how the Egyptians destroyed it, and how Solomon rebuilt it in a distinctive style.

Another of Solomon's close allies was Hiram, king of Tyre. The Phoenicians had widespread trading links throughout the Mediterranean Sea, and they gave Solomon assistance to develop his own sea trade in the Red Sea and the Indian Ocean. They also probably helped him with the expertise necessary to build and operate his own copper refineries on the Gulf of Aqabah. Solomon was also a horse dealer on a grand scale, trading with the Egyptians in the south and the Hittites in the north.

The temple

2 Samuel 7:1–17

2 Samuel 24:18–25; 2 Chronicles 3:1

The profits from all this activity helped to finance the erection of many buildings in Jerusalem – Solomon's own palace, a palace for his Egyptian wife, a hall of audience for state occasions, a smaller judgement hall. And, of course, the temple.

David had originally wanted to build a permanent temple to house the ark of the covenant. He had been unable to do so, but that did not stop him securing a site and gathering together items to go into a temple. Solomon was remembered by later generations of

Israelites largely because of his completion of this project. Like everything else that he attempted, the work was carried out on a lavish scale. The best materials were imported at great cost, and skilled craftsmen were brought in from Phoenicia. Naturally, they used their own art forms in its construction, and the general design of the temple they produced was thoroughly Canaanite. Though it was to contain the ark of the covenant, which symbolized the presence of Israel's God Yahweh, the actual plan of the temple was identical to temples of Baal that have been discovered elsewhere in Palestine.

1 Kings 5—7

Some have also suggested that Solomon adopted the same attitude to the temple as the rulers of Ugarit took to their own temple of Baal. They point out that the Jerusalem temple was consecrated at exactly the same time in the year as the Baal temple at Ugarit, just before the beginning of the all-important autumn rains. And it is beyond doubt that Solomon took upon himself some of the most important religious functions. He offered sacrifices and he blessed the people. Yet Saul and David had been expressly forbidden to do both these things – and Saul's attempt to do so had led directly to his downfall. Because of the central importance later attached to Jerusalem and its temple, the writer of the book of Kings makes no comment on these particular features of Solomon's kingship. But he does criticize what many saw as Solomon's active promotion of the interests of 'foreign gods'. His careless disregard for the faith of the tribes must have been a major factor in his eventual downfall. Solomon may have been renowned for his wisdom, but it was not the kind of practical wisdom that led to a sympathetic understanding of his own people, or to an appreciation of the kind of king that Israel's faith would tolerate.

1 Kings 6:1, 37–38; 8:2
1 Kings 3:15; 8:62–66
1 Kings 8:14–61
1 Samuel 15:10–35

1 Kings 11:1–13

Arts and sciences

The 'wisdom' attributed to Solomon was in fact not just common sense and insight. It was rather part and parcel of a great international intellectual movement of the day that is often simply referred to as the 'wisdom movement'. The writer of 1 Kings explicitly compares Solomon's 'wisdom' with that of other ancient rulers: 'Solomon was wiser than the wise men of the East or the wise men of Egypt. He was the wisest of all men . . . ' And the nature of this intellectual endeavour becomes clearer when we learn that 'He composed three thousand parables and more than a thousand songs. He spoke of trees and plants . . . he talked about animals, birds, reptiles, and fish'. This is comparable with the intellectual pursuits of kings and philosophers in ancient Egypt and Mesopotamia, who compiled encyclopedic descriptions of the world and all its affairs – from astrology to botany and politics. The knowledge thus gained was sometimes distilled into pithy sayings, such as we find in the Old Testament book of Proverbs, parts of which are said to have been composed by Solomon himself. In a later period, professional 'wise men' could be found as religious advisers whose position was comparable to that of a priest. But at this stage the pursuit of 'wisdom' was probably a secular interest.

1 Kings 4:30–31

1 Kings 4:32–33

Proverbs 10:1; 25:1

Jeremiah 18:18

Solomon's temple

Winged creatures
Ark of the covenant
The Most Holy Place

Store rooms
The Holy Place

Porch

Free-standing pillars

Bronze tank

In building the temple, Solomon used the best and costliest materials. He bought timber from Hiram, King of Tyre, who supplied the famous Lebanon cedarwood, used also for temple building in Egypt and Assyria.

All.this activity stimulated the development of other literary skills in Israel. We know that Solomon had his own official archivists who recorded the events of his reign. It is also widely believed that the stories of Samuel, Saul and David were written down in a continuous narrative at this time. It is certainly not unlikely that a successful king would want to record the events that led up to his accession to the throne. Many scholars also believe that as a reaction against all this self-centred artistic and intellectual endeavour, other writers during Solomon's reign wove the traditional stories handed down by the tribes into a great epic account of Israel's earliest history – to emphasize again how Abraham, Moses, and the early tribes had prospered not because of their own efforts, but because of their humble dependence on the love and goodness of God in choosing them to be his own people.

1 Kings 11:41

Balancing the books

There was certainly a strong build-up of ill feeling and resentment against the style of Solomon's rule. It was bad enough that his actions should violate so many of the old tribal ways. But the people saw no reason why in addition they should actually pay for his extravagance through taxation. Yet it was inevitable, for Solomon's trading activities could not generate sufficient funds to finance the life of his court. On occasion, he could try to pay off his creditors by offering them land. This is what he tried to do with Hiram of Tyre, but the towns he offered were refused. So the people had to pay for their king.

1 Kings 9:10–14

The administrative framework for the collection of taxes already existed, for David had inaugurated a modest system whereby twelve

The wealth of Solomon's kingdom and his extended alliances made Israel into a major trading nation.

different districts of his territory would support his court with provisions for one month each year. Solomon extended this to provide the means for collecting taxes, and each district was placed in the charge of a single officer. The idea did not appeal to the people. It was not just that they were reluctant to pay their dues. To them, the very idea of a privileged elite being served and paid for by the ordinary citizens was a fundamental denial of the traditions of their people. At Mt Sinai, their ancestors had stood as equals before God. They had all been slaves. And the development of Israelite tribal society in the days of the judges had sought to express that. But now the old ways were being eroded: instead of twelve tribes serving God, there were twelve districts serving the king. And the fact that the worshippers of Baal at Ugarit had a very similar way of supporting their own royal house can only have served to emphasize the essentially pagan nature of the idea.

1 Kings 4:7–19

But there was worse to come. The taxation raised in the districts was still not enough to balance Solomon's books. So he introduced what the Old Testament euphemistically calls 'forced labour' – in other words, slavery. This was the last straw, and a coup was planned by one of the officers in charge of the taxation districts – a man called Jeroboam. His plot was uncovered, and he fled into exile in Egypt for a while. But the movement that he started could not be stopped. The tribes in the northern part of Solomon's kingdom – the original tribes who had chosen Saul as their leader – had had enough. Not only did they regard Solomon's demands as excessive, but they believed them to be unfair, for the southern tribes – who first made David their king – appear to have been excluded from the taxation districts altogether.

1 Kings 5:13; 11:28

1 Kings 11:26–40

1 Kings 4:7–19

So the seeds of Solomon's destruction were sown. Judged by the standards of world powers, Solomon was outstandingly successful, the greatest of all Isael's rulers. But judged by the moral and spiritual standards of the covenant, he was a miserable failure.

The stories about David and Solomon

The books of Samuel and Kings belong together. They are a compilation of different stories, brought together by an editor or editors to make one great account of Israel's history, that probably included the books of Joshua and Judges as well. Quite often, the editors refer to their sources of information (e.g. 1 Kings 11:41). At other points, modern scholars have tried to uncover the origins of their stories. This can often be an unprofitable exercise, but in the case of the stories of David and Solomon many people believe that such 'source analysis' can show that we are actually reading a kind of 'court history' that was written down more or less at the same time as the events themselves happened.

The stories in 2 Samuel 9 — 20 and 1 Kings 1 — 2 are undoubtedly among the most vivid narratives in the whole Old Testament. They are well written and excitingly presented, with the kind of psychological appreciation of human relationships that gives an added plausibility to what they say. In this respect they are quite different from what precedes or follows them – and even from the final chapters of 2 Samuel itself (21 — 24).

In 1926, the German scholar Leonhard Rost suggested that this section of Samuel and Kings was originally a self-contained story, and that it was originally written to prove that Solomon was the legitimate heir to David's throne. There is no doubt that the accession of Solomon is surprising, for he was a relatively minor son, and apart from a short notice of his birth in 2 Samuel 12:24–25 there is no mention of him before he became king. He also came to power through a court intrigue, and by murdering his opponents – and, Rost suggested, many loyal Israelites must have been asking awkward questions about the morality of all this. So a supporter of Solomon set out to justify his position – and,in the nature of things, he must have done so at an early date in Solomon's reign.

There was a well established tradition of such political apologetic among other nations at the time, especially the Hittites. So, encouraged by international contacts, and the new opportunities for artistic endeavour provided by Solomon's court, Solomon's friend took the older traditional stories about David's reign, and showed how the elder sons Amnon, Absalom, and Adonijah, had all disqualified themselves by their disregard for the covenant traditions (2 Samuel 13:8–14; 16:22; 1 Kings 2:13–17). This was why Solomon emerged as David's successor – and the brutal events which brought him to power were a regrettable but necessary evil.

Rost hailed this narrative as the beginning of real history writing in the ancient world. But more recent scholars have qualified his judgement. They point out, for example, that these stories contain much that is unfavourable to David and Solomon – and therefore, perhaps what we now have is a kind of expurgated version of a series of stories that originally disapproved of the Davidic dynasty. But this carries no weight if the original intention was apologetic: in such a situation, unfortunate facts have to be faced, and explained away in some way or another. But it has also been suggested that much of the material is more like a novel than real history. It certainly includes some surprising details – like the conversation that Amnon had with Tamar when he raped her (2 Samuel 13:1–21). But this does not call into question the general veracity of the narrative. It simply shows that it was written in the first instance by a journalist rather than an annalist. This in turn perhaps suggests that it was not really the official court record of David, but a popular account of Solomon's origins, designed to win the support of the average person in the street for the new king.

After Solomon

When Solomon died he was succeeded by his son, Rehoboam. But by then an irreversible change of mood had come over the northern tribal grouping. They had had enough of dynastic kingship, and they were looking for a return to the old ideal in which the people, and not an elite ruling class, would decide their own fate.

So when Rehoboam went north from Jerusalem to Shechem to secure the allegiance of the northern tribes, their local leaders announced the terms on which they would be prepared to acknow-

1 Kings 12:1–7

ledge him as their king. Rehoboam's oldest and most experienced advisers told him to listen sympathetically. But he rejected their advice, and told the northern leaders that worse was to come: 'My father placed heavy burdens on you; I will make them even heavier.

1 Kings 12:14

He beat you with a whip; I'll flog you with a horsewhip!' He regarded them as rebellious subjects, and got ready to force them

1 Kings 12:21–24

back into line. But it was too late. Jeroboam had already returned from Egypt, and the people had accepted him as their king.

It was an irreversible change. From this point onwards, the northern tribes had their own king and their own kingdom – Israel. And the descendants of David in Jerusalem ruled over a much smaller kingdom in the south – Judah. Israel's golden age was past. She had asked for 'a king like the other nations' without fully appreciating the distinctive nature of the society that God had established in the covenant at Mt Sinai. And in a choice between king and covenant, the covenant must come first.

Society and religion in the days of the kings

The years between Saul and Solomon saw the establishment of a distinctively Israelite society for the first time. Despite the problems that it caused, the idea of a monarchy was accepted, and even when the ten tribes broke away under Jeroboam they did little to change the outward forms of the society established by Solomon: they simply explained them in a different way.

So it is to be expected that the events of these difficult years should have set the pattern for Israel's life for many years to come. As we read the Old Testament books, that is precisely what we find. Perhaps nowhere is this more obvious than in the case of the Psalms and the 'wisdom literature' of the Old Testament. For though the editors of Israel's history books could see much to be ashamed of in the activities of David and Solomon, both of them soon came to be revered in the religious tradition of their people. David was credited with the authorship of much of the Old Testament book of Psalms, while Solomon was thought of as the founder of the 'wisdom movement' in ancient Israel. Not many scholars today would accept such traditions at their face value. But in the last fifty years or so, many people have been convinced that these kings and their successors in Jerusalem exerted a considerable influence on the religious and cultural life of their people.

It is not our intention here to consider in any detail the important religious message of these Old Testament books. That is dealt with more exhaustively in the companion to this book, which is entitled *The Old Testament Faith*. But it is appropriate here to notice some aspects of the picture they provide of religious life and culture in ancient Israel.

The divided kingdom

ISRAEL

• Samaria

Jerusalem •

JUDAH

The Psalms

The Old Testament book of Psalms consists of 150 separate pieces of religious poetry or songs, arranged in five separate sections, or 'books'. As a collection, they were probably brought together for use in the worship of the restored temple that was built in Jerusalem about 520 BC, after the Jewish exile in Babylon (see chapter seven).

Psalm 137

Naturally, some of the psalms were written at that time. But the majority were not, and it is widely agreed that they originated in the worship of God by ancient Israel during the period from about 1000 BC to 586 BC. Many of the psalms have titles, but these were not a part of the original compositions, and are rightly relegated to footnotes in modern versions such as the *Good News Bible* . Some of these titles contain musical directions, indicating the tune to which particular compositions were to be sung, or the musical instruments used to accompany them. Others indicate that a particular psalm was connected with David, the sons of Korah, Sons of Asaph, and others. The precise meaning of such ascriptions is often unclear. Even the term 'A psalm of David' could just as easily mean 'A psalm for David', and may not necessarily have been intended as a claim that he was its author. Such a title could also indicate that the psalm in question originally belonged to a collection of songs issued by the Davidic royal house in Jerusalem, or that it was written for the king there, who was of course always David's descendant. Most scholars today would not rule out the possibility that some of these psalms could go back to David himself. But we really have no way of being sure.

Life is always a kaleidoscope of conflicting experiences and emotions – and we find this variety reflected in the contents of the Old Testament psalms. Not all psalms are the same. Some of them are majestic hymns of praise to God, reflecting the joy of the

Psalms 145—150

jubilant worshipper who is at peace with God and with the world. By contrast, others reflect the darker moments of human experience. Sometimes the worshipper recognized his or her own guilt as

Psalms 51;130

the cause of the trouble. But on other occasions the worshipper protests that he is truly innocent, and ought not to be suffering in

Psalms13;71

the first place. Such emotions are familiar to us all, for they are part and parcel of life in every place and at every time.

In other psalms, we can see how the whole nation might react in a

Psalms 44; 74; 80; 83

time of national disaster or uncertainty. We can also share in the great ceremonial events of national life, like the coronation or

Psalm 45

wedding of a king – while yet other psalms give us a glimpse into the heartfelt gratitude to God felt by an individual worshipper who

Psalms 30; 92; 116

had been delivered from some personal trial.

In the early years of this century, the psalms were classified along these lines by a German scholar, Hermann Gunkel. These psalms, he suggested, fall into five main categories: Hymns of Praise, Individual Songs of Lament, Community Laments, Individual Songs of Thanks, and Royal Psalms. His classification has stood the test of time, though it is in some respects unsatisfactory. For example, Gunkel tended to make too sharp a distinction between individual and community psalms. A number of psalms that begin

Psalms 51; 102; 130

as the words of a single person go on to speak not just of an individual, but of the whole nation of Israel. The category of 'Royal Psalms' can also be questioned. For all the Royal Psalms could easily be fitted into other categories, and the only thing that binds them together is their apparent reference to the king.

The psalms must have been used in a number of different ways. Gunkel, for example, assumed that they were mostly personal expressions of piety – the sort of poetry that any worshipper would use to express his or her deepest feelings about life and about God. Others have argued that the psalms do not reflect individual experiences, but the experiences of the whole nation of Israel over a long period of time. It has even been suggested that they are a kind of spiritual temperature chart of Israel's history from the earliest days up to the time after the exile. Both these elements are no doubt present. But what is fundamental to the varied thoughts of the psalms is a deep religious experience that their authors knew to be relevant to the whole of life. For the sense of God's reality can come as readily from nature as from Israel's history or from the writer's own private experiences.

Psalms 8; 104
Psalms 78; 105
Psalms 31; 130

The Psalms and Israel's worship

Some scholars have suggested that the psalms were more fundamental to Israelite worship than we have suggested here, and that in them we have a detailed account of the religious activites at the Jerusalem temple in the period before the exile to Babylon. Two points in particular have contributed much to our understanding of this subject:

● Many of the psalms can be understood not just as hymns, but as more comprehensive liturgies. Not only do they reflect the praise and penitence of the worshippers – they also contain God's response to that worship (e.g.Psalms 2, 12, 20, 21, 45, 50, 81, 89, 91, 95, 108, 110, 132). These responses are often similar in both style and substance to the messages of the Old Testament prophets. And so it has been suggested that there was in the temple at Jerusalem a group of prophets whose job it was, alongside the priests, to lead the people in worship. When it was first made, this claim was a surprise to many Old Testament scholars. In the nineteenth century it had often been taken for granted that in Old Testament times the prophets and the priests were firmly opposed to each other, with the priests being concerned with the mechanical performance of rites of 'religion', while the prophets concerned themselves with true revelation – bringing a living word from God to their people. It is certainly true that most of the prophets had hard things to say about the meaningless

performance of empty religious rituals. But this sharp division between priest and prophet often owed more to the intense anti-Catholic views of the scholars who made it than it did to the evidence of the Old Testament. Even Amos, who is often thought to be one of those most fiercely opposed to religious rituals, apparently delivered his messages in the course of organized worship at Bethel. And the book of Jeremiah not only lists prophets and priests together as leaders of the community (Jeremiah 18:18), but also gives other indications of the association of prophets with the Jerusalem temple (e.g. Jeremiah 5:30–31; 23:11; 26:7,16; 27:16; 29:26). These prophets are often called 'cult prophets' to distinguish them from people like Amos or Jeremiah. In Jeremiah's time, most of them were giving false reassurance to the people, and as a result their office disappeared after the Babylonian exile. But the book of Psalms gives some indication that at an earlier period they had a full and perfectly legitimate part to play in the worship of God at the temple.

● A number of scholars have also claimed on the basis of the psalms that the king played a significant role in the worship at the temple. They observe that elsewhere in the ancient world, kings were often thought of as divine or semi-divine beings, whose well-being was crucial to the continued prosperity of their people. His involvement in religious ritual was often connected with the cycle of the seasons – as, for example, in Babylon where the king appeared in the annual New Year Festival as the personification of a god, whose ritual death and resurrection symbolized the death and renewed vitality of nature. We have already noticed a number of occasions when David and Solomon played an important part in Israelite worship – and no doubt their successors continued to do so. Of course, neither they nor their people ever thought they were divine, though they did have a special position as a result of God's blessing upon them (Psalm 2:7). Yet some still insist that there was an annual festival in Israel at which the king underwent a ritual humiliation and restoration along the lines of the Babylonian festival. The Scandinavian scholar Sigmund Mowinckel is on safer ground when he argues that the annual celebration of the New Year in Israel centred more on the enthronement of God himself, and the celebration of his continued lordship over the forces of chaos and disorder. Others however have denied this, preferring instead to see the New Year festival in Israel (the Feast of Tabernacles) as an occasion for solemn renewal of the covenant made at Mt Sinai – or even as an annual celebration of the establishment of the royal family of David. Certainly it is difficult to accept that the king in ancient Israel was exclusively, or even mainly, a religious functionary. There is no evidence to show that the Babylonian idea of kingship was widely held in the ancient world. And in addition, much of the theory relies on intelligent guesswork that lays too much emphasis on the psalms and not enough on the rest of the Old Testament. Admittedly, there is everywhere an insistence that the king of Judah has been appointed and chosen by God himself. But much of this is a theological comment on a simple fact of life, and the overall impression the Old Testament gives of the kings is of men whose activities (naturally and inevitably) had some interaction with religious worship, but whose main sphere of operation was elsewhere, in the judicial and diplomatic functions of the ancient monarch.

Wisdom

Just as David was traditionally associated with the types of religious poetry we find in the book of Psalms, so Solomon was often linked with the so-called 'Wisdom' books of the Old Testament in Jewish tradition. One such book (now contained in the Apocrypha) is actually called The Wisdom of Solomon.

Paradoxically, there is only one book in the Old Testament proper that mentions Solomon in its title – and that is not a wisdom book at all! This is the Song of Solomon. It probably has no direct connection with Solomon, other than the fact that his name occurs in it a number of times. Indeed, the way he is mentioned in these passages suggests very strongly that he was not the author of it. Its exact origins are uncertain. It contains at least one Persian word and one word that may be Greek, which would suggest it was written some time after the rise of the Persian empire in 539 BC. But it also has features that suggest a much earlier origin, while there is much evidence of similar poetry from the nations surrounding Israel, dating from long before the time of Solomon himself. It is quite likely therefore that it is really an anthology of poetry, rather than a continuous composition written at one particular point in time.

Its subject is certainly timeless – human love. It is a collection of erotic love poems, in which a woman and her lover encourage one another in their sexual relationship. Many readers of the book, both Jewish and Christian, have been alarmed by its frankness, and they have often given it a symbolic meaning – asserting that it represents

Song of Solomon 1:1,5; 3:7–11; 8:11–12

Song of Solomon 4:13

Song of Solomon 3:9

The Song of Solomon is a collection of love poems, in which a young bride and groom celebrate their love with great beauty and frankness.

the relationship between God and his people Israel, or between Christ and the church. But such ideas were certainly not in the mind of those who first included it in the Old Testament. For them, God was the creator of all things, including sexual relationships – and a collection of love poems was no more out of place than the story of God's dealings with his people in the great events of their history.

Solomon's name and influence has more often been connected with two other Old Testament books: Proverbs and Ecclesiastes. Along with the book of Job, and two other Jewish works, Ecclesiasticus and Wisdom of Solomon, these are usually classed together as 'wisdom' books.

What is wisdom?

1 Kings 3:9
1 Kings 3:9
1 Kings 5:7,12

There is no short, simple answer to this question. When Solomon is described as a 'wise man', the description seems to include many different characteristics. To be wise was 'to know the difference between good and evil'. But it also included political skills to deal with his own people and diplomacy in international relations, as well as the possession of the sort of knowledge we would associate

1 Kings 4:33
1 Kings 4:32
1 Kings 3:16–28

with a botanist or zoologist. In addition to all that, Solomon's wisdom also included the ability to write poetry and sensitivity in resolving legal disputes.

From this, it seems that when the ancients spoke of 'wisdom' they included all those elements in a person's character and upbringing that enable them to be a mature and successful member of society. In order to find a meaningful place alongside our fellow human beings, there are certain things we need to know. Nowadays, we often place most emphasis on educational achievements. We spend much time and effort in becoming proficient at particular skills, which will fit us to carry out a particular job. No doubt vocational training had its place in the life of the ancient world. But being fully equipped for life involves much more than that – and it is this that forms the substance of the wisdom literature of the Old Testament. These wisdom books reflect a broad cross-section of moral and intellectual thinking in the ancient world, and we can trace the influence of several specific life situations in their pages:

● **The Family** Many modern western people feel that it is the job of the state to prepare their children for life, both in terms of vocational training and in moral and religious teaching. But for most people elsewhere, it is in the context of the family that children can learn by both precept and example the distilled wisdom of previous generations. Here, they learn how best to relate to other people, and what not to do if they want to have a happy and fulfilled existence. All of this is based on the experience of their parents, and before them of the grandparents, who in turn learned much from their own forebears. And it was always the same in ancient Israel. Many of the sayings in the book of Proverbs certainly originated in this context and have the form of advice given by a parent to a child, such as: 'Listen to what your father teaches you, my sons . . . When I was only a little boy, my parents' only son, my father would teach me . . . Pay attention to what I say, my son. Listen to my words . . . they will give life and health to anyone who understands them. Be careful how you think; your life is shaped by your thoughts.'

Proverbs 4:1, 3–4, 20, 22–23

● **The Village** As well as being a part of a family, we are all part of a larger community in the place where we live, and much of the 'wisdom' that equips us for life is derived from our relationships in that context. Again, this is something that is becoming increasingly alien to many western peple, who live in isolation from others, often relying on the television to provide them with a sense of 'community'. But even in the west, there are still many places which have the sense of community that is widespread elsewhere in the world. In my own village in Scotland, I know where to go if I want to meet the local worthies and get their advice and opinions on the issues of the day. And this is precisely what happened in ancient Israel. Everything happened at the city or village gate. Justice was dispensed there – and it was also the forum where the great issues of life were debated. It was the place where people went to exchange views and ideas – and some of this 'wisdom' is undoubted-

The books of Proverbs and Ecclesiastes are concerned, in their very different ways, with how to find wisdom in everyday life. Though centred on life in God, much of their teaching is rooted in the practicalities of daily affairs.

ly contained in the wisdom books of the Old Testament. Job says in one of his speeches that he himself had regularly taken his place at the city gate with those who went to debate and ponder on life's

Job 29:7 great mysteries – and we can be quite sure that much of the argument contained in that book had been well rehearsed in that setting in many an Israelite settlement. Proverbs also refers to the discussions at the city gate, and no doubt much of the advice of that

Proverbs 24:7; 31:23, 31 book came from the same context.

● **The Royal Court** The sort of advice that was given in the family and at the city gate wold not be unique to Israel. People of all cultures have their equivalents, and the ancient world was no different from ours in that respect. One of the results of Solomon's great expansion of trade and international diplomacy was that the people of Israel became familiar with the 'wisdom' traditions of the surrounding nations. Just as the Queen of Sheba came to Jerusalem

1 Kings 10:1–13 to find out about Israelite wisdom, Israelites were no doubt busy discovering the wisdom of other races. There was a good deal of such wisdom literature available elsewhere, especially in Egypt. One Egyptian text has many striking similarities with parts of the

Proverbs 22:17—23:11 Old Testament book of Proverbs. It was probably in such international circles that the knowledge of 'trees and plants . . . animals,

1 Kings 4:33

birds, reptiles, and fish' was handed on. Solomon specialized in such 'wisdom', and it must have been a more intellectual pursuit than the moral advice that was evolved in the family and the village community. The more intellectual nature of such knowledge has led to the suggestion that from the time of Solomon onwards there may have been in Israel a group of professional 'wise men', whose job it was to study and teach such subjects in specialized schools. We certainly know of the existence of such people at a very much later date (about 180 BC), though their main subject of study was the Old Testament itself. But at a slightly earlier date, Jeremiah mentions 'wise men' alongside priests and prophets as leaders of the nation – and of course in the time of Solomon there were many professional diplomats, who must have been taught reading, writing and other intellectual skills by someone. So there may have been schools in ancient Israel in which knowledge was pursued for its own sake, though we cannot be certain.

Ecclesiasticus 38:24; 39:1–4

Jeremiah 18:18

The wisdom books

Like the Psalms and most of the messages of the prophets, the wisdom books are written in poetry. In Hebrew poetry the most important feature is not its metrical form, but a device known as 'parallelism', in which the ideas that are communicated are the most important thing. In the simplest form of poetry ('synonymous parallelism'), the second line of a typical couplet simply repeats in different words the thought of the first line:

> Who has the right to go up the
> Lord's hill?
> Who may enter his holy Temple?
> Psalm 24:3

'Antithetic parallelism' can make the same point by placing one part of the couplet in a positive form, and the other expressed negatively:

> Good people will be remembered
> as a blessing,
> but the wicked will soon be
> forgotten.
> Proverbs 10:7

There are many other more subtle and intricate forms of verse, and sometimes there is a parallelism just of form, and not of meaning.

Many other literary devices are used in the wisdom books. Riddles and parables, autobiographical advice, as well as dialogue (as in Job). The acrostic is also occasionally used. This is a poetic composition in which each couplet or section begins with a diffferent letter of the alphabet, starting with the first letter and working through to the end. Psalm 119 is the most striking example in the

Old Testament, but Proverbs 31:10–31 also uses the same device.

Proverbs

This book is a collection or anthology of practical wisdom. The title (1:1) attributes the book to Solomon, though it is only in one section (10:1—22:16) that Solomon is explicitly connected with its teaching. Other sections are attributed to Agur (30:1–33) and Lemuel (31:1–9), both characters of whom we know nothing. And yet other sections are presented as anonymous compositions, which is what we would expect in view of the likely origins of the kind of practical advice that the book contains.

Many of the wisdom sayings in Proverbs go back a long way into Israel's history, and were obviously composed long before the book itself was edited in its present form. The earliest date we could possibly give to this final editing would be the sixth century BC, since Hezekiah, king of Judah from 715 to 687 BC, is mentioned (25:1). But it is more likely that the final editing of Proverbs was not completed until around the third century BC.

The book is mostly concerned with advice about relationships in different areas of life. As such, it is the kind of advice about good manners and sensible behaviour that could have originated in any society. But the editor has gone out of his way to emphasize that the true meaning of such wisdom could only be found in a living relationship with God himself: 'To have knowledge, you must first have reverence for the Lord' (1:7).

Ecclesiastes

This is a very different kind of book from Proverbs. Whereas Proverbs takes an optimistic view of life, and makes a positive assessment of its potential, Ecclesiastes is essentially negative and sceptical. This need not surprise us if the wisdom books are indeed based on the distilled experiences of real people. For there can be few of us who have not stood alongside the author of Ecclesiastes and asked whether life has any real meaning, or whether instead it is not 'all useless' (1:2). The author vacillates between these two. Though he believes in God, he finds that his faith seems to give little meaning to the details of everyday life. There is no mention of Israel's history here, nor of the nation's experiences in events like the exodus, which could well have provided some sort of answer to the writer's questions. Instead, like many a modern believer in his position, he felt that the mere reiteration of traditional religious dogmas would not solve his immediate problems. But he was prepared to accept that the meaning of life could be known to God, even if it was not possible for the human mind to comprehend it all. In practical terms, 'all we can do is to be happy and do the best we can while we are still alive. All of us should eat and drink and enjoy what we have worked for. It is God's gift' (3:12–13).

The apparent unbelief of Ecclesiastes has often caused problems for Jewish and Christian readers of the book. But it does bear witness to two facts that are of fundamental importance. For it reminds us that there is a dimension of human life which we cannot understand by the exercise of our own reasoning. And it testifies to the reality of doubt and uncertainty about God and his ways, even in the midst of a community of believing people.

Ecclesiastes identifies its author as 'David's son, who was king in Jerusalem' (1:1). This was probably meant to indicate Solomon. But there are compelling reasons against supposing that he had any connection with it:

● The writer often writes from the point of view of an oppressed subject rather than that of an absolute monarch like Solomon (4:1).

● He also seems to have lived in a province of a great empire like that of the Persians, for he gives a warning against the spies of the rulers (5:8).

● Political upheavals are mentioned, but of a kind that were not experienced in Solomon's time (4:13–16).

● The Hebrew of Ecclesiastes shows clear Aramaic influences. Aramaic was the language of the Persian Empire, which suggests a date in the third or second century BC. A date in this period seems the most likely.

Job

The book of Job falls into two parts, with a prologue and epilogue written in prose (1—2, 42:7–17) and the rest in poetry. The prologue and epilogue contains an old story about Job. He was an upright and God-fearing man, who was also 'the richest man in the East' (1:3). But then in a series of inexplicable calamities he lost all that he had and was himself afflicted with a dreadful disease. This part of the story depicts God as the president of a heavenly court, and explains Job's sufferings by reference to an accusation brought against Job by the prosecutor, Satan. The charge was that Job was pious only because he found that piety paid. So he was put to the test to verify his faith – and, at the end of the story (42:7–17), Job's proverbial patience was rewarded by renewed prosperity and happiness. Some features of this story (such as the part played by Satan) suggest a fairly late date in Jewish history. But other features seem to set it in a very early historical context. Perhaps it was an ancient story that was adapted by a later wisdom writer, to provide an opportunity for the exploration of the place of suffering and evil which forms the major part of the book.

Job is clearly not a wisdom book in the same sense as Proverbs. Indeed, it seriously questions the easy-going optimism found in much of that book, with its assumption that doing good will lead to success and prosperity. For Job it had led to just the opposite, and though his friends tried to convince him of the truth of the conventional view, he would have none of it. But this was not the only problem with which Job contended. For in the midst of his suffering, he was also wrestling with the same problems as the writer of Ecclesiastes. Far from finding God in these adversities, Job felt abandoned by the very God whom he had so diligently served. Where was God, he asked – indeed, what sort of a God was he to leave his servant apparently at the mercy of a meaningless and evil universe?

Job's friends had no answer to that question. Nor is any answer given to it. For when the writer records God's answer to Job, there is no question of his

The book of Job deals in dramatic form with the universal problem of sorrow and suffering. How can the just God allow us to experience so much pain?

giving an explanation either of Job's suffering or of the apparent meaninglessness of life. Instead he emphasizes in majestic poetry the grandeur and greatness of both God and the world – and in doing so he turns Job's thoughts away from himself and directs them to the majesty of God and his creation (38—41). And in the face of this self-revelation of God's character and personality, Job recognizes that the only response to make is one of trust and worship. The 'why' of human suffering was not answered as an intellectual question. It is never answered in that way anywhere in the Bible. Job's friends held a common view. They believed that a person whose life was full of suffering

must be a great sinner. But the writer of the book of Job had no time for such easy assumptions. No one could *explain* the presence of evil in God's world. But they could face up to it in the strength that God gives. For the book of Job does have a message to those who suffer undeservedly. As Job realized he could never resolve his own predicament, and was forced to rely on God alone, he found his broken heart was healed as God burst into his life and assured him again of his constant care and love.

In recent years a number of scholars have suggested that writings originating from wisdom schools can be traced elsewhere in the Old Testament. They point to some of the oracles of the prophets, especially in Amos and Isaiah, which seem to propound similar views. We have already noted the theory that the 'Succession Narrative' (2 Samuel 9—20; 1 Kings 1—2) could have been a moralistic 'wisdom' writing, and the same idea has been put forward regarding the stories of Joseph (Genesis 37, 39—50). Here again it is suggested that Joseph is portrayed as an ideal example of a person who lived his life according to the kind of rules we find in the book of Proverbs. It has also been suggested that the portrayal of the heroine of the book of Esther may owe something to such motives. There is nothing to prove any of these speculations, and it is unlikely that any of these stories came into existence purely as a means of demonstrating the value of practical wisdom. At the same time, the book of Job gives us one example of an older story that was taken up and reinterpreted in this way, and if the concerns of the wisdom books were, as we have suggested, deeply embedded in the very fabric of Israelite society, then it would be surprising if the same lessons were not hammered home in other types of Old Testament literature.

5 The two kingdoms

1 Kings 12:21—22:53
2 Kings 1:1—18:12
Amos
Hosea

Israel in exile
(Assyria)

JUDAH

Ahaz 735-715

Uzziah 783-742

Joash 837-800
Athaliah 842-837
Ahaziah 842

Jehoshaphat 875-851

Isaiah

Rehoboam 930-908

Jeroboam I 930-910

• Battle of
Qarqar 853

Amos
Hosea

Omri 885-874
Ahab 874-852

Jehu 842-815

• Fall of
Samaria 722

• Shoshenk
attacks
Palestine

Jeroboam II 786-746

ISRAEL

Elijah

Hoshea 732-722

EGYPT
Shoshenk 945-924

ASSYRIA

Shalmaneser III 859-824

Adad-Nirari III 810-783

Tiglath-Pileser III 745-727
Shalmaneser V 727-723
Sargon II 722-705

DAMASCUS

Hazael 843-796

• Fall of Damascus 732

| 950 | 900 | 850 | 800 | 750 | 700 |

A kingdom divided

WHAT HAPPENED after Solomon's death is often referred to as 'the division of the kingdom'. As a statement of fact, that is what happened: the extensive empire ruled over by Solomon was split into two. But in reality, this split was nothing more than the concrete political expression of an ideological division that had existed for much longer. The northern tribes, led by Ephraim, and the southern tribes led by Judah, had only ever been truly united by their common allegiance to David. Both groups looked on him as a leader following in the footsteps of the judges. His position was assured only because God had chosen and equipped him, and his continued rule was valid only in so far as he lived up to the responsibility that involved. But Solomon's reign was different. He had been part of an established dynasty, and that in itself raised new questions about his relationship to the old order of things. The fact that Solomon had violated so many of the ancient traditions, together with the fact that he was not a northerner, helped considerably to revive the old rivalries and suspicions between the two groups of tribes.

Back to the old ways

So when the tribes in the north saw their chance to opt out of the vast bureaucratic state centred on Jerusalem, they lost no time in doing so. They were not motivated just by political expediency, nor even primarily by a feeling of outrage at the injustices which Rehoboam promised to impose on them. Over and above all this, they had a deep desire to get back to the old ways, to retrace their national footsteps and go back to their roots. They wanted to recapture the spontaneity of belief and action that characterized the generation that escaped from Egypt. Of course, they saw clearly enough that they could not return precisely to those early days. Then, the judges had been leaders of their own tribes, and it was exceptional for them to unite all the tribes. In the new political climate, that was impractical. The new leader must be a national figure. But equally, he must never succeed to the throne just because his father had been king. Every king must demonstrate that he had been called and equipped by God for the job at hand – and he would stay as king only if he was seen to be carrying out God's will among his people.

This view was accepted in theory by the people of the southern state of Judah: they too believed that God should be the ultimate ruler of his people. But the political context in which they found themselves had led to the emergence of a permanent royal family, and they were firmly convinced that God's rule would now be exercised only through the royal house of David. The old ideals of the days of the judges had found their fulfilment in the promise to David and his successors, and therefore it was both pointless and unnecessary to try to ascertain God's direct will in each different generation. This view doubtless owed a great deal to the social and political situation of the southern kingdom, especially the position of its capital Jerusalem. For it is striking that once Omri, king of Israel, had founded his own royal capital in Samaria, the northern state too came to accept the concept of a royal family – first in Omri's own family, and later in Jehu and his successors.

Political changes

A casual reading of the Old Testament books of Kings may suggest that Judah was by far the more important of the two kingdoms – and, in its lasting religious influence, it has certainly proved to be. But in the two centuries following the death of Solomon, the northern kingdom of Israel had more territory, a larger population, and was in every way the more wealthy, more civilized, and even at times the more religious of the two. Israel was therefore a greater force in the international politics of the time. But by the same token, she was also less secure than Judah. Judah's capital, Jerusalem, was well away from all the main trade routes, and the kingdom's strategic importance was consequently less. So, despite her greater prosperity, the kingdom of Israel had a shorter and more troubled history than the kingdom of Judah, and almost exactly 200 years after Jeroboam was first acclaimed as king of Israel, the whole of his kingdom was wiped out, and its subjects taken away to Assyria to become the so-called 'ten lost tribes'.

In the shorter term, too, the decision of the northern tribes to go their own way led to considerable social and economic changes in the life of the people of the two kingdoms.

● **Lost territory** The people of Israel and Judah were no longer able to hold separately the large empire that they had held together under David and Solomon. The province of Aram (Syria) in north-east Palestine had already been lost in part during the reign of Solomon, and it soon became a powerful nation in its own right, based on the city-state of Damascus. It was a serious rival to the Israelite kingdoms, and frequently invaded the Israelite territory to the east of the River Jordan. All but one of the Philistine city-states regained their freedom from Judah in the south, though they were no longer a military threat. The Ammonites also took this chance to throw off Israelite rule, and the Moabites probably did

The cobbles of an ancient street in Dan, town of the most northerly of Israel's twelve tribes. Israel was said to extend 'from Dan to Beersheba'. But from the time when the kingdom was divided, and the northern tribes separated from Judah and Benjamin in the south, Israel never refound its unity as one territory.

the same. Judah fared slightly better than Israel, for she still retained some kind of control over the trade routes through the Gulf of Aqaba in the south. And Rehoboam built new fortifications in many of his cities.

2 Chronicles 11:5–12

But the loss of all this territory left both Israel and Judah as very second-rate powers. In the time of David and Solomon, the united kingdom had been the major power centre in the whole area. From now on, the two kingdoms were little more than pawns in the political games of the superpowers based in Egypt and Mesopotamia. The strength of both kingdoms was considerably weakened by the invasion of Shoshenk I, king of Egypt (called Shishak in the Old Testament). He moved in about five years after the separation of the two states, eager to re-establish the authority that Egypt had enjoyed in Canaan before the arrival of the Israelite tribes. The Old Testament only mentions this campaign in relation to Judah, and relates how Rehoboam was forced to give him treasure from both the temple and palace, to stop Shoshenk actually attacking Jerusalem.

1 Kings 14:25–28

This seems to have worked, for in an inscription in the temple of Amun at Thebes, Shoshenk makes no mention of towns in Judah being taken. He does however mention a number of towns in Israel, and an Egyptian inscription found at Megiddo suggests he must have overrun most of Palestine. In an interesting detail of his temple-list, he mentions a place called 'the Field of Abram', which is the only reference outside the Bible to connect a person of that name with Palestine. Of course, Shoshenk did not want to occupy the country, though no doubt he left troops at strategic places. A later king of Judah, Asa, faced an attack from the same quarter led by a man called Zerah. He is described as a Sudanese, but was probably an Egyptian officer left in charge of troops in south Palestine at the time of Shoshenk's invasion.

2 Chronicles 14:9–15

● **Petty squabbles**   The two kingdoms were incapable of keeping all their territory partly because they were also fighting each other. They were at war for something like fifty years, fighting over the border territory that was just to the north of Jerusalem.

1 Kings 14:30; 15:16–22

This was perhaps inevitable. Jerusalem's original appeal to David had been its unique position midway between the two groups of tribes. But now what had been a tactical advantage became a strategic liability. Judah's capital was too near the border with the northern kingdom, and that made it especially vulnerable to attack. Rehoboam, Abijam, and Asa, kings of Judah, and Jeroboam, Nadab, and Baasha, kings of Israel, were squabbling over the land in this area for a considerable time. Baasha, king of Israel, managed to move in as close as five miles to the city of Jerusalem and when it looked as if he would advance further, Asa of Judah appealed for help to Benhadad, king of Damascus. This king already had a treaty with Baasha. But Asa must have made him a very attractive proposition, for he sent an army to attack the towns in the north of Israel. This forced Baasha to withdraw his army from the frontier with Judah. It was not the last time that Judah adopted such tactics, but she eventually discovered to her cost that it was a very short-sighted policy.

● **Social unrest** The northern kingdom of Israel also turned out to be politically unstable. In theory, they thought it was right to go back to the old idea that every leader of the people should be chosen and equipped directly by God. But as a political and social institution, this was simply unworkable. At best, it meant that Israel was 'a kingdom based on revolution by the will of God'. In practice, it often meant that the nation was torn apart over the issue of the kingship. For one thing, it was open to any military adventurer to try to sieze the throne, whether or not he had any religious support. And in addition, it was only natural that those kings whose reigns had been properly accredited should in due course want their own sons to succeed them. So Israel was in constant turmoil. In the first fifty years, the throne was seized three times by a usurper who assassinated his predecessor. Jeroboam reigned for twenty-one years, but only one of the eight kings who followed him reigned for more than ten years (Baasha), and some lasted only a matter of months.

There were many problems. But this was also a constructive period. The evidence of archaeology shows that at this time the Hebrew people really were the settled, permanent occupiers of their land, and the Canaanites were quite definitely their subjects.

Religious problems

It was all very well for Jeroboam to come to power in the north on a wave of popular enthusiasm, but he soon needed to get down to the business of running his kingdom. In doing so, he had many formidable obstacles. Not least of them was that in the north, there was no obvious capital city that could form the centre of his government. The Old Testament mentions three capitals where he operated in turn: Shechem, Penuel, and Tirzah. Various reasons have been suggested for this. Possibly he was forced to retreat from one to the other in the face of Shoshenk's invading armies. More likely, there was a popular resistance to the idea of having a capital, on religious grounds. For it had been through the possession of his own personal city that Solomon had been able to behave with such disregard for the tribal traditions. At least if Jeroboam had no fixed capital, there was no chance that he would build up a state apparatus to work for his own personal benefit.

1 Kings 12:25; 14:17

But it was essential that at least one of the functions of the city of Jerusalem should be located at a permanent site in the north. For the temple built at Jerusalem to house the Ark of the Covenant was an important link with the people's past. It was natural that the tribes in the north, with their fierce devotion to all that the Ark symbolized, should want to go on pilgrimages there. Yet politically, it was essential that Jeroboam should stop them from doing so. To allow this would have been tantamount to an acknowledgement that Jerusalem still had some sort of power over the northern tribes – and the free passage of pilgrims from one state to the other would only increase the risk of subversive action to undermine

1 Kings 12:26–27

Jeroboam's position as king.

On top of that, Jeroboam had a considerable Canaanite element in the population of his territory, and he needed to try in some way to unite them with the native Israelites. He hit on an idea that he believed would solve both problems at once. He would displace the old loyalties to the temple in Jerusalem by building his own new religious centres. The sites he chose were at Dan in the extreme north, and Bethel in the south near to the border with Judah. These had been old centres of Canaanite worship, but both of them also had important connections with events in the earlier history of the people of Israel.

Genesis 12:8; 31:13; Judges 18:30; 20:18–28; 1 Samuel 7:16

But Jeroboam's actions in setting up these places of worship were to earn him the lasting condemnation of the Old Testament writers. For at these two shrines, Jeroboam placed golden bulls. This was a bold effort to bind the different elements of the population together, and to reconcile Canaanite beliefs with the distinctive faith of Israel. The Canaanite elements of the population would have no difficulty in associating these bulls with their own fertility god Baal, who was often represented as a bull. And, in theory, the Israelites could regard the bulls as thrones for their own invisible God Yahweh, just as the ark of the covenant in Jerusalem represented his invisible presence. In the event, it was a foolish move. Jeroboam's people regarded these bulls as their god, and worshipped them just as the Canaanites did. Like Saul before him, Jeroboam had overstepped his authority. He had moved against the very convictions that had brought him to power in the first place. And the prophet who announced his accession now pronounced his

1 Kings 12:28–33

A golden bull from ancient Egypt. Jeroboam placed golden bulls at the shrines of Dan and Bethel.

doom. Though he had been God's choice, Jeroboam had lost God's approval, and he would have to go, to be replaced by a king who would obey God.

1 Kings 14:1–16

New alliances

1 Kings 15:25–32

1 Kings 15:34
1 Kings 16:1–7

1 Kings 16:8–14
1 Kings 16:15–20

Jeroboam's immediate successor was his son Nadab. But he was not accepted by the people, and had the approval of no religious leaders. He lasted for just a few months, and then Baasha came to power. The people recognized him as the right man, and he had a relatively long reign of twenty-four years. But he too followed in Jeroboam's footsteps, and 'led Israel into sin'. Like Jeroboam, he was rejected by a prophet speaking in the name of God. When he died, his son Elah tried to succeed him. He reigned for less than two years, but had no popular backing and Zimri assassinated him in a military coup and seized the throne for himself. He was not the right man either, and he lasted for only seven days.

This kind of chaos naturally weakened the position of Israel. But the man who got rid of Zimri was to be one of Israel's greatest kings. Not only did he re-establish much of the nation's prestige, but he did it so successfully that when he died his son was recognized as the most appropriate person to follow him. The father was Omri, and the son was Ahab.

Prosperity again

1 Kings 16:21–28

1 Kings 16:29—22:40

1 Kings 22:41–50; 2 Kings 8:25–27

1 Kings 16:31

The Old Testament says very little about Omri for, in the view of the writer of 1 Kings, he was even more wicked and irreligious than any of his predecessors. As in so many cases, his social and political achievements are mentioned only briefly, and we are told that 'Everything else that Omri did and all his accomplishments are recorded in *The History of the Kings of Israel*' – which, of course, is a book we do not possess. By contrast, his son Ahab features very prominently in the Old Testament story. But even there, we are told far more about his religious outlook than about political affairs during his reign.

Yet there can be no doubt about the greatness of Omri and his son. For under their rule, Israel once again became a force to be reckoned with.

● **Internationally,** Omri and Ahab strengthened the kingdom's position with a number of new alliances and fresh conquests. They put an end to the long-standing but stupid warfare with Judah, and this led to a new period of prosperity and peace in the southern state also. Jehoshaphat, king of Judah, took control of many trading routes in the south, and the new friendship between the two states was eventually sealed by the marriage of Ahab's daughter, Athaliah, to Jehoshaphat's son, Jehoram. Israel made peace in the same way with the Phoenicians of Tyre. This alliance was also sealed with a marriage: this time, Ahab himself married a Phoenician princess called Jezebel. Omri also managed to gain control over Moab again. The Old Testament tells us nothing of this, but we know of it from a large black stone inscription erected by king Mesha of Moab after he had finally managed to release his

2 Kings 3

kingdom from Israel's grasp following the death of Ahab. Naturally, much of this inscription dwells on Mesha's victory rather than on his previous submission to Omri. But it says quite plainly that 'Omri, king of Israel, humbled Moab for many years'.

● **Internally,** Omri secured his own position by building a new capital. This is what David had done by capturing Jerusalem. Omri went one better, and chose an entirely new site, with no previous settlement on it. It is almost certain that he was trying to imitate David's success. For just as Jerusalem had been chosen because of its central position between the northern and southern tribes, so Samaria was roughly midway between the mainly Canaanite cities nearer the coast, and the predominantly Israelite towns further inland. This was to be Omri's own city, just as Jerusalem had been David's own city. Under Omri and Ahab it was built up into a fine place, well fortified and with many elegant buildings. Like Jerusalem, it also had a temple – for Baal. This came to be seen as Ahab's greatest mistake: 'He sinned against the Lord more than any of his predecessors. It was not enough for him to sin like King Jeroboam; he went further . . . and worshipped Baal'. But Ahab's religious observance was probably more concerned with politics than religion as such. Like Jeroboam before him, he had the problem of uniting the Canaanite and Israelite elements of his population. What went on in Samaria was mainly, if not exclusively, for the benefit of the Canaanites. It was, after all, organized like a Canaanite city-state. But the city of Jezreel was still

1 Kings 16:32; 2 Kings 10:18–27

1 Kings 16:30–31

Below: The Moabite Stone, put up by King Mesha of Moab in Omri's day. Its inscription contains information not included in the Old Testament account.

Below right: The ruins of Ahab's palace look down from the hill on which once stood the city of Samaria, capital of the northern kingdom of Israel.

of great importance, and it could well be that Ahab had in effect two capitals: Samaria for the Canaanites, with a temple for Baal, and Jezreel for the Israelites, with a temple for their God, Yahweh. It is certainly significant that both Ahab's sons had distinctively Israelite names (Ahaziah and Joram) – and that is more than could be said even for a great hero like David!

Decay and collapse

The tensions that Omri and Ahab created between their state and the covenant faith of their people soon became overpowering. In the normal course of affairs, Ahab would have discovered, like Solomon, that it was impossible to accept the worship of foreign gods and still keep the loyalty of the tribes. But matters were brought to a head even sooner by Jezebel. For she was not content with the easy-going tolerance of Ahab. She wanted Baal to become the god of Israel. There may have been a political reason for this – to show that Israel was subject to her own kingdom of Tyre. But more likely it was in the honest conviction that hers was a religion of a more civilized people. In addition, she was devoted to

The city of Megiddo was one of Ahab's chariot cities. Ahab's water tunnel and a pagan altar have been excavated. Built to guard the pass through the Carmel range on the main north-south coastal highway, Megiddo reflects layer after layer of Bible history.

The kings of Israel and Judah

Solomon's kingdom divides ●

Shoshenk attacks Palestine ●

ISRAEL

920

910

900

890

880

870

JUDAH

Elijah

860

Battle of ● Qarqar 853

850

THE HOUSE OF DAVID

REHOBOAM 930-908 was the son of Solomon. At the beginning of his reign the northern tribes broke away from the south to form their own kingdom

ABIJAH 908-906

ASA 906-875

JEHOSHAPHAT 875-851 Judah was prosperous again during his reign, and there was peace between Israel and Judah

JEHORAM 851-842

AHAZIAH 842 was assassinated by Jehu of Israel

ATHALIAH 842-837 seized power when her son Ahaziah was killed

JOASH 837-800 was the son of Ahaziah. He came to power when Athaliah was deposed in a palace coup

AMAZIAH 800-783

Jerusalem, capital of the southern kingdom of Judah.

JEROBOAM I 930-910
became king of the northern tribes
after Solomon's kingdom was divided

THE HOUSE OF JEROBOAM

NADAB 910-909

BAASHA 909-886
assassinated Nadab and
usurped the throne

THE HOUSE OF BAASHA

ELAH 886

ZIMRI 886

OMRI 885-874
was one of Israel's greatest kings.
He strengthened the kingdom through alliance and
conquest, and built Samaria as Israel's capital

THE HOUSE OF OMRI

AHAB 874-852
attempted to unite the Israelite and
Canaanite elements of the population, and
compromised Israel's covenant faith

AHAZIAH 852-850

JORAM 850-842

Samaria, capital of the northern
kingdom of Israel.

JEHU 842-815
originally an army officer,
he assassinated Joram and purged
Baal worship from Israel

THE HOUSE OF JEHU

JEHOAHAZ 815-801

JEHOASH 801-786

JEROBOAM II 786-746
under his rule Israel
enjoyed prosperity

MENAHEM 746-738 **THE HOUSE OF MENAHEM**

PEKAHIAH 738-737

PEKAH 737-732

UZZIAH 783-742
reigned during a time
of peace with Israel.
He strengthened and
extended his kingdom

Amos

Hosea

HOSHEA 732-722
was the last king of Israel.
In 722 Samaria fell to
the Assyrians and a mass
deportation took place

Fall of
Damascus 732

Fall of
Samaria 722

Isaiah

JOTHAM 742-735

AHAZ 735-715
appealed to the Assyrians
for help against Syria and
Israel. This move made Judah
dependent on Assyria

830
820
810
800
790
780
770
760
750
740
730
720
710
700

her husband – and the worship of Baal gave far more power to the king than did the covenant religion of Yahweh, God of Israel.

It was at this point that things were disrupted by the emergence of a man called Elijah. He was a fierce spokesman for the covenant traditions of his people, and he realized that this institutionalized worship of Baal was something very different from the local and casual worship of Baal that still went on in village shrines throughout the land. It was a direct threat to the very fabric of the nation.

Elijah and the religion of Baal

On Mount Carmel, overlooking the plain of Jezreel, Elijah had his great confrontation with the prophets of Baal.

Elijah is a significant character in the Old Testament. In some ways, he is a member of that line of ecstatics whose influence can be traced in the early stories of Saul. He certainly had some connection with a group of prophets like those whom Saul encountered (1 Kings 18:4,13) and his movements could at times be unpredictable and beyond human apprehension (1 Kings 18:12). But these are not the most distinctive marks of his personality. For he was first and foremost a man with a message. He believed that the God whom he knew and worshipped was not just a God who had lived and worked in the past: he was a God who was present with his people here and now, and who had his own understanding of the important issues in their national life. In this respect, Elijah was the forerunner of the great prophets whose messages are preserved in the books of the Old Testament that bear their names – men like Amos, Isaiah, Jeremiah, and others.

The precise nature of the conflict between Baal worship and the ancestral faith of Israel is made clear in three stories from the life of of Elijah:

● Elijah came from Gilead, from the very edge of the desert in the east of the country (1 Kings 17:1–7). His life-style was spartan, and his clothes were rough. He was immediately recognizable as a devotee of the style of life followed by the tribes with Moses in the desert. He was a miracle worker (1 Kings 17:8–24), but his miracles were mostly concerned with the fertility of the land, especially the holding back or sending of rain. This, of course, was supposed to be the special function of the Canaanite Baal. But Elijah was determined to prove that it was really his own God, Yahweh, who controlled the rain. So he challenged 450 prophets of Baal and 400 prophets of Asherah to a contest on Mt Carmel. This was a high ridge near the territory of the Phoenicians. It had originally belonged to Israel during the days of David and Solomon. But the altar to Yahweh erected there then had now been displaced by an altar to Baal. Elijah was determined to sort out once and for all the religious priorities of his people. He challenged the prophets of Baal and Asherah to bring fire from heaven – presumably he meant the lightning that would normally come before a rain storm. After much religious ecstasy, they were exhausted – and unsuccessful. But where they failed, Elijah succeeded – not by following their bizarre ecstatic practices, but by a simple prayer to his own God. As a result, the long period of drought ended with deluges of rain (1 Kings 18:1–46). It was Yahweh, not Baal, who controlled the weather!

● In spite of that, Jezebel still held the power, and she was all the more determined to track down the elusive Elijah. He felt (mistakenly) that he alone was left as a faithful spokesman for the God of Israel. In fear of his life he ran away from Jezebel right to the south of Judah, then south again from Beersheba to Mt Sinai. This was the place where Moses had taken the escaping slaves. It was the very centre of his people's faith, where the covenant had been made, and where God's people could still gain fresh inspiration. And that was what Elijah found. In an experience of deep emotion, he was reminded that though God indeed had power over nature, his supreme activity was to be seen in the events of everyday life. He had delivered the slaves from Egypt, and was still active in his people's lives. Elijah was sent back to stir up a political ferment in both Syria and Israel, that would lead to the overthrow of the house of Omri and its allies (1 Kings 19:1–18). Commitment to the covenant faith did not make him a mere reactionary: it transformed him into a political activist, reminding his people by his social

involvement that the God of Mt Sinai was still their only true king.

● The story of Naboth's vineyard brings out the meaning of all this in social terms (1 Kings 21:1–29). When Ahab wanted to have this piece of land to extend his own garden, he knew it was impossible. For the land of Israel belonged not to individuals, but to God – and particular people only held it in trust because God had given it to them. This was quite different from the Canaanite notion, as Ahab well knew. After all, his father Omri had been able to buy the site of Samaria outright from a Canaanite. But Ahab was still too much of an Israelite to accept that land could be seized by the king just to suit his own inclinations. So he sulked for what he knew he could never rightly possess. His wife, Jezebel, on the other hand, took a different view. She regarded the life and property of every subject as belonging to the king, and so she had no hesitation in having Naboth killed, and confiscating his property for her husband's use. It was Elijah who so boldly denounced the queen's action – just as Nathan had done when David acted on the same principles (2 Samuel 12:1–15). For Elijah, religious belief was concerned with common life and politics, and even the queen was not above the law of the covenant from Mt Sinai. For in the covenant community, every man and woman stood equal. This meant that economic and social justice were a concern of God and his representatives just as much as ritual and worship. This theme was taken up by all the great prophets of the Old Testament. But it first emerges in the testimony of Elijah, who pronounced the death sentence on Jezebel and the whole house of Omri, and declared that God would ultimately intervene to restore justice and freedom to his people.

1 Kings 22:51–53; 2 Kings 3:1–27

2 Kings 9:1–13

Ahab managed to survive, and he was succeeded in turn by his two sons Ahaziah and Joram. But there was nothing they could do to prevent the disintegration and eventual collapse of the royal house of Omri. It was not long before a revolution was instigated by devotees of the covenant faith of Israel. They had chosen an army officer by the name of Jehu to be the next king of Israel, and he was anointed in the aftermath of a great battle between Israel and Syria, at Ramoth-Gilead. Joram had been wounded in the battle and had returned to Jezreel to recuperate. Jehu therefore left the battlefield, and with a band of his own men headed straight for Jezreel. When he got there he found that by a stroke of luck Ahaziah, the king of

2 Kings 9:14–37

2 Kings 10:1–11

2 Kings 10:18–31

2 Kings 13:6

Hosea 1:4–5

2 Kings 10:23–24

Jeremiah 35:6–10

Judah, was also there visiting Joram. Since he was a relative of Ahab too, Jehu had no hesitation in assassinating both of them, along with Jezebel the queen mother. He followed up this bloodbath with an appeal to the city rulers of Samaria to come over to his side – which they did, and signified their allegiance to him by presenting him with the heads of seventy members of Ahab's family who were left there. Not content with that, Jehu managed to trick all the priests of Baal into coming to the temple in Samaria, and there had them all butchered on the spot.

But Jehu's purge cannot have been all that extensive, for by the time his son Jehoahaz became king all the paraphernalia of the Baal worship had been reinstated in Samaria. Jehu was not as loyal to the covenant faith as his supporters had hoped – and 100 years later the prophet Hosea declared that the violence that accompanied his rise to power was quite incompatible with the faith that Jehu professed to uphold.

Yet it is not difficult to see why Jehu's revolution succeeded. For though Omri's dynasty had been so successful, it was suffering from so many tensions that its collapse was inevitable:

● The strongest opposition had been evoked by the Baal worship at Samaria, instigated by Jezebel and encouraged by Ahab. The fact that Jehu joined forces with a fanatical religious movement led by Jehonadab, son of Rechab, shows just how strong the reaction was. For these Rechabites were trying to opt out of civilized, settled life altogether. They neither built houses, nor cultivated the soil, nor drank wine. All these things were typical of the life of Canaan, but they wanted to get back to the kind of life the escaping slaves had with Moses in the desert. They were convinced that the settled life of farming could never be reconciled with Israel's ancestral faith, and so it must be abandoned.

● There was also a certain amount of social unrest and injustice in the land, much as there had been towards the end of Solomon's reign. This time it had been caused partly by a great famine during the time of Ahab. This had increased the number of poor people, and led to a radical division in society between the rich merchants and the poor peasants. The story of how Ahab took over Naboth's vineyard was by no means unique, and many small farmers found themselves being displaced by rich and powerful princes at this time.

● Externally too, Israel was under pressure. New enemies were making their presence felt, especially Assyria (based in Mesopotamia) and Syria (based in Damascus). The Assyrians had pressed as far west as the Mediterranean Sea during Ahab's reign. A casual alliance against them was formed by the king of Damascus, along with Ahab and the king of Hamath. They met Assyria at the Battle of Qarqar, just north of Hamath in 853 BC, and managed to repel the Assyrians. Ahab's military strength can be judged from the fact that though he could provide only half as many troops as Syria (but the same as Hamath), he had 2,000 chariots, which was more than Syria and Hamath put together. Israel obviously had fewer people than Damascus, but far greater material resources. But Benhadad, the king of Damascus, was not interested in a lasting peace with Ahab, and according to the Old Testament Ahab was killed in battle with the Syrians at Ramoth-Gilead. His sons were powerless to regain this lost territory, and no doubt lost the support of the army for that reason. This is perhaps why the military Jehu, fast driving and ready for desperate action, was readily accepted by them as their new king.

2 Kings 20:1–34; 22:29–40

Growing insecurity

As things turned out, Jehu himself was relatively powerless in political terms. He naturally lost the support of the powerful alliance with Phoenicia – and he also lost the support of Judah, whose king he had killed. Power was seized in Judah by Athaliah, the queen mother, who was Ahab's sister. She murdered all the other possible claimants to the throne, except for one child, Joash, who was rescued by the priest Jehoiada. Athalia reigned in Jerusalem for six years, and encouraged Baal worship. But she was deposed in a palace coup led by Jehoiada, and Joash was installed as king.

2 Kings 11:1–21

During this period of uncertainty and weakness, Israel could easily have been overcome by the Syrians of Damascus, had they not been fully occupied resisting the armies of the Assyrian king Shalmaneser III. He had a deliberate plan for extending his own empire, and he made annual military expeditions, of which he kept detailed records. Some territories he conquered altogether, but

Countries in conflict

from most he simply took tribute. This was the king who had been successfully repelled by the coalition of which Ahab had been a part. But shortly after Jehu came to power, he was back with a vengeance. In 841 BC he moved through the whole area. Damascus was besieged, and much of the Syrian kingdom was invaded. Both Phoenicia and Israel had to pay tribute to keep the Assyrians at bay. Shalmaneser describes all this in great detail. Not only does he mention that he took tribute from Jehu of Israel; he also lists what he was given, and depicts Jehu himself bowing down low to present these gifts. This is a most interesting record, for the picture of Jehu

This Assyrian obelisk, the famous 'Black Obelisk' from the time of Emperor Shalmaneser, depicts King Jehu of Israel paying tribute as leader of a vassal state. It is the only known portrait of an Old Testament figure.

preserved on Shalmaneser's Black Obelisk is the only contemporary portrait we have of any named Israelite in the Old Testament.

Before the end of Shalmaneser's reign, a revolt back in Nineveh weakened Assyrian power. But this was of no advantage to Israel. It simply gave Hazael, king of Damascus, another chance to get even, and under Jehu's son Jehoahaz, Israel became almost a province of Syria. The whole of Israel east of the Jordan was occupied, and the Syrians pressed into Judah in the south. Joash, the king in Jerusalem, prevented Hazael from attacking the city only by offering him a part of the treasure from the temple.

2 Kings 13:1–9, 22–23

2 Kings 12:17–18

In little more than 100 years, the states of Israel and Judah had been reduced from the great empire that Solomon held to become the satellites of the city-state of Damascus.

New prosperity and false security

International relations were in such turmoil at this period that by the time Jehu's grandson, Jehoash, came to the throne in Israel things were quite different. The power of Assyria was building up again under Shalmaneser's grandson, Adad-Nirari III, and his renewed interest in Palestine was to enable both Israel and Judah to regain some of their former glory. According to the Assyrian annals, Israel was again forced to pay tribute, along with the Edomites and Philistines – but not, apparently, Judah. Damascus was worst hit by this renewed Assyrian advance, and when the Old Testament describes how 'the Lord gave Israel a saviour, so that they escaped from the hand of the Syrians', some scholars believe that he was

2 Kings 13:5

referring to the Assyrian king Adad-Nirari III.

In any event, the Assyrian attack on Damascus gave Jehoash the chance he was looking for, and he soon began to recover Israel's lost territory to the east of the River Jordan. Amaziah, the king of Judah, also recovered lost territory from Edom at this time. But then, he foolishly declared war on Israel, and as a result Judah was so decisively defeated that Jehoash of Israel actually raided Jerusalem itself. With this, Amaziah lost the confidence of his own people and was soon assassinated. But, as had always been the case in Judah, his place was taken by his son Uzziah.

2 Kings 14:1–16
2 Kings 14:17–22

National revival

There followed then two of the longest and most prosperous reigns in all Israelite history: Jeroboam II of Israel, and Uzziah of Judah. They reigned for over forty years each, and though the Old Testament gives no specific details of their military activities, the two kings between them extended their borders almost to the original extent of Solomon's united kingdom.

2 Kings 14:23—15:7

Uzziah repaired the fortifications of Jerusalem, reorganized his army, and equipped it with new types of armoury. He introduced new agricultural practices to the land, and was even able to reopen part of Solomon's copper refineries on the Gulf of Aqaba. This led to a revival of trade through the Red Sea, and since the two kings of Judah and Israel were at peace with one another, between them they must have controlled all the major trade routes of the area.

2 Chronicles 26:1–15

The splendid buildings erected by Jeroboam II in Samaria demonstrate well enough the prosperity of the northern state. Many people became very rich as a result of the increased opportunities for international trade. They also became very religious, for they concluded that their new-found wealth must be a sign of God's favour upon them. They came to believe that their position was assured, and their kingdom was impregnable, and began to look forward with eager anticipation to the coming of a great 'Day of the Lord', when Israel would finally be victorious over all her enemies.

But not everyone thought like that. For during the reign of Jeroboam II many people once again began to ask if all this high living was compatible with the covenant faith of Israel. Some scholars believe that in reaction against all this, a new edition of Israel's early history was written, reflecting the memories that had been handed down in the northern tribes. They believe that many of these stories, which emphasized the work of Moses, later came to form a part of the Old Testament, especially in the books of Genesis and Exodus. But whether it took that precise form, there can be no doubt that there was strong disapproval of Israel's style of life at this time. For it was towards the end of Jeroboam II's reign that the prophet Amos delivered his striking messages, in which he declared that Israelite society was rotten to the core. Though many were rich and prosperous, others were penniless and oppressed. The great shrines like Bethel were full of worshippers, but it was all just empty ritual – and for people like that 'the day of the Lord', when it came, would not be a time of triumph but a day of doom.

Amos 8:4–6

Amos 5:18–27

The book of Amos

Nowadays we commonly think of a prophet as a person who predicts the future. But this was not the way the great Old Testament prophets saw themselves. They were essentially God's messengers, sent to remind their people of the covenant made at Sinai, and to apply it to the everyday life of their towns and villages. They were not fortune tellers, but politicians and preachers.

They did occasionally write some parts of their message down (e.g. Jeremiah 30:2; 36:1–2). But it is unlikely that any prophet actually wrote the books now found in the Old Testament. Indeed, these writings are not really 'books' in the sense of having a connected argument from start to finish. They are much more like an anthology of a great person's thoughts. That is why modern translations of the Bible make a clear division between the various sections, for the messages of these prophets were gathered together by editors, and they often did not place them in any sort of chronological order. The same people occasionally added historical and biographical passages, explaining the prophet's situation, together with stories of incidents in his life. The book of Amos contains all these types of material.

The man and his message

Amos himself came from the town of Tekoa, which was just south of Jerusalem in Judah (1:1). But his message was for the people of the northern kingdom, and he delivered it in one of the religious sanctuaries set up by the first Jeroboam, at Bethel (7:10–17), and possibly also in Samaria itself (3:9—4:3). While he was in Bethel, Amaziah, the priest of the sanctuary, tried to send him back to Judah, telling him that his own people should pay for his services. He obviously thought Amos was some kind of professional prophet, who was looking for a full-time job attached to a permanent place of worship. We know that there were such full-time prophets in both Israel and Judah. Some of them seem to have had an official position alongside the priests (Jeremiah 35:4–5), while others were court officials who would say anything the king wanted to hear (1 Kings 22:1–28).

But Amos was not this kind of man. He had been a simple shepherd and he was not delivering his challenging messages to tickle the ears of his political masters, but because God had shown him the rotten state of Israelite society – and he was impelled to do something about it (7:10–17; 3:3–8). Amos saw a complete breakdown of morality and covenant faith, not only in

The prophet Amos, the earliest whose words are systematically recorded in the Old Testament, was a shepherd. His message to Israel was an uncompromising warning that God's judgement would come unless they brought back justice into their society.

Israel but also in the nations with whom she was most closely associated. Syria, the Philistines, Tyre, Edom, Ammon, (1:3—2:5). Of course, all but Judah had never been a part of the covenant faith. But Amos condemned them in God's name. They had refused to treat each other as people. They had disregarded the elementary principles of human dignity: acting with great cruelty, taking whole communities into slavery, breaking treaties, and exacting merciless revenge on neighbouring states.

All this was just a prelude to God's judgement of Israel. Israel might not have done any of these things, but she had broken the covenant relationship with her God in very fundamental ways. Though the northern state had ostensibly been founded on a conviction that all members of the community were of equal worth and value, this had never become a social reality. Instead, some had become rich on the back of others – and they were increasing their wealth at the expense of the rest. People were selling themselves into slavery because they could not repay trivial debts (2:6–8). The rich were feasting themselves and playing in idle luxury, while others were homeless (3:9—4:1; 5:10–13).

Judgement–and hope

Paradoxically, in the middle of all this there was great religious fervour. The shrines were full of worshippers, all carrying out their ritual observances with meticulous care. They would make sure they did not violate the weekly day of rest – but as soon as it was over, they could hardly wait to get back to the legalized robbery that went on in every market-place. This false religious confidence incensed Amos more than anything. The rich believed they were prospering because they were very religious. But if only they had the eyes to see it, they would have realized they were wealthy because they had disregarded the basic requirements of their covenant faith.

So Amos declared God's total lack of interest in this kind of empty ritual: 'Go to the holy place in Bethel and sin, if you must! Go to Gilgal and sin with all your might! Go ahead and bring animals to be sacrificed . . . offer your bread in thanksgiving to God . . . This is the kind of thing you love to do' (4:4–5). But God had other ideas: 'The Lord says, "I hate your religious festivals; I cannot stand them! . . . I will not accept the animals you have fattened to bring me as offering . . ."' (5:21–22). These had not been the things that characterized Israel's experience of God in the desert. The covenant relationship forged at Sinai was concerned not with religious ritual, but with a personal relationship between God and his people — a relationship of love and concern that should have created a new society marked by the same qualities. So Amos pleaded in God's name: 'Stop your noisy songs; I do not want to listen to your harps. Instead, let justice flow like a stream, and righteousness like a river that never goes dry' (5:23–24).

Not that Amos expected to be heard. For the real trouble was that the worship at Bethel and Gilgal was not the worship of Israel's covenant God at all: it was the worship of Canaanite gods and goddesses, with their rather different view of society (2:7–8; 5:26–27; 8:14). Israel had gone too far. Her leaders were unable to tell the difference between truth and lies. But it would all come to an end – and soon. Just as God had intervened in Israel's history before, he would do so again – and Israel would be totally destroyed, her people taken away into exile, and her cities devastated (5:1 — 9:10). The prosperity of the day of Jeroboam would indeed culminate in 'the day of the Lord'. But instead of a day of great blessing, it would be a day of judgement and despair (5:18–20).

The last paragraph of Amos (9:11–15) gives just a slight ray of hope, and because of this some scholars believe it was added later by the book's editor, to alleviate the blackness of Amos's message. But it does not really contradict what he says. Amos knew that the nation was heading for a great disaster. But he also knew that events were in God's control: 'I will give the command and shake the people of Israel like corn in a sieve. I will shake them among the nations to remove all who are worthless' (9:9). Because of that, an element of mercy and love would always be found even in judgement. For Amos's God was the one who had rescued his people from Egypt, and who had shown his overpowering love for them in so many ways throughout their history. It was inevitable, therefore, that though the present looked bleak, beyond the storm clouds of God's anger Amos could still dimly see the clear rays of God's love.

Assyria on the move

It was not long before Amos's dire predictions were to become a dreadful reality. The moral disintegration that began in Jeroboam II's reign led to social and political disintegration in the years after his death, with a rapid succession of weak kings, assassinations and revolts. At the same time, the power of Assyria was increasing again with the accesssion to the throne of Tiglath-Pileser III. He had a new expansionist policy that he hoped would avoid the failures of his predecessors. Instead of merely taking tribute from defeated nations, he would incorporate conquered states into the Assyrian empire. To ensure that they did not revolt, the leading elements of the population would be moved away to other parts of the empire, and replaced with settlers similarly displaced from elsewhere.

2 Kings 15:17–22

The first mention of an Assyrian invasion of Israel occurs in the account of Menahem's reign. He tried to keep the kingship within his own family by paying tribute to Tiglath-Pileser, but his son Pekahiah reigned for only two years before he was removed by an anti-Assyrian revolt led by Pekah. He went on to form a new alliance against the Assyrians with Rezin, king of Syria. They tried to persuade Jotham, king of Judah, to join them. He refused, and when a new king came to power in Jerusalem, they declared war on Judah.

Isaiah 7:1–17

This move struck terror into the people of Jerusalem, and brought into prominence one of the Old Testament's greatest prophets: Isaiah. He advised the new king, Ahaz, that this threat to his security would come to nothing – and before the new born child Immanuel could tell the difference between good and bad, both

Isaiah 7:10–25 Syria and Israel would collapse. As it turned out, Isaiah was right. But Ahaz did not believe him. It was perhaps on this occasion that in desperation he offered his son as a sacrifice to try to change the course of events. He certainly went out to get the Assyrians on his side – and in response to his appeal, they attacked Damascus, killed Rezin, and took away his people.

2 Kings 16:3–4

2 Kings 16:5–9

But it was a foolish move, for by doing this Ahaz had given up his own independence. He went to Damascus to pay homage to Tiglath-Pileser, and brought back from there the plan for an altar that was erected in the temple at Jerusalem, as a sign of submission to the Assyrian Empire and its gods. As Isaiah had warned, it was a short-sighted policy to go to the Assyrians for help.

2 Kings 16:10–18

Meanwhile in Israel, things were going from bad to worse. Pekah's positon was weakened because the Assyrians took over yet more of his territory, and he was assassinated by Hoshea. Hoshea realized that the kingdom was in grave danger of disappearing entirely, and so he surrendered – unwillingly – to the Assyrians. But once the immediate danger was past, he soon began plotting against them again. He saw his chance when Shalmaneser V replaced Tiglath-Pileser III, and appealed for support to the king of Egypt.

2 Kings 15:29

2 Kings 17:1–4

But Egypt was powerless to help, and when Shalmaneser moved his armies against Israel no one could stop him. Samaria fell after a siege lasting two years, and in his annals Sargon II (Shalmaneser's successor) tells how he deported 27,290 people from Israel and replaced them with others from elsewhere in his empire. An Assyrian officer was put in charge of the land, and Israel was finished.

2 Kings 17:5–6

The Assyrians

The Assyrian Empire was based in northern Mesopotamia, chiefly around the cities of Nineveh, Asshur and Kalah. The people of this area had exerted a strong influence in that region for a long time, and we can trace their existence back to a time long before the Israelites emerged as a nation. But it was not until the early days of the Hebrew monarchy that the Assyrians began to take an interest in the lands that lay to the west of their home.

Tiglath-Pileser I (1115–1077 BC) was the first king to try to move westwards. But he had not thought out his strategy with sufficient care, and though he got as far as the northern part of Syria he was unable to establish a firm power base there. In the next few centuries, the Assyrians concentrated on setting up a strong administrative structure, into which conquered territories could easily be incorporated. They also developed a well trained and highly disciplined army, ready to move at a moment's notice. The description

of them in Isaiah 5:26–29 clearly reflects the impression that these troops made on those who saw them: ' . . . here they come, swiftly, quickly! None of them grows tired; none of them stumbles. They never doze or sleep. Not a belt is loose; not a sandal strap is broken. Their arrows are sharp, and their bows are ready to shoot. Their horses' hooves are as hard as flint, and their chariot-wheels turn like a whirlwind. The soldiers roar like lions that have killed an animal and are carrying it off where no one can take it away from them.'

Ashurnasirpal II (883–859 BC) renovated the Assyrian capital at Kalah, and established a firm control over his Mesopotamian territories, and this new security gave his son Shalmaneser III (858–824 BC) the chance to expand his empire to the west. He was the emperor whose forces met Ahab and his Syrian allies at the battle of Qarqar in 853 BC. But it was almost another 100 years before the toughest emperor of them all came to the throne: Tiglath-Pileser III (745–727 BC). He was also acclaimed as king of Babylon in southern Mesopotamia, and he was an expert military strategist. He saw that the key to imperial expansion was the establishment of a clearly defined policy. Though many of the records from his reign are confused and uncertain, he obviously had a clear strategy for annexing other states.

First of all, he would try to make a treaty with other rulers, persuading them to acknowledge his sovereignty in exchange for certain limited privileges. But any hint of revolt by such vassals would be dealt with at once – usually by direct invasion, followed by the taking over of a good deal of their territory, and the installation of a new king to rule over what was left in accordance with Assyrian instructions. Any more revolts would lead to the whole state being taken over and turned into an Assyrian province – with its native leaders being deported to other parts of the empire.

We can see how this happened in stages in the case of Israel – though it was not an unchangeable procedure, for neither Judah nor the Philistine city-states were ever dealt with in precisely this way.

Tiglath-Pileser III represented the zenith of Assyrian power. Some of his successors still had expansionist ideas. Indeed, Esarhaddon (681–669 BC) actually annexed Egypt itself. But by the end of his reign, Assyria's imperial power was spent. The reign of his successor, Ashurbanipal (669–627 BC) saw the establishment of a remarkable library of cuneiform texts at Nineveh. But it also witnessed an extended civil war in Babylon, and revolts in other parts of the empire. By the end of his reign, the empire was beginning to disintegrate and its collapse was inevitable.

Hosea and the fall of Samaria

The indecision and opportunism of the last few kings of Israel is all reflected in the book of Hosea. Hosea began his work as a prophet after Amos, but probably before the end of Jeroboam II's reign, and he continued until after the Assyrians had captured Samaria.

The disorders and constant revolts of the people against their kings are all vividly described here: 'In the heat of their anger they murdered their rulers. Their kings have been assassinated one after another, but no one prays to me for help.' (7:7). Israel thought she could do without God, and so she 'flits about like a silly pigeon; first her people call on Egypt for help and then they run to Assyria! But I will spread out a net and catch them like birds as they go by. I will punish them for the evil they have done.' (7:11–12). Yet in spite of her impending doom, Israel seemed to be quite unaware of what was happening: 'The Lord says, "The people of Israel are like a half-baked loaf of bread. They rely on the nations around them and do not realize that this reliance on foreigners has robbed them of their strength. Their days are numbered, but they don't even know it."' (7:8–9).

The man and his message

We know very little about Hosea himself. But he was obviously a countryman. He refers with the knowledge of experience to the morning mist and the dew (13:3), to the fragrance of the cedar trees of Lebanon (14:6), to corn and wine and olive oil (2:8), and to the work of ploughing and harvesting (10:11–13). Along with all this, Hosea has a strong nostalgia for the life of the desert. For he loved not only his own countryside, but also its history, and he could look back with excitement to the old stories of Jacob and Moses and the Exodus (11 — 13). Amos was logical and impartial. He saw God's dealings with Israel as just one example of his dealings with other nations. But Hosea could never be like that. He was too deeply attached to his own homeland. He loved the land, he loved his people, and he was sure that God loved them too.

Hosea received his message for the nation from God through a personal tragedy in his own life. The story begins with Hosea's marriage to a woman called Gomer. Some interpreters believe that this woman was a temple prostitute whom Hosea tried to win over to his own understanding of God's relationship with his people. But it is just as likely that her sexual promiscuity was quite unexpected. In any event, Hosea and Gomer had three children, each of them given symbolic names that would convey a message about the fate of the nation. The first was called Jezreel, as a reminder that God would still avenge Jehu's massacre there; the second was called Unloved, to declare that Israel seemed to have gone beyond God's love and forgiveness; and the other was called Not-my-people. Gomer subsequently left Hosea to live

Amos had been. Amos denounced the great public evils of the people – but Hosea saw behind them the breakdown of morality in homes throughout the land, all of which sprang ultimately from unfaithfulness to the God of the covenant.

God and Israel

The people of Israel believed they would get prosperity and good harvests by observing the fertility rites of Baal worship. But these rituals involved the very same sexual indulgence that had ruined Hosea's own home life. Just like Gomer, Israel was saying, 'I will go to my lovers – they give me food and water, wool and linen, olive-oil and wine' (2:5). This was the typical thinking of the worshippers of Baal. They worshipped him for what they could get out of him, like prostitutes making love for money. But in fact, Hosea knew that it was Israel's own God Yahweh who provided all these things: 'She would never acknowledge that I am the one who gave her the corn, the wine, the olive-oil, and all the silver and gold that she used in the worship of Baal' (2:8).

This was not how Israel should love her God. She must love him for what he is and in gratitude for what he has done. So Hosea returns over and over again to what God had done for his people Israel. Sometimes he uses the picture of his own relationship to Gomer. At other times, he thinks in terms of God as the father of his people: ' . . . the more I called to him, the more he turned away from me. My people sacrificed to Baal; they burnt incense to idols. Yet I was the one who taught Israel to walk. I took my people up in my arms, but they did not acknowledge that I took care of them. I drew them to me with affection and love. I picked them up and held them to my cheek; I bent down to them and fed them.' (11:2–4).

Amos had little hope in his message. For him, 'the Day of the Lord' was almost entirely a day of punishment. But Hosea speaks of God making 'Trouble Valley' into 'a door of hope' (2:15). God still loved his people, and in due course Israel would come back to him: 'She will respond to me . . . as she did when she was young, when she came from Egypt. Then once again she will call me her husband – she will no longer call me her Baal.' (2:15–16). To be sure, Gomer had suffered the consequences of her action – and so would Israel: 'Samaria must be punished for rebelling against me. Her people will die in war; babies will be dashed to the ground, and

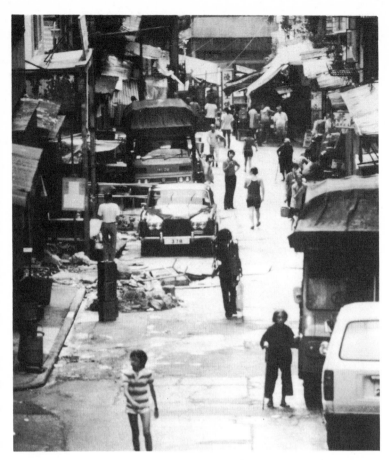

Hosea was as concerned for social justice as his predecessor Amos. In the true prophetic tradition, he saw the oppression and inequality of his day as an offence against God.

with another man (1:2—2:5).

In the next recorded event from Hosea's life, he goes to the market place and sees a prostitute who has fallen into some sort of slavery from which she can be released for a small payment. And he is so moved by her plight that he buys her and takes her to live with him (3:1–5). Some interpreters believe this was a different woman altogether from Gomer. But if we compare the details of the story with the message that Hosea brought about God's relationship to his people Israel, it makes more sense to assume that this prostitute was in fact Gomer, who had presumably therefore been abandoned by the man she was living with.

Certainly this personal tragedy was the key to Hosea's message for the nation. Just as his love for Gomer had been rejected and despised, so had God's love for Israel. And if a man like Hosea felt so deeply grieved when his wife left him, how must God feel over the unfaithfulness of Israel? Because of his personal involvement in this way, Hosea was able to see deeper into the nature of Israel's wrongdoing than pregnant women will be ripped open' (13:16). But God would never give up Israel, any more than Hosea could give up his own wife: 'How can I give you up, Israel? How can I abandon you? . . . My heart will not let me do it! My love for you is too strong . . . ' (11:8).

In return, God was looking for the unreserved commitment of his people. Unlike Baal, he was not primarily interested in religious rituals. Instead, he was seeking a personal relationship between his people and himself: 'What I want from you is plain and clear: I want your constant love, not your animal

sacrifices. I would rather have my people know me than burn offerings to me.' (6:5–6). What was required was a return to the old simplicity that had characterized the life of the slaves who escaped from Egypt. They knew how much God had done for them, and because of his faithfulness and love they knew they could unreservedly commit themselves to his care. Israel had come a long way since those days, but God's love was unchanging – and that message was to become increasingly important to the Bible writers as time went by.

Dating the Old Testament story

Some incidental details in the Old Testament have been strikingly confirmed by recent discoveries. The note in 1 Kings 6:7 that 'no hammer, chisel or any other tool was heard at the temple while it was being built' is explained by the fact that 'Solomon's quarry' is deep under old Jerusalem, where the stone for the building was quarried and dressed. Though so near to the temple, no sound of the underground quarrying would carry to the construction site above.

At first glimpse, it might seem easy to give dates to the events recorded in the Old Testament. There are certainly many lists of ancestors and descendants of prominent peole, as well as complicated comparative datings at a number of points in the narratives. But it is extraordinarily difficult to condense all this material into one consistent chronological system. There are a number of significant problems:
● Different ancient versions of the Old Testament actually have different figures at many points. The Hebrew version (the Massoretic Text) is not always the same as the Greek version (the Septuagint).
● We do not fully understand the basis on which the Old Testament's dating system operates. For instance, it usually refers to numbers of years within a given king's reign. But do these years include the year in which he became king – or is 'the first year' of a reign actually the first full year after the king's accession? Lack of certainty on this point can lead to considerable differences in dating, even over a short period of time.
● In the earlier Old Testament books, people are often credited with amazingly long life spans, regularly running into hundreds of years. There are similarly extravagant claims in many records from ancient Mesopotamia, but we do not know precisely how to understand them in relation to our own calendar. It seems likely that such calculations were based on a shorter year than our twelve month period, but in the absence of certain knowledge we can deduce very little from them.
● Many scholars feel that the figures given in the Old Testament are stylized, and perhaps even symbolic. For example, the whole time scheme of the Hebrew Old

Testament seems to be designed so as to give special prominence to four important events in Israel's history: the exodus, Solomon's building of the temple, the end of the Babylonian exile, and the Maccabean reconsecration of the temple. We also find the frequent use of the number forty, which perhaps suggests that it stands for something – maybe just indicating a long time, or a generation (though a literal generation would be much shorter than that). This figure occurs frequently in the stories of the judges, and if we add all the time indications up there, we have a period in excess of three hundred years. Yet we know from other evidence that the time between Moses and Samuel can hardly have been more than half that length.

There are obviously many uncertainties in trying to assign accurate dates to events in the Old Testament. But from the time of the great empires founded by the Assyrians and the Babylonians, we have detailed records written by their own annalists, and these often mention people and events also described in the Old Testament. Moreover, the Assyrian and Babylonian records can be easily dated in absolute terms. This means that it has been possible to work out a general chronological framework for the Old Testament, by using these other materials and combining them with the dating methods found in the Bible story.

Naturally, different scholars make their own judgements on such complex issues. But the dates given in this book are widely recognized as being accurate to within about ten years or less for the earlier Old Testament stories – while the dates given for events and people during the Assyrian and Babylonian periods (and later) are much more accurate than that.

6 Judah and Jerusalem

2 Kings 18:13—25:21   **Nahum**
Isaiah 1—39   **Habakkuk**
Micah   **Jeremiah 1:1—39:10**
Zephaniah

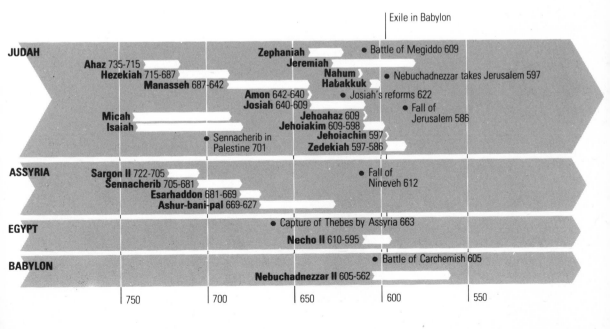

Danger and uncertainty

WITH ISRAEL gone, and Samaria reduced to a heap of ashes, life in Judah changed dramatically. Jerusalem was no longer protected from Assyria by its remote location. The border of the Assyrian Empire was now less than twenty miles away, and Judah's security was threatened. Ahaz had only made things worse by actually offering to subject himself to the Assyrians, in exchange for protection against the kings of Damascus and Israel. Isaiah had been unable to prevent this, but he had no doubt of the likely outcome of such political madness. In a characteristically picturesque message, he declared that the people of Jerusalem 'have rejected the quiet waters from the brook of Shiloah' (near Jerusalem), in exchange for 'the flood waters of the River Euphrates, overflowing all its banks. They will sweep through Judah in a flood, rising shoulder high and covering everything'. Instead of trusting in God, Ahaz and his people had deliberately courted disaster by their cowardly submission to the Assyrians.

Isaiah 8:5–8

Ahaz himself was too cautious to allow that to happen during his reign. But he was sowing the seeds of eventual collapse.

● **Politically,** Ahaz's acceptance of Assyrian rule was inept. But it also had immediate and serious social repercussions for his people. The halcyon days of Uzziah were gone for ever. Much of Judah's territory had been lost – and along with it, a large slice of the royal income. That in itself would have been bad enough to lead to a major economic recession for Ahaz. But his problems were increased by considerable numbers of refugees from the northern kingdom of Israel. He was forced to extend Jerusalem, building new houses and defences to settle these people. It was perhaps inevitable that people should be tempted to get whatever they could for themselves, with no thought of the wider social and moral consequences.

● **Religiously,** Ahaz was encouraging this. Not only was he officially promoting the worship of Assyrian gods – even in the

Isaiah warned King Ahaz that his servility towards the Assyrians would lead to disaster: 'the waters...will sweep through Judah in a flood.'

temple itself – but he also allowed many other forms of native Canaanite religions to prosper. The arrival of northern refugees probably just made this worse. But it meant that the distinctive message of Israel's own faith was once again in danger of being lost.

Isaiah was deeply concerned about all this. He knew that the social and political collapse of the northern kingdom had been caused by its failure to pay due attention to the demands of the law from Mt Sinai. And he could see the same things happening in Judah. There was plenty of religious activity, but little evidence of its impact in everyday life. Isaiah's messages at this period bear a remarkable resemblance to the dire warnings that Amos had given: 'Listen to what the Lord is saying to you . . . He says, "Do you think I want all these sacrifices you keep offering to me? . . . I am tired of the blood of bulls and sheep and goats . . . I am disgusted with the smell of the incense you burn . . . I hate your New Moon Festivals and holy days; they are a burden that I am tired of bearing . . . Stop all this evil that I see you doing . . . and learn to

The prophet Micah asked: 'Shall I acquit the man with wicked scales, and with a bag of deceitful weights?' The prophets were concerned with the ordinary dealings of society, and with the honesty without which social and commercial life begins to break down.

Isaiah 1:10–17

do right. See that justice is done – help those who are oppressed, give orphans their rights, and defend widows.'"

The same message was emphasized by the prophet Micah. But whereas Isaiah belonged to the upper classes, Micah was a farm worker. He saw even more clearly what was wrong with society, because he had experienced its injustice for himself. Judah, he said, was rotten from top to bottom. Even her leaders 'hate justice and turn right into wrong . . . building God's city, Jerusalem, on a *Micah 3:9–10* foundation of murder and injustice'. They might manage to persuade their own prophets to promise that 'wine and liquor will *Micah 2:11* flow' for them, but messages like that were just 'lies and deceit'. People had got their standards mixed up. They believed that God's approval and support could be secured by religious observances. But Micah knew that the real basis of the covenant society was not empty ritual, but justice and equality: 'What shall I bring to the Lord, the God of heaven, when I come to worship him? Shall I bring the best calves to burn as offerings to him? Will the Lord be pleased if I bring him thousands of sheep or endless streams of olive-oil? Shall I offer him my first-born child to pay for my sins? No, the Lord has told us what is good. What he requires of us is this: to do what is just, to show constant love, and to live in humble *Micah 6:6–8* fellowship with our God.'

Like Amos before him, Micah saw little hope for people whose view of God's nature was so twisted. 'Twist and groan, people of Jerusalem, like a woman giving birth, for now you will have to leave the city and live in the open country. You will have to go to

Isaiah described Judah as God's vineyard. He expected a good harvest, but the grapes it bore were sour.

Babylon . . . Zion will be ploughed like a field, Jerusalem will become a pile of ruins, and the Temple hill will become a forest.'

Micah 4:10; 3:12

There were times when even Isaiah felt the same. In a dramatic picture, he describes Judah and Jerusalem as God's vineyard – a vineyard from which he had great expectations. Instead, all he got was sour grapes. So the vineyard must be destroyed: 'I will take away the hedge round it, break down the wall that protects it, and let wild animals eat it and trample it down.'

Isaiah 5:5

But Ahaz was not disposed to listen to messages like these. He believed he had already secured a measure of prosperity for his people. But in reality, he was undermining the foundations of society. Instead of trusting in God, he was terrified of the Assyrians, and insisted in trusting his own political judgement. Judah had lost her independence to Assyria, and Isaiah could see no hope as long as Ahaz was king. So he withdrew from public life, and until the death of Ahaz he gave his teaching only to a small group of his own personal friends.

False confidence

Ahaz was succeeded by his son, Hezekiah. By the time he came to power, the Assyrian emperor Sargon had become preoccupied with other problems in the east and north of his empire. This meant the states in Palestine had a little more freedom, and they lost no time trying to turn that freedom to real political advantage. Egypt's power was also increasing at this time, and the Philistine city-states were soon plotting with the Egyptians to get rid of Assyrian domination once and for all.

Naturally, they tried to get the support of Judah. No sooner was Hezekiah enthroned in Jerusalem than Philistine ambassadors came to ask for his help. But Isaiah warned them that Assyria's power was far from broken: 'Howl and cry for help, all you Philistine cities! Be terrified, all of you! A cloud of dust is coming from the north – it is an army with no cowards in its ranks.'

Isaiah 14:31

Undaunted, the Egyptians tried to persuade Hezekiah to join their revolt – and Isaiah repeated his message. In a dramatic anticipation of what would happen to the rebels, the prophet took off all his clothes and walked naked round the streets of Jerusalem. This, he said, was 'a sign of what will happen to Egypt and Sudan. The emperor of Assyria will lead away naked the prisoners he captures from those two countries. Young and old, they will walk barefoot and naked, with their buttocks exposed, bringing shame on Egypt.'

Isaiah 20:3–4

Hezekiah had more sense than his father, and listened carefully to Isaiah's advice. It was just as well he did, for in a short time the Assyrian army had moved in strength against the Philistines and the Egyptians. They were unable to defend themselves, let alone Judah, and their power collapsed just as Isaiah had predicted.

Reform in Jerusalem

Hezekiah was still tempted to make his own bid for freedom. But he now realized that he would need to move carefully. So he began surreptitiously by reforming the religious practices of his people.

2 Kings 18:1–8

Isaiah and Micah had both complained that the worship of their own God Yahweh was being mixed up with the worship of other gods. Some of these gods were certainly the local Canaanite Baals that had caused such havoc in the northern kingdom of Israel. But in addition, Ahaz had erected an altar to the Assyrian gods in Jerusalem as a sign of his political allegiance. Hezekiah soon saw that if he got rid of these things, he could please religious fanatics like Isaiah, but he could also make a start on establishing his own independence from Assyria. A number of features of Hezekiah's reforms indicate the clear political intention behind it:

● As well as clearing the Jerusalem temple of all the paraphernalia of alien worship, he also tried to close down even legitimate places of worship elsewhere in the country. That would ensure the temple in Jerusalem would be the only place where the people could worship God. Of course, this temple had always been Judah's national shrine. But when Solomon first built it, it also became an instant symbol of the king's own power. Hezekiah knew that if he could persuade his people to worship only in his own temple, that was bound to strengthen their loyalty to him and to his successors.

● Hezekiah's own people were not the only ones who were invited to worship in Jerusalem. He also sent a message to those who were left in what had been the territory of northern Israel. This

2 Chronicles 30:1-12

King Hezekiah faced a constant military threat from Assyria. As part of his preparation for a possible siege, he had a water tunnel dug to bring water from outside the Jerusalem city well to the Pool of Siloam inside the city. This constant water supply stood the city in good stead when Sennacherib's army invaded.

state was now part of the Assyrian Empire, and therefore had no official ties with Israel's national faith. But Hezekiah knew that many of its inhabitants were still descended from the old Israelite tribes – and if they could be tempted to come south and worship in Jerusalem, that may begin to undermine the Assyrian power on his doorstep. Hezekiah certainly made strenuous efforts to link his reign with the corporate memory of the old kingdom in the north, even calling his son Manasseh, which was the original name of one of the ten northern tribes.

● As well as reorganizing religious worship, Hezekiah also made military preparations for the inevitable Assyrian backlash. He built new defences in Jerusalem and many other cities. He reorganized

2 Chronicles 32:5; Isaiah 22:9-11

2 Chronicles 32:5–8
2 Chronicles 32:27–29

2 Kings 20:20;
2 Chronicles 32:30;
Isaiah 22:9–11

the army, built new store cities, and rationalized his civil service. In Jerusalem itself he built the Siloam Tunnel, to make sure the city would have plenty of water in the event of a siege. Hezekiah was determined that, when the right opportunity presented itself, he would have a good chance of siezing a real and lasting independence from the Assyrians.

His chance came with the death of Sargon. Soon afterwards, both the king of Babylon and a new Egyptian king sent a message asking Hezekiah to help overthrow the Assyrians. Isaiah warned Isaiah 30:1–7; 31:1–3 against this, but his warnings feel on deaf ears. The only ruler in Palestine who was opposed to this plan was the Philistine king of Ekron. But Hezekiah soon overcame his opposition, by arranging some sort of revolt among his own officials. The Assyrian king Sennacherib describes how 'the officials, the politicians, and the people of Ekron, had thrown Padi, their king, into fetters . . . and handed him over to Hezekiah the Jew'. After this, all the Philistine city-states seem to have fallen in with this new anti-Assyrian alliance.

The Assyrians move in

The inevitable happened. The Assyrian king Sennacherib could not allow this kind of revolt, even on the edge of his empire. He marched south through Palestine, and Egypt and the Philistines

'Sennacherib's prism', an Assyrian document inscribed on stone, describes the siege of Jerusalem from the invaders' point of view. Sennacherib speaks of shutting Hezekiah in Jerusalem 'like a bird in a cage'.

collapsed at once. Then he moved against Judah, using the same tactics as his predecessor Shalmaneser had adopted against the northern kingdom of Israel. First, he would weaken Hezekiah's position by taking over much of his territory. Instead of making the towns and villages of Judah a part of his own empire, he handed them over to various Philistine kings. But the result was the same: Hezekiah had no supporters to whom he could appeal for help. And so Sennacherib moved in the direction of Jerusalem. In his own vivid account, he describes how he had Hezekiah shut up in his own capital city 'like a bird in a cage'.

Hezekiah could see there was no chance of escape. The best he could hope for was to save the city itself by paying Sennacherib a huge tribute. The Assyrian king was prepared to accept this, and so Hezekiah sent large quantities of gold and silver treasures to the town of Lachish, where Sennacherib was encamped with his army.

2 Kings 18:13–16

It is not altogether clear what happened next. The Old Testament continues with the story of a siege of Jerusalem which ended in complete failure. The Assyrian army apparently camped outside the city in force, in the hope that the people would depose Hezekiah and so save themselves from the hardship of a siege. Then, just as the fall of the city seemed imminent, the Assyrian army suddenly withdrew, after many of its soldiers had died in some mysterious way.

2 Kings 18:17—19:37

The Assyrian records have a detailed account of Sennacherib's activities in Judah, but they do not mention this event. That in itself is not too surprising, for their official annals often ignored defeats. Most scholars believe that the Old Testament story is authentic enough, but they differ about when it actually happened. Some think it must have been a part of Sennacherib's campaign in 701 BC. But he is hardly likely to have besieged Jerusalem immediately after receiving such a large payment of tribute. Others have noted that the story mentions 'King Tirhakah of Sudan'. A king of that name ruled in Egypt from about 689 BC, and it is therefore possible that this incident took place later, perhaps as a result of another attempted revolt by Hezekiah. On the other hand, we have no knowledge from Assyrian sources of a second expedition by Sennacherib into Palestine.

2 Kings 19:9

Assyria's final fling

2 Kings 19:37; Isaiah 37:38

We know comparatively little of what was going on in Judah in the years immediately following Sennacharib's invasion. Sennacherib himself was murdered, and his successor was Esarhaddon, who was to be one of Assyria's most powerful rulers. When he died, his empire was divided between his two sons. Ashur-bani-pal reigned at Nineveh, and Shamash-Shanakin at Babylon.

During this period, Assyria eventually achieved her greatest ambition. Ashur-bani-pal finally managed to crush Egypt, and captured its capital city, Thebes. Assyria now dominated the whole of the Fertile Crescent, including the rival superpower of Egypt. But Ashur-bani-pal was not primarily a great warrior. He had no

Ashurbanipal, depicted on this relief killing a lion, was emperor of Assyria in the time of Manasseh's reign in Jerusalem. He collected a library of historical documents at his capital, Nineveh, mostly in the form of clay tablets written on in cuneiform script. A great many of these documents have been pieced together and give a remarkably full record of Assyrian civilization.

need to be: his predecessors had already established the empire on a firm foundation.

He was able to turn his attention instead to the enrichment of Assyrian culture, and his palace at Nineveh became a great centre of both the literary and the visual arts. His artists produced some of the most striking work of the ancient world, and his scribes gathered an amazing library of literature. Not only did they catalogue the events of recent history with great precision, but they also collected the ancient traditions of Mesopotamia, which went back right to the very dawn of civilization. Their writing methods may seem primitive to us today, for they used the material that lay ready to hand: river mud. First they formed the mud into conveniently-sized blocks, then they wrote on them with wedge-shaped sticks while the mud was still wet. Once the writing was complete, the blocks could be baked solid in the heat of the sun. This meant their books were bulky, but they were also virtually indestructible, and even today it is still possible to piece together mud blocks that have been broken for centuries. It is due to this royal library at Nineveh that we have so much detailed knowledge of the ancient civilizations of the area and of their national traditions.

There was little to say about life in Jerusalem and Judah at such a time as this. Hezekiah's successor, Manasseh, had no room to flex his nationalistic muscles. He was no match for Assyria's power, and was in complete subjection to it. The Assyrian records mention him only as a source of building materials and troops, and confirm that he continued to pay regular taxes. The Old Testament makes no direct mention of Assyrian power during Manasseh's long reign, but it shows quite clearly the reality of it in its description of events

2 Kings 21:1–18 in the Jerusalem temple. Judah's own national faith was once more neglected, and all sorts of pagan ceremonies were promoted, including star worship. Like Ahaz before him, Manasseh was forced to express his subservience to the Assyrians by worshipping their gods. But this time he made sure there would be no protests from people like Isaiah: those who disagreed with his policies were

2 Kings 21:16 put to death. Because of all this, the Old Testament writers regarded him as the most wicked of all the kings. And his son Amon

2 Kings 21:19–26 continued the same unhappy policies.

Reform and renewal

Then came an unexpected opportunity for change. Things suddenly began to move on the fringes of the Assyrian Empire. The Egyptians regained their independence. The kingdom of Lydia in the north-west, and the Medes in the east, began to harrass the Assyrians. At the same time, hordes of Asian raiders (Scythians) swept down from the north. All of this had an unsettling effect on the empire. Indeed, its internal stability had already been shaken by feuding between Ashur-bani-pal and his brother. And within a few years of Ashur-bani-pal's death, the Assyrians were fighting for survival against the Babylonians and the Medes.

As before, the weakening of Assyrian power led to the revival of national hopes in Judah. This time, they centred around Amon's son, Josiah, who became king in Judah while he was still only a boy.

2 Kings 22:1–2 As soon as he grew up, Josiah set about re-asserting his country's independence. Assyria's problems now looked serious, and he saw a real chance of restoring the kingdom to something like the glory of the days of David and Solomon. He did not quite manage that, but nevertheless Josiah had considerable success in extending his territory. Archaeological evidence shows that he controlled land as far north as Galilee, and his influence extended east of the River Jordan into Gilead. He also had some power over the Philistine states in the west – and all this was consolidated with at least two

2 Kings 23:31, 36 marriages.

This territorial expansion went hand in hand with a thoroughgoing religious reformation. This was only to be expected, for the terms of Assyrian rule had closely integrated religion with politics. Ahaz and Manasseh had both demonstrated their allegiance to Assyria by worshipping Assyrian gods in Jerusalem. Hezekiah's move for independence had started with the removal of the paraphernalia of Assyrian religion, and Josiah had to do the same. In the event, he was far more successful than Hezekiah had ever been: he even managed to ban the symbols of Assyrian domination in the territories of the former northern kingdom of Israel. The sanctuary established at Bethel by Jeroboam I was destroyed, along with many local shrines and their priests.

2 Kings 23:15–20

But the central feature of Josiah's reform was the discovery of a long-forgotten book in the temple at Jerusalem. This book was not the cause of the reform, for it only came to light after the workmen had started to renovate the temple. But once discovered, it played a significant part in the subsequent course of events. The Old Testament story does not directly identify this book. But three main ideas seem to have dominated it:

2 Kings 22:3–20

● Israel was a united people, and therefore the political division between Judah and Israel was meaningless.

● The central plank of Israel's faith must be belief in only one God.

● Israel's one God must be worshipped in only one place.

A lost book Up to this point, Josiah's reform had probably been more concerned with getting rid of Assyrian objects than with promoting the worship of Israel's God Yahweh for his own sake. But this book provided a new, positive impetus. At times of political crisis and uncertainty, people often try to go back to the old ways, even today. And in Josiah's time, many nations in the ancient world were taking a new look at their own national heritage for the same reasons. So when an ancient book was discovered in Jerusalem, it was naturally treated with special reverence. As it happened, this book also played right into Josiah's hands, for its main ideas seemed to give a

The Assyrian Empire

religious backing to the political moves he was already making. He was trying to restore Judah's control over the former territory of the whole of the united nation of Israel. He was getting rid of Assyrian gods. And he needed to strengthen his personal position by insisting that the religious allegiance of the people should be given to his own royal temple in Jerusalem.

There can be no doubt that this book was the Old Testament book of Deuteronomy. Some scholars have occasionally suggestd that, far from being an ancient book, Josiah had actually arranged to have it written for precisely the reasons just mentioned. But this is highly unlikely. If Deuteronomy had been written in Josiah's time, it would have reflected his own situation much more clearly. In particular, it would have identified the one place where God should be worshipped as the temple in Jerusalem. But in fact, Deuteronomy does not do this – and in any case, Josiah was not the first king of Judah to try to strengthen his position by this stratagem: Hezekiah had already tried it before him.

Deuteronomy does not in itself support the centralization of worship in Jerusalem, and it actually has many close links with the dynamic view of kingship that had been followed more self-consciously in the northern kingdom of Israel. For this reason, many scholars believe that the 'one sanctuary' mentioned in **Deuteronomy 12:5** Deuteronomy was not Jerusalem, but the place where the ark of the covenant had been kept during the earliest period of Israel's settlement in the land. The whole book clearly emphasizes the lessons that had been forcefully presented by northern prophets like Amos and Hosea: that the nation's prosperity could only be assured if they were willing to return to the old ways, and recognize the demands for justice and equality that had been so important in the covenant made at Mt Sinai.

This is something that the people of Judah had forgotten. They were laying more emphasis on the promises given to David and to his successors. Instead of asking what they had done to deserve the punishment that was being handed out to them by Assyria, they reassured themselves with the belief that Jerusalem was God's chosen city – Zion – and so nothing could ever happen to it. It was impregnable, and would always be that way. Even Isaiah had agreed with this point of view. Though he saw Assyria's iron hand as the **Isaiah 1:10–20; 2:6–21; 5:26–30** agent of God's punishment, he still could not believe that Judah's **Isaiah 9:1–7; 11:1–16; 14:1–2** day was finished. But now, as Josiah and his people read this old book, they could see very clearly that unless they changed their ways, Judah and its people were indeed finished. So in a solemn ceremony reminiscent of the events of Mt Sinai, the people of Judah pledged their allegiance once again to the long-forgotten **2 Kings 23:1–3** ideals of their ancient faith.

The Babylonians

While all this was going on in Judah, the Assyrians were fighting desperately to hang on to the tattered remains of their once great empire. The Babylonians were more powerful than ever, and they soon captured all the main Assyrian cities. The defeated Assyrians tried to re-establish themselves at Harran, but they were soon ejected from there as well. Some thirteen years after Josiah's reformation in Judah, the Assyrians made a last-ditch effort to regain this town. This time, their old enemies the Egyptians came to help them. Necho II, now king of Egypt, could see that his real rival was no longer the king of Assyria but Nabopolasser, king of Babylon. Judah had no reason to be involved in all this. But for some inexplicable reason Josiah decided that he would try to stop

A representation of a demon from Babylon. Unlike Israel to the north, Judah survived the years of Assyrian dominance. But the Babylonian Empire took over control of the region, and none of the Judean kings after Josiah could resist their influence.

the Egyptians from reaching the beleaguered Assyrian army. He was unable to do so, and died in the atttempt at Megiddo. As a result, Judah came under Egyptian domination for a while.

But nothing could stop the advance of the Babylonians now. Four years after the final collapse of Assyria the Babylonian army met the Egyptians in battle at Carchemish, and decisively defeated them. At this Jehoiakim, a king of Judah who had been put in power by the Egyptians, was forced to transfer his allegiance to the Babylonian Nebuchadnezzar. But like his predecessors, he was

2 Kings 24:1

always searching for a suitable opportunity to reassert his own independence.

When Babylon was defeated by the Egyptians some four years later, he decided to take his chance. But he had seriously misjudged the situation. The Babylonian Nebuchadnezzar moved in strength through the whole of Palestine, and besieged Jerusalem with his army. He was determined to replace Jehoiakim with a king who could be trusted. As it happened, the job was done for him, for Jehoiakim died during the course of the siege, and was replaced by his son Jehoiachin. He could see that resistance was futile, and surrendered to Nebuchadnezzar. But the Babylonian did not trust him. Instead, he took him off into exile in Babylon, along with many of the leading citizens and a large quantity of the treasures from both palace and temple.

Three prophets

Three of the shorter Old Testament books seem to have originated during the reigns of Josiah and Jehoiakim: Zephaniah, Nahum, and Habakkuk. We know virtually nothing of the prophets whose messages they contain, but they were all concerned with one subject: the way that God was using nations like Assyria and Babylon to achieve his own ends.

● **Zephaniah** is identified as a descendant of Hezekiah (1:1), and he probably delivered his messages in the earliest days of the reign of Josiah. Judah and Jerusalem, he declared, were being brought to ruination by the worship of Canaanite gods like Baal, as well as the astral deities of the Assyrians (1:4-6). But Zephaniah did not blame Josiah himself for this state of affairs. Instead, he singles out his court officials (1:8-9), which suggests that Josiah was still a boy and his great religious reforms were a thing of the future. Probably therefore Zephaniah delivered his messages some time between 640 and 622 BC, and this date would also fit in well with the theme of the poem which ends the book (3:14-20). For this is a celebration hymn, following the deliverance of Judah and Jerusalem from some particular enemy – possibly the Scythians, who were advancing south towards Egypt at about this period. But the jubilation with which the book closes is not reflected in the rest of the prophet's messages.

Zephaniah warned his people against a false confidence in the security of Jerusalem just because of God's promises to David. The 'Day of the Lord' would be coming soon enough – and it would not be a day of rejoicing for the people of Judah, any more than it had been for the people of Samaria (1:7-18). They would experience God's anger, just as other nations would. Even Assyria, which God had used to punish his own people, would in turn be destroyed themselves because of their pride and self-satisfaction (2:13-15). But like Isaiah before him, Zephaniah saw that God could both punish his people, and yet still show his love for them. Though Jerusalem was doomed, 'a humble and lowly people' would survive (3:12), and through them God's promises would come true.

● **Nahum** belongs to a period nearer the end of Josiah's reign, either just before or just after the collapse of the Assyrian capital Nineveh in 612 BC. Nahum too saw that, though Assyria had been the instrument of God's punishment for his people, they had over-reached themselves – and they would be punished in their turn. The collapse of Nineveh (Nahum 2—3) is described in such vivid language that some scholars have argued that the prophet must actually have witnessed the scene. But others believe that his apparent realism is a purely imaginary – though remarkably accurate – description of the city's fall, and was probably written even before the Babylonians finally moved in. Either way, the message of the book is the conviction that God himself, and not the Assyrians, is the Lord of history. He can use nations to achieve his own ends, but he is the one who is in control. This was obviously an important issue for the people of Judah, who had suffered so much at the hands of Assyria. Because of the poetic form of the book, and the dramatic content of it, some have suggested that Nahum's messages were put together in this form to be used as a

Habakkuk's prophecies were given at a time when Babylonian military power was dominant and no other army would resist them. This time of warfare brought great suffering and humiliation on the people, and Habakkuk tried to understand how God could be found at such a time.

part of the worship in the temple at Jerusalem, to celebrate Nineveh's downfall, and to remind the worshippers of God's great power.

● **Habakkuk** tackled the same problem, but this time from a more reflective perspective. He lived slightly later than Nahum, in the reign of Jehoiakim. By the time he delivered his messages, Egypt had been defeated at the battle of Carchemish (605 BC), and Habakkuk now had a chance to reflect on the Babylonian style of government. He was not impressed with what he saw. Things in Judah were bad enough, and society was collapsing in moral and political anarchy (1:2–4). God was rightly using superpowers like Babylon to discipline his people. But were the Babylonians any better? They 'catch people with hooks, as though they were fish. They drag them off in nets and shout for joy over their catch! They even worship their nets and offer sacrifices to them, because their nets provide them with the best of everything.' (1:15–16). So, asked Habakkuk, how could God tolerate this kind of inhuman wickedness, while dealing so sternly with the lesser evil that was going on in Jerusalem?

He found the answer to that in the conviction that the Babylonians would themselves be punished by God. Like Nahum, he could see that God himself was in charge of history. And though he could use even evil nations to accomplish his intentions, he would never allow them to get away with their wrongdoing: 'You are doomed! You founded a city on crime and built it up by murder. The nations you conquered wore themselves out in useless labour,

and all they have built goes up in flames. The Lord Almighty has done this. But the earth will be as full of the knowledge of the Lord's glory as the seas are full of water . . . The Lord will make you drink your own cup of punishment, and your honour will be turned to disgrace.' (2:12–14, 16).

Of course, Habakkuk realized that this kind of answer to the problem of evil in the world is not much direct use to those who are actually suffering. But he also included some practical advice for his people: 'Those who are evil will not survive, but those who are righteous will live because they are faithful to God' (2:4). There is some debate as to the precise meaning of these words, but almost certainly we should translate the Hebrew to refer to the faithfulness of God himself, first experienced by his people in the events of the exodus, and repeated many times since then. It was in these words that Paul and Luther found the heart of Christianity, and of course the commitment of which they spoke is essentially a human response to the faithfulness of God himself. This confidence in God was eloquently expressed by Habakkuk in the closing verses of his book – and it was to be needed in the dark days that were ahead for Judah: 'Even though the fig-trees have no fruit and no grapes grow on the vines, even though the olive-crop fails and the fields produce no corn, even though the sheep all die and the cattle-stalls are empty, I will still be joyful and glad, because the Lord God is my saviour. The Sovereign Lord gives me strength. He makes me sure-footed as a deer, and keeps me safe on the mountains' (3:17–19).

Jeremiah's early life

Even before Josiah's reformation in 622 BC, another young prophet called Jeremiah had already begun his work. He belonged to a family of priests from Anathoth, a village about four miles north east of Jerusalem. Like the other prophets, he was convinced that God himself had spoke to him, and given him a message for his people. He was to be 'a prophet to the nations', communicating the will of God in the midst of much international turmoil (Jeremiah 1:4). This was certainly an appropriate time for the emergence of such a person. For by the year of his call, 627 BC, Assyria's power was crumbling and independence for Judah once more seemed a real possibility.

But Jeremiah could not share in the mood of national optimism. He saw many things wrong in his nation. They had ignored the covenant laws of God, and would have to pay the price for their disobedience. One day he saw an almond tree in blossom. Now the

Hebrew word for 'almond' sounded rather like another Hebrew word that meant 'watching' – and Jeremiah saw this tree as a sign that God was watching over his people, looking for the appropriate time to carry out his sentence of destruction (1:11–12). When he saw a pot of boiling water on a fire that was fanned by a wind from the north, he realized that this too had a message in it. God's anger was about to boil over against Judah: 'Destruction will boil over from the north on all who live in this land, because I am calling all the nations in the north to come. Their kings will set up their thrones at the gates of Jerusalem and round its walls, and also round the other cities of Judah. I will punish my people . . . ' (1:13–16).

Of course, things soon began to change with the religious reforms instituted by Josiah. And Jeremiah was almost certainly in favour of all this. He certainly wanted to get rid of foreign religious influences, and some of his

Jeremiah's picture of an almond tree in blossom was not a comforting one. The Hebrew word for 'almond' sounds like 'watching'. Jeremiah was convinced that the Lord was watching over his people, against the time when he should bring on them the judgement due for generations of disobedience to the covenant.

Jerusalem finally fell to the Babylonians, and most of its people either became refugees or were taken into exile. It seemed that the history of Judah had come to an end.

messages may well have been delivered in support of Josiah, for they angered his relatives in Anathoth, who decided to try to kill him (11:1–23). Their reaction would make sense if Jeremiah was supporting Josiah's closure of all the sanctuaries except the temple in Jerusalem, for as priests they would presumably be in danger of losing their jobs.

But Jeremiah soon saw that Josiah's reform was not going to have much lasting effect on the way of life of the people. By the time of Jehoiakim things were as bad as they had ever been. But he also believed that Josiah's emphasis on the Jerusalem temple had actually undermined the faith that was emphasized in the ancient book found there. For instead of facing up to their responsibilities under the covenant law, his people developed a pathetic and misguided confidence in their religious institutions. They came to believe that as long as they performed all the religious rituals in the temple, God would actually preserve them from their enemies and all would be well.

In the end, events proved Jeremiah was right. But in the short term, he was disappointed and depressed. The people refused to listen to his message. And he was puzzled himself, because it was not coming true. Instead of the doom that Jeremiah had predicted, Judah was enjoying a period of great prosperity. Under Josiah her territory was enlarged and there never seemed any shortage of money for grand new building projects. Under the circumstances, people like Jeremiah were unlikely to be taken seriously. When Nineveh was destroyed in 612 BC, his message seemed to be quite discredited.

But the picture soon changed. Three years later, Josiah was dead and the Egyptians had taken over the land of Judah. The prosperity that had gone before had been attributed to the fact that things had been set right in the temple at Jerusalem. So what had gone wrong now? Why had God not saved his apparently faithful people from the power of Egypt? In this situation, Jeremiah's messages did not look so unrealistic. And when under Jehoiakim the reforms of Josiah virtually disappeared, the stage looked set for the scenario of disaster that Jeremiah had so vividly described. Even Jehoiakim himself could see that, and he made a concerted effort to get rid of opponents like Jeremiah. At least one prophet, Uriah, was killed (26:20–23), and Jeremiah himself was brought to trial

(26:7–24). He escaped death, but he still continued his messages of doom and destruction, and was beaten up and put into the stocks for a night (20:1–2).

Even that did not stop him. God had spoken to him, and he could not refuse to communicate the message: 'When I say, "I will forget the Lord and no longer speak in his name", then your message is like a fire burning deep within me. I try my best to hold it in, but can no longer keep it back' (20:9). But he was banned from delivering his messages in public at the temple. So he withdrew from public life for the rest of Jehoiakim's reign, and sent out his messages in a new way. This time he got his friend Baruch to write them down, and then he took them into the streets and read them out.

In the reign of Jehoiakim, Jeremiah's messages were no longer general declarations of disaster, but definite predictions of the impending end of Jerusalem, and especially of the destruction of its temple. Jeremiah was sure that the idea that God was bound to protect his own temple and city was false.

But Jeremiah's challenge came not just from his enemies. He had his own problems with the message God had given him. If it was so correct, why did no one else accept it? After all, Jeremiah had not refused God's call, even though he wanted to do so. He had laid himself open to disbelief and ridicule, and had become involved in endless arguments (15:10–21). He had given up the ordinary human joys of home and family to be a spokesman for God – and he felt that God had deceived him (20:7–18). He had to learn some hard lessons, and some of the most striking parts of his book are taken up with this kind of self-examination. But he was also learning an important new lesson, for out of the crisis of his own life he discovered what it meant to trust God in a personal and living way.

Dark days in Jerusalem · When Nebuchadnezzar captured Jerusalem in 597 BC, he placed a new king, Zedekiah, on the throne there. But things did not change. Instead of learning their lesson, the people of Jerusalem concluded that they were specially favoured by God, because they had not been carried off into exile. The prophet Jeremiah had no time for all this. He knew that what had happened was a just punishment for the people's wrongdoing – and worse was to come. He pointed to two baskets of figs in the market. One contained good figs, the other was full of rotten figs. The good ones, said Jeremiah, were the

The people of Jerusalem were deported to Babylon in stages. At first only the leaders were taken in the days of King Jehoiachin, while Zedekiah was put on the throne as a puppet ruler. Only after his revolt was the city fully crushed. Jeremiah characterized this intervening time as being like a basket of figs, of which the good ones stood for those already in exile, and the bad ones for the leaders who remained.

Jeremiah 24

exiles in Babylon. The bad ones were the people left in Judah, and they would suffer the same fate as figs that were too bad to eat.

Zedekiah did not know which way to turn. Jeremiah told him the only sensible thing to do was to accept Babylonian domination, and he wanted to listen. But he was a weak man. When the Egyptians tried to persuade him to join a revolt against Babylon, many prophets advised Zedekiah to do so. But Jeremiah would not change his mind. He appeared with a wooden yoke on his

Jeremiah 27

shoulders. He was confronted in the temple by a prophet called Hananiah. This prophet poured scorn on Jeremiah's message, and to prove his point he smashed Jeremiah's yoke. Jeremiah knew this was a false message, and he quickly replaced the wooden yoke with

Jeremiah 28

an iron one.

In the event, Jeremiah was right. The Babylonian army moved up to crush the rebellion masterminded by Egypt, and Judah was finished. After a siege of eighteen months Jerusalem fell to Nebuchadnezzar. Zedekiah tried to escape, but he was captured. His family was killed before his eyes, and then he was blinded and carried off to Babylon along with most of the leading people of the land. This time the Babylonians made sure of their victory. They systematically destroyed all the main buildings in Jerusalem, including the temple. A palace official named Gedaliah was made governor of Judah. There would never be a king again.

2 Kings 25:1–26

Jeremiah's dreadful predictions had come true. The temple was gone. But he knew that God's promises could not be overthrown so easily. Like Habakkuk, Jeremiah knew that God could be trusted to keep his word, and there would be a future for his people. Even while Jerusalem was under attack, Jeremiah had bought a piece of land in his native village, as an expression of his confidence for the future. The action nearly cost him his life, for he was arrested as a traitor while leaving the city to go and view the property.

Jeremiah 32:1–25
Jeremiah 37:11—38:13

Yet his trust in God was not founded on a crudely materialistic expectation. He had already made it plain that his people's future and the real meaning of the faith from Mt Sinai was not to be found in the temple. All the institutions connected with that were only of limited value. God was not truly to be found in the ritual of sacrifice, but in a personal and living relationship of trust and commitment. The exiles in Babylon were to learn that soon enough. But it was an insight that had already been given to Jeremiah. For he saw beyond and through the disaster and destruction, to a new relationship that God would establish with his people. God himself had remained faithful to the covenant made at Mt Sinai, but his people had been unable to respond to his love. They had not managed to live up to the high ideals. What they needed now was a 'new covenant', that would repair the omission of the old – a covenant that would not just ask them to be obedient to God, but that would actually give them the moral power to be so.

'The new covenant that I will make with the people of Israel will be this: I will put my law within them and write it on their hearts. I will be their God, and they will be my people . . . all will know me, from the least to the greatest. I will forgive their sins, and I will no longer remember their wrongs. I the Lord have spoken.'

Jeremiah 31:31–34

The Lachish Letters

The last days of Judah are depicted vividly in the book of Jeremiah, where the prophet's message reflects the disarray and confusion of the people. They could see the Babylonians coming, and were powerless to do anything about it. The picture we get from Jeremiah has been supplemented by one of the most remarkable finds ever made by archaeologists in a Bible city: the Lachish Letters.

The city of Lachish lay to the south-west of Jerusalem, and its history began long before the Israelite tribes ever came into the land. It was an important city from the time of Joshua onwards, and has been more thoroughly excavated than most Israelite towns. The material found there by archaeologists has been of great importance for our understanding of the development of the Hebrew language, and the discovery of Canaanite altars and other religious objects has added to our knowledge of the kind of practices so often denounced by the prophets in the Old Testament. The city was destroyed by Sennacherib in 701 BC, and then later Nebuchadnezzar captured it in about 587 BC, just before the final collapse of Zedekiah's Jerusalem. The Lachish Letters relate to this sequence of events.

They are actually what archaeologists call 'ostraca', that is, scraps of broken pottery with messages written on them. A total of twenty-one of these ostraca were found, mostly in what appears to have been the guardroom of the city gate. Not all of them are now legible, but the majority of them that are were addressed to a man named Yaush, who was probably the military commander of Lachish at the time. Many of the messages were written by a man called Hoshayahu, who seems to have been the

Fragments of a letter, written on pottery by a military commander at an outpost near Lachish, bear witness to a desperate state of affairs as the Babylonian army advanced.

officer in charge of a military outpost to the north of Lachish. The same name is found in Jeremiah (42:1; 43:2), but there is no reason to think they were the same person. Yet the letters do give us a fascinating insight into the same situations as were described by Jeremiah:

● Jeremiah 34:1–7 reports a message given by Jeremiah to Zedekiah while Nebuchadnezzar's army was moving against Jerusalem. At the same time, 'the army was also attacking Lachish and Azekah, the only other fortified cities left in Judah' (Jeremiah 34:7). Azekah was almost half-way between Lachish and Jerusalem, and in one of the Lachish ostraca Hoshayahu writes 'we are watching for the signals of Lachish . . . for we cannot see Azekah'. Azekah was perhaps midway between Hoshayahu's post and Lachish, and was therefore used as a signalling station . But at the time of writing, it had apparently fallen to the Babylonians.

● The name Jeremiah is found in two of the letters, though there is no reason to identify this person with the Old Testament prophet in either case. But there is a clear reference to 'the prophet' in at least two of these letters, and the term may be found in a further two. Some have suggested that the person referred to so clearly as 'the prophet' must have been Jeremiah himself. Others argue that it could be Uriah, since the same letter also refers to 'Coniah, son of Elnathan' going to Egypt – and according to Jeremiah 26:22, Jehoiakim sent a man called Elnathan to bring Uriah from Egypt to face death in Jerusalem. This identification is highly questionable, for the letters did not originate in Jehoiakim's reign, but later in the time of Zedekiah. Nevertheless, even these uncertain references do indicate that such prophets as Jeremiah were performing an important role in national affairs at this period in Judah's history.

The first scholar actually to decipher these letters thought that the story behind them was closely linked with the prophetic movement in Jerusalem. Hoshayahu was apparently trying to justify his actions in some matter connected with confidential letters. According to Professor Torczyner, Yaush, the commander, was a supporter of the prophets, and Hoshayahu had been responsible for betraying Uriah when he fled to Egypt. This explains why Yaush was storing the letters in his guardhouse, so they could be used as evidence in Hoshayahu's trial later.

But this is only a conjecture (and perhaps not a very likely one). The greatest value of these letters is the insight that they give us into the people of Jeremiah's day, and their reactions as they faced the inevitable end of their nation at the hands of the Babylonian army.

7 Dashed hopes and new horizons

2 Kings 25:22–30	Isaiah 40—66	Joel	Ruth
Jeremiah 39:11—52:34	Haggai	Malachi	Jonah
Lamentations	Zechariah	Nehemiah	1 and 2 Chronicles
Ezekiel	Obadiah	Ezra	

Exile in Babylon | Return to Judah

JUDAH
Jehoiachin 597
Zedekiah 597-586
Jeremiah
Sheshbazzar
Zerubbabel and Joshua • Jerusalem temple rebuilt 520-515
Haggai
Zechariah
Obadiah
Joel
Malachi
Nehemiah
Ezra
• Nehemiah appointed Governor of Judah 445

BABYLON
Ezekiel
Isaiah of Babylon
Nebuchadnezzar II 605-562
Amel-Marduk 562-560
Nabonidus 556-539
• Fall of Babylon 539

PERSIA
Cyrus 539-530
Cambyses 530-522
Darius I 522-486
Artaxerxes I 464-423

| 650 | 600 | 550 | 500 | 450 | 400 |

THE PERIOD following the Babylonian invasion of Judah was one of the most important in the entire history of the Jewish people and their religion. The previous millennium had seen many striking changes, as Israel first emerged as a nation, soon to become a world power, and then to sink into political and spiritual decay, so that in the years immediately prior to the fall of Jerusalem, the state of Judah had become a relatively unimportant middle-eastern kingdom. Politically, the nation was finished. Yet by the time of Jesus, the religious beliefs based on the life of this ancient people had achieved a world-wide influence, and large groups of their descendants were making a significant contribution to the life and culture of major cities throughout the known world.

This amazing transformation, in which Judaism arose phoenix-like out of the ashes of the old kingdom of Judah, can only be explained after a careful analysis of the new currents of thought that swept through the Old Testament faith in the centuries immediately following the Babylonian exile. These centuries were an intensely creative time, as the lessons of the past were assessed and their spiritual power was harnessed to a new cause. But unfortunately for us, we know comparatively little about this period in Israel's history. We certainly know a good deal less than we do of the earlier years of the Old Testament story. There are many decades in the exilic age about which we simply know nothing at all – and even those scraps of information which we do get from the Old Testament and elsewhere are often confused and incomplete. Interpreting them is sometimes a matter of pure guesswork, and it is always a process of painstaking deductions from partial and incomplete evidence.

Facing up to disaster

2 Kings 25:18–24; Jeremiah 40:7–12

We can see the nature of the problem right away, when we ask what life in Judah itself was like immediately after Nebuchadnezzar's invasion. The general outline of events is reasonably clear: the royal family was deported to Babylon, along with most of the leading citizens, after which a palace official called Gedaliah was made governor of Judah, with his capital at Mizpah. This fact suggests that neither the destruction nor the deportation was as extensive as has often been imagined. There would have been little purpose in appointing Gedaliah if there were no territory and no population over which he could rule. But at the same time, it is not at all clear what his status actually was. Was he, for example, regarded as a Babylonian official, and Judah a Babylonian province? Or was the social structure much less rigid than that? We simply do not know.

2 Kings 25:25–26; Jeremiah 40:13—41:3

What we do know is that his existence soon provoked opposition, and it was not long before he was assassinated by a member of the former royal family, a man called Ishmael. He was certainly one member of the Jerusalem aristocracy who had escaped the Babylonians, by fleeing to the neighbouring state of Ammon. He was not the only one to have escaped Nebuchadnezzar's invasion

2 Kings 25:22–24;
Jeremiah 40:7–12
Jeremiah 40:10

Jeremiah 41:11–15

2 Kings 25:26; Jeremiah 41:16–18
Jeremiah 42—43

like this, and once the Babylonians had gone, such people came out of hiding and allied themselves with Gedaliah. The life-style that they anticipated for themselves was hardly at subsistence level. But it was never realized. For though Ishmael himself was put to flight after his murder of Gedaliah, those who were left at his headquarters now feared a Babylonian reprisal, and so they decided to go and live in Egypt, where they would be able to obtain employment as mercenary soldiers. Jeremiah did not want to go with them. When he had been offered a choice earlier, he had decided to stay in Judah rather than go to Babylon – and this is what he wanted to

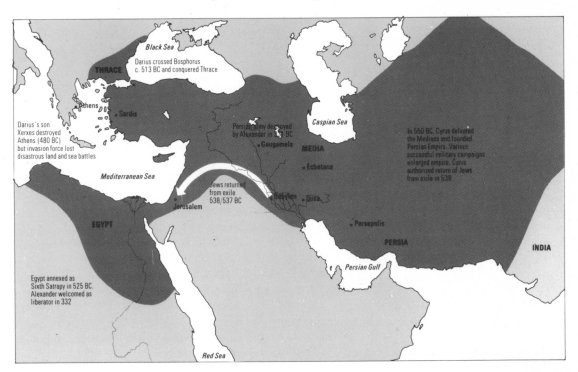

The Persian Empire

do now. He felt that his people had suffered enough, and God would soon restore their fortunes. But to be sure of that they must stay in their own land. By going abroad they would forget the God of their ancestors. Jerusalem was the place where they had lost their true faith, and it was where they must try to regain it.

Nevertheless, Jeremiah was forced against his will to join the exiles in Egypt, and he spent the rest of his life there. No doubt those who took him to Egypt felt they had done the right thing, for it seems that the Babylonians did indeed return to Judah, and a further deportation in 582 BC may well have been a reprisal for the chaos that followed the murder of Gedaliah.

Jeremiah 52:30

We know virtually nothing of life in Judah for at least the next forty years. What little we do know suggests that its people were disillusioned by what had taken place. This is hardly surprising when we recall the high expectations they had held. They never believed that Jerusalem could fall to an alien army at all: it was

God's city, and he had given it his own seal of approval through the covenant with David's family. As they faced up to the realities of their predicament, it must have seemed to these people as if very little was left of Judah's great national heritage.

The book of Lamentations

In the book of Lamentations, the full weight of Judah's grief can be felt as they experience the destruction of Jerusalem. What makes it so much more acute is that the Lord himself has turned against them in judgement.

The depth of feeling about this national tragedy is reflected with great pathos in the Old Testament book of Lamentations. The book consists of five poems, the first four of which are arranged in an acrostic pattern based on the letters of the Hebrew alphabet. This is an unusual literary device in the Old Testament, and though it may have been used here simply as an aid to the memory, it is more likely to be connected to the deeply felt message of these poems. They are essentially an adaptation of the mourning songs that were sung at every funeral, and their literary form may well be intended to reflect the all-embracing character of the tragedy which left the people emotionally and morally distraught.

The people were forced to accept the truth of what prophets like Jeremiah had been saying all along: the havoc wrought upon Jerusalem was the work of God, and it had been brought about by the disobedience and unfaithfulness of his people. Though 'No one has ever had pain like mine, pain that the Lord brought on me in the time of his anger' (1:12), nevertheless 'the Lord is just, for I have disobeyed him' (1:18). This first poem could well refer to the situation in Jerusalem after 597 BC, but before its final destruction. But the whole book gives us a striking insight into the despair of those whose arrogance and vanity are depicted so clearly in the book of Jeremiah. His message of doom had been opposed by false prophets, but their teaching now lay exposed for what it really was: 'Your prophets had nothing to tell you but lies; Their preaching deceived you by never exposing your sin. They made you think you did not need to repent' (2:14).

The pitiful trust of the people in the sanctity of their capital city and its institutions is clearly reflected here too: 'No one anywhere, not even rulers of foreign nations, believed that any invader could enter Jerusalem's gates. But it happened because her prophets sinned and her priests were guilty of causing the death of innocent people. Her leaders wandered through the streets like blind men, so stained with blood that no one would touch them.' (4:12–14). Jeremiah had seen all this coming long before the final tragedy; now those who opposed him had been forced to agree. And their unbridled despair and grief knew no boundaries.

Yet even in the midst of such shattered dreams, the tattered remnants of a once proud nation could still see cause for hope: 'The thought of my pain, my homelessness, is bitter poison; I think of it constantly and my spirit is depressed. Yet hope returns when I remember this one thing: The Lord's unfailing love and mercy still continue, fresh as the morning, and sure as the sunrise. The Lord is all I have, and so I put my hope in him. The Lord is good to everyone who trusts in him, so it is best for us to wait in patience – to wait for him to save us . . . ' (3:19–26). That in itself could never relieve the anguish that these people felt. But it did give them the confidence to pray for restoration – and that prayer is the theme of the fifth and final poem in the book: 'Bring us back to you, Lord! Bring us back! Restore our ancient glory' (5:21).

Author and date

The Old Testament itself presents this book as an anonymous work. But other traditions, mostly within Christian circles, have attributed it to Jeremiah himself. The reason for this is to be found in 2 Chronicles 35:25, where it is stated that 'Jeremiah composed a lament for king Josiah . . . The song is found in the collection of laments.' But Lamentations has no connection at all with this early period of Jeremiah's life, and it in fact makes much better sense when viewed as a product of those elements of Jerusalem society that had been originally opposed to all that Jeremiah stood for. Various aspects of

the political outlook reflected in Lamentations seem to suit Jeremiah's opponents rather than the prophet himself. It is anti-Babylonian (1:21–22; 3:59–66), and suggests dependence on Egypt (4:17), something that Jeremiah consistently opposed (Jeremiah 37:5–10). It is also difficult to imagine Jeremiah referring to Zedekiah as 'the source of our life, the king the Lord had chosen, the one we had trusted to protect us from every invader' (4:20). To the prophet, he had been one of the 'bad figs' (Jeremiah 24:8–10).

Nevertheless, the book certainly stands as a vindication of Jeremiah's message, as we see how even those who had been implacably opposed to him were forced to admit their guilt in the face of God's judgement. These five poems probably reflect the ways they did this in Judah itself, in the period immediately following 586 BC, and before the collapse of the Babylonian Empire in 539 BC.

Not everyone, however, accepted that Israel's national faith could explain the tragedy. Some people lost their faith altogether. They came to think of these sad events as a battle between Israel's God and the Babylonian gods, and they were forced to admit that the gods of Babylon had apparently won. Others felt they had been misled all along by the very prophets who claimed to speak in the name of their own God. Those who took Jeremiah to Egypt believed that the Babylonian invasion had been the fault of prophets like him. They had encouraged them to abandon the worship of the gods and goddesses to whom the land of Palestine had belonged for centuries – so why should they be surprised that the land had met with such disaster? They were convinced that the way to renewed prosperity must therefore be found in an enthusiastic return to the old ways of the Baal religion: 'We will offer sacrifices to our goddess, the Queen of Heaven, and we will pour out wine-offerings to her, just as we and our ancestors, our king and our leaders, used to do in the towns of Judah and in the streets of Jerusalem. Then we had plenty of food, we were prosperous, and had no troubles. But ever since we stopped sacrificing to the Queen of Heaven . . . we have had nothing, and our people have died in war and of starvation.'

Jeremiah 44:17–18

Jeremiah would have none of this. He argued again that it was precisely this kind of worship that had led to the disaster. But who could they believe? This was a crucial question for the restructuring of Jewish society. Eventually, it was Jeremiah's argument that won the day, for his interpretation of Israel's history was embodied in the stories of the Old Testament itself. The idea that obedience and loyalty to Israel's own God led to success and prosperity is the organizing principle of the books of Joshua, Judges, Samuel and

Jeremiah 44:23

Kings, and many scholars believe that these books were issued in a new edition in Judah itself in the years immediately following the Babylonian invasion. In previous times of national crisis, the people had often looked to their past to re-define the nature of their society, and so now they began to rebuild their shattered lives by trying to see where they had gone wrong.

The Deuteronomistic History

It was the German scholar, Martin Noth, in a book originally published in 1943, who first suggested that the books of Joshua, Judges, 1—2 Samuel and 1—2 Kings were gathered together to form an epic history of Israel at this time. He also suggested that the book of Deuteronomy, which immediately precedes these historical books in the Old Testament, was a part of them, acting as an introductory section to explain the theological basis on which Israel's history was to be understood. This is why he called these history books as a whole 'the Deuteronomistic History'. He believed that this great reassessment of Israel's history took place sometime after 561 BC (the year when Jehoiachin was released from prison, 2 Kings 25:27–30), but before the Persians came to power in 539 BC, and the subsequent rebuilding of the temple in Jerusalem in about 520 BC.

This is a bold hypothesis to explain the origin of these Old Testament books. But it is also an attractive one, and a number of facts seem to speak in its favour:

● It is not at all unlikely that those who survived the destruction of Jerusalem would begin to look at their past history as a way of making sense of their present predicament. We can see the same tendency among the exiles in Egypt, mentioned in the book of Jeremiah, and we have no reason to suppose that the same thing did not happen in Judah itself. Not only that, but in the immediate aftermath of the fall of Jerusalem there must have been an added incentive to gather together the traditions of the nation for their own sake, simply as a means of preserving the ancient records for posterity. All these books refer to other ancient sources of information from which their own stories have been extrapolated or summarized, and all of these other records have subsequently disappeared with the passage of time.

● At the same time, these Old Testament history books are more than just an anthology of extracts from older historical materials. For they also present a clear and coherent view of the meaning of the events that are recorded.

We have already mentioned the prominence of such an interpretation in the book of Judges. But it is present in many other passages too. It has not been superimposed on every detail of the narratives, but at strategic points the lessons of history are made plain: Israel was committed in a covenant relationship to God, and this placed upon her certain responsibilities. Accordingly, if she was willing to accept these responsibilities and obey the law of the covenant, she could expect the blessing that God had promised. On the other hand, deliberate disobedience would lead to failure and destruction. This message is often conveyed in the form of speeches at strategic points in the story (Joshua 23; 1 Samuel 12; 2 Samuel 7; 1 Kings 8:22–53), a device that is found in much ancient history writing.

● The fact that the covenant forms the basic framework within which Israel's history is understood in these books also gives a certain plausibility to Noth's claim that Deuteronomy was a preface for the whole work. For the literary structure of Deuteronomy is closely linked to the covenant pattern which has been traced in Hittite and Assyrian sources. In addition, the speech with which the book opens (Deuteronomy 1–4) is almost a classic exposition of the theological perspective of the so-called Deuteronomists. What is more, it sems to contain an explicit appeal and reassurance to the people for whom the exile was such a great crisis: 'The Lord will scatter you among other nations, where only a few of you will survive . . . There you will look for the Lord your God, and if you search for him with all your heart, you will find him. When you are in trouble and all those things happen to you, then you will finally turn to the Lord and obey him. He is a merciful God, he will not abandon you or destroy you, and he will not forget the covenant that he himself made with your ancestors' (Deuteronomy 4:27–31).

Noth's theory has not been universally accepted by scholars, but it has won a large measure of support. Four major issues have arisen in recent discussion of it:

● Noth regarded the Deuteronomistic History as simply an explanation of the tragedy that had befallen the people of Israel, and he therefore understood it as an essentially pessimistic work. But this is not the whole story. The main emphasis is certainly on Israel's past, but this is not simply an antiquarian interest. Indeed, there never was such a thing in ancient Israel, for the past was always seen as the theatre of God's activity, and therefore it inevitably became a mirror of the future, and a challenge to the people to face up to that future. The prophets had seen the failures of the past as an invitation to renewed obedience, and the history writers had the same perspective. Perhaps that is why they ended with the story of Jehoiachin's release, for that in itself must have generated renewed hope in the hearts of the people.

● Some have questioned whether there is such a thoroughgoing, unified presentation of the meaning of Israel's history in all these books. They point out, for example, that some passages of Samuel and Kings (like the Succession Narrative, 2 Samuel 9—20; 1 Kings 1—2) seem to have very little trace of the Deuteronomic point of view. They also ask whether the simple viewpoint of Deuteronomy itself, related to the earliest stages of Israel's history, is truly compatible with the complex position of the king and the Jerusalem temple in the later books. But these observations have more bearing on the complex way in which the various stories were gathered together. It is quite likely that the long job of writing a continuous history of Israel had already been started long before the dark days of the exile. Many scholars think that even before the time of Josiah, the outline for such a history was already in existence, and even in the earliest parts of the history, it is universally agreed that some of the stories were first written down more or less as they happened. For the later editors were not concerned to rewrite the stories (still less to invent them, as has very occasionally been suggested): they simply wanted to present them in a way that would be most meaningful to the people of their own day.

● Scholars have often asked just who these so-called Deuteronomists actually were. They have been identified in turn with groups of priests, prophets, and wise men. But they seem to have most in common with the great

A great theme of the book of Deuteronomy is that the land will be blessed if the people obey God's Law, but cursed if they disobey. This theme re-appears frequently in the history books that follow the same tradition.

prophets. Though Isaiah is the only one who is actually mentioned by name in the Old Testament histories (2 Kings 19—20), the message of these books is the same as theirs: the facts of Israel's history were taken as proof that the prophets were right. There are also a number of passages in the books of the prophets which are quite similar to parts of the Deuteronomistic History. Indeed, it is quite possible that these prophetic books were first gathered together by the same people who issued this great historical work. It is perhaps more than accidental that the Jews themselves came to regard the books of Joshua—Kings as 'the former prophets'.

● If Noth's theory is correct, then of course Deuteronomy must be detached from the Old Testament Law, or Torah, and linked instead to this Deuteronomistic History. On this, see further the special note on the Pentateuch.

By the rivers of Babylon

We know far more about the life of the exiles who were taken off to Babylon than we do about those who were left behind in Judah. They seem to have settled in a kind of Jewish ghetto in Babylon, and they evidently enjoyed considerable freedom to organize their own affairs, both socially and religiously. The fact that Jehoiachin was there no doubt helped to generate this community spirit. He was one of those taken from Jerusalem in the first deportation of 597 BC, but since he was the last true member of the royal family of David, it was to be expected that the exiles would focus their national allegiance on him. His exact position is not absolutely clear. The Old Testament states that Nebuchadnezzar's successor, Amel-Marduk, released Jehoiachin from prison and gave him a distinctive position at the Babylonian court. That was in 561 BC, but even before that the Babylonian annals describe Jehoiachin as 'king of Judah'. Perhaps therefore his imprisonment was little more than a nominal house arrest. His presence in Babylon was certainly important for the exiles. They counted the years of their exile in relation to him, and his sons and grandsons continued to play an important part in Jewish affairs for a considerable time. But he seems to have been a figurehead rather than a ruler in any sense, and the Jewish community itself was organized by groups of elders.

On the whole, life in Babylon was probably quite comfortable – even prosperous – for the exiles from Judah. From a slightly later period than this, we have detailed business records relating to the activities of a Jewish firm run by the Murashu family in Nippur, and the Old Testament itself suggests that about 100 years

2 Kings 25:27–30

Ezekiel 1:2; 33:21; 40:1

Ezekiel 14:1–11; 20:1

'By the rivers of Babylon...' The exiles from Judea found the city of Babylon and the banks of the Euphrates alien territory, where they could not bring themselves to 'sing a song to the Lord'. Through the years of exile they were to discover that it is possible to worship the Lord even away from the temple and David's city.

Ezra 1:6; 2:68–69 later many of the exiles were quite rich. But they were not always happy. No matter how comfortable life in Babylon might be, it was not the same as the homeland they had left behind. The despair and dereliction felt by these people made such an impression on them that, like the story of their slavery in Egypt centuries before, it achieved a permanent place in their national consciousness:

'By the rivers of Babylon we sat down;
there we wept when we remembered Zion.
On the willows nearby we hung up our harps.
Those who captured us told us to sing;
they told us to entertain them:
"Sing us a song about Zion".
How can we sing a song to the Lord in a foreign land?
May I never be able to play the harp again
if I forget you, Jerusalem!
May I never be able to sing again if I do not remember you,
Psalm 137:1–6 if I do not think of you as my greatest joy!'

By the standards of international justice, the Babylonians had been relatively benevolent. Their predecessors, the Assyrians, would never have allowed deported peoples to live in their own communities like this. But the exiles still hated them, and the same poem which contains such a moving expression of Jewish anguish ends on a note of hatred that is unparalleled anywhere else in the Bible: 'Babylon, you will be destroyed. Happy is the man who pays you back for what you have done to us – who takes your babies and Psalm 137:8–9 smashes them against a rock.'

We get the same bleak picture in the messages of the prophet Ezekiel. He himself was one of the exiles, and he knew that this dreadful experience had knocked all spiritual vitality out of his people. They were, he said, like a valley full of dead bones, with no Ezekiel 37 life in them at all. They were quite powerless to do anything to help themselves: their only hope for new life now lay with God himself.

Ezekiel

Ezekiel's career was roughly contemporary with that of Jeremiah. Both of them came from priestly families, but Ezekiel was far more conscious of his background, and he had much greater interest in the Jerusalem temple than Jeremiah ever had. Ezekiel was one of those who were taken to Babylon in the first deportation of 597 BC, and his carefully dated messages were given between 593 and 571 BC.

The Old Testament book of Ezekiel falls neatly into four sections:

- Messages concerning the people of Jerusalem before the city was destroyed in 586 BC (1:1—24:27)
- Oracles against foreign nations (25:1—32:32)
- Messages given in Babylon, mostly relating to the return of the exiles to Judah (33:1—39:29)
- A priestly blueprint for a future Jewish state (40:1—48:35)

This neat literary structure belies the complexity of the book and its message. Its contents are so diverse that it is not difficult to imagine many different people involved in its composition. At one time the prophet is a person who has strange visions of winged animals and of wheels with eyes (Ezekiel 1:4–28). At another he seems much more like Jeremiah, pronouncing doom on a wicked Jerusalem and laying a new emphasis on a personal relationship between God and his people (15:1–8; 20:1–49). Then there is a prophet whose messages to other nations reflect an extensive grasp of the intricacies of international politics (25:1—32:32). And there is a priest, who plans with great detail for the operation of a new temple with even stricter ritual than it had before (40:1—48:35). Because of this, some scholars have regarded the book as a compilation of the work of different people. As long ago as the first century AD, the Jewish historian Josephus mentioned 'two books' of Ezekiel (*Antiquities of the Jews X.v.1*). But it is more likely that all these messages originated with just one person.

Ezekiel was called to be a prophet in Babylon in 593 BC. He had a vision of a fiery cloud from the north containing a chariot drawn by four winged creatures of a kind familiar from many Babylonian sculptures and inscription (1:4–28). There was a throne on this chariot, and on the throne was the God of Israel, Yahweh himself. In the vision, Ezekiel was given a scroll to eat, which contained his message: 'cries of grief . . . and wails and groans' (2:10).

These messages are contained in the first section of the book. They were addressed to the people of Jerusalem in the dark days of the reign of Zedekiah. Ezekiel depicts the moral and spiritual decline of Jerusalem society with such realism that it is hard to believe he was not there, but in Babylon. Indeed, some scholars think Ezekiel must have paid visits to Judah at this time. But it is more likely that he had some kind of clairvoyant second sight. Ezekiel's experiences as a prophet are much closer to those of the other great prophets to the behaviour of those bands of ecstatics who are mentioned in the early period of Israel's history. He obviously had a psychic personality, for after receiving his initial vision, he lay in a trance for a full week (3:15). In view of all this, his extraordinary accuracy in portraying life in Judah could well have been due to visionary experiences rather than to actual observations made on the spot.

But Ezekiel was not an irrational prophet, and his essential message was not all that different from Jeremiah's: Jerusalem would be destroyed shortly, and its people taken off into exile. He saw no immediate hope of a return, though there are hints that the exile might be limited to about forty years (4:6).

In spite of his declaration of doom and destruction, Ezekiel's message to the exiles in Babylon after the events of 586 BC was a positive one. He had no doubt that the nation had brought ruin on itself, but he was equally convinced that the nation's fate was not in their own hands. It was God's loving actions that had made them a nation in the first place, and it was his power that would restore them, even giving them the ability to repent and start afresh: 'I will give you a new heart and a new mind. I will take away your stubborn heart of stone and give you an obedient heart. I will put my spirit in you and I will see to it that you follow my laws and keep all the commands I have given you. Then you will live in the land I gave your ancestors. You will be my people, and I will be your God.' (36:26–28). God was personally concerned for his people, just like a good shepherd caring for his sheep. They might be scattered, but he would retrieve them and lead them to a new life: 'I will take them out of foreign countries, gather them together, and bring them back to their own land . . . I myself will be the shepherd of my sheep, and I will find them a place to rest' (34:11–15).

Two distinctive features of Ezekiel's messages are worth special notice:

● When he looks forward to the restoration of a kingdom of Israel under a prince of the royal family of David, he often describes it in terms that clearly go beyond a literal nationalism. The earlier prophets had often hoped for better things to come, but they generally believed that it was at least theoretically possible that the new and better age would come through a new king in Jerusalem, who would actually obey God's will, unlike his predecessors. Ezekiel, however, implies that the inauguration of a golden age, when God and his people would live in complete harmony, could not be achieved by any ordinary king. It would have to be the direct work of God himself. Thinking of this kind led eventually to the development of a new type of Jewish religious literature: the so-called apocalyptic books, and we can see traces of its beginning in passages like Ezekiel 38—39. Here the prophet describes how the enemies of Judah under a mysterious leader called Gog would attack Palestine, only to be annihilated with torrents of fire and brimstone raining down from the sky. After that the exiled Jews would be restored to their own land, and the spirit of God would be poured out on them. The same kind of extravagant language is used when Ezekiel describes a wonderful life-giving stream flowing from the restored temple in Jerusalem out to the Dead Sea, and changing the

Judean desert into a land of great fertility (47:1–12).

● Ezekiel's messages also contain a detailed plan for a renewed temple in Jerusalem (40:1—48:35). Not only does he describe the building itself, but he also lays down the rules that should regulate its worship. Some scholars have seen this as the symptom of an arid legalism which they believe to have been rampant in the exilic age. The same influences are said to be found in other prophets of the period, and this interest in religious ritual is often contrasted with the convictions of the truly 'great' prophets like Amos and Hosea, who declared that God's will was not fulfilled through religious mumbo-jumbo, but through ordinary everyday behaviour. But this kind of view misrepresents Ezekiel's message. It owes more to modern Protestantism than it does to the Old Testament, and as a result the significant features of Israel's cultic worship are often misunderstood. Ezekiel was not emphasizing the performance of religious ritual for its own sake. But he knew that the exiles could never renew their own spiritual life. Even in the halcyon days immediately following the exodus from Egypt, obedience to God's covenant law had not been easy. Sin and disobedience were an inescapable reality. It was not the goodness of the tribes that had made them a great nation, but the unchanging presence of God. And right from the start, that presence had been represented by the formal institutions of worship – from the simple tent of worship in the desert to the elaborate temple in Jerusalem. Far from being an aberration, these things were a permanent symbol of the centralities of Israel's faith, representing not only God's own faithfulness and power, but also the way to forgiveness for his wayward people. It was for this reason that the same symbols must be an essential part of the restored community.

Ezekiel was not the only one who saw the situation in these terms. For it is widely believed that during the exile in Babylon, the Jewish leaders began to re-assess the state of their people by looking back into their past. We have already seen how the Deuteronomistic History may have been written down in Judah itself at this time, for precisely the same reasons. But the emphasis of that History on a close connection between the people's obedience and the blessing of God could easily lead to the false conclusion that the exiles themselves were responsible for their own destiny. The message of prophets like Amos and Hosea, and even Jeremiah, could easily be misunderstood to suggest that good behaviour was a way of blackmailing God into giving Israel his blessing. But when we look back to the very earliest period of Israel's history, we can see that this was only one side of the story. The prophets' demand for obedience to God's law had itself been based on the unsought goodness of God's love in events like the calling of Abraham and the exodus from Egypt. The prophets had rightly declared that the nation's religious problems had started once they settled in the land of Canaan. But the time before that had hardly been perfect. Perhaps, then, there was a lesson here for the exiles as they struggled to come to terms with their national disaster.

With thoughts like these before them, religious leaders in Babylon probably set out to write a history of the earliest experiences of their nation, starting from creation itself. They did not compile their story from nothing, any more than the Deuteronomic historians did. They had at their disposal the full riches of their nation's heritage, going back over many centuries. But as they re-told these familiar stories, they could see that the problem of human disobedience was an old one. It was part and parcel of life

Facing page: 'The Law' (*Torah*) is very holy to the Jew. He is educated in it from childhood, and it is his rule of conduct. Sometimes 'the Law' refers to the whole Old Testament, but more commonly it is applied to the first five books, the 'books of Moses', the Pentateuch.

itself. Yet in spite of that, God's living presence had been with their people. Right from the very earliest days in the desert, God had been there, even at times of disobedience. The thing that had brought the tribes from Egypt to their own land was not their own goodness, but the love of God. So a new hope and concern began to emerge from the lessons of history. As they looked at their own resources, they could see no hope. Instead, they must trust God, for his power was still supreme and all-powerful.

The Pentateuch

It is widely believed that the historical re-assessment that took place among the exiles in Babylon had strong connections with the writings of the first five books of the Old Testament, the Pentateuch. If we accept the idea that Deuteronomy was a preface to the Deuteronomistic History, then we should more accurately speak of a 'Tetrateuch', consisting of Genesis, Exodus, Leviticus, and Numbers.

In Jewish thinking, the Pentateuch was always traditionally regarded as the work of Moses. But most scholars today consider this to be impossible. At least five reasons can be given:

● **Anachronisms** Deuteronomy 34 tells the story of Moses' death, which at least makes it unlikely that he wrote this section – though both Philo (*On the Life of Moses* II.291) and Josephus (*Antiquities of the Jews* IV viii.48) claimed that he did! More significantly, however, a number of other incidental features of some of the stories in these books reflect the perspective of a later age. For instance, Genesis 36:31–39 lists the kings of Edom who ruled 'Before there were any kings in Israel'. Or again, a couple of incidents in Abraham's life took place when 'the Canaanites were still living in the land' (Genesis 12:6; 13:7). And part of the land of Canaan itself is given the name 'Philistia', though it did not have that name until after the arrival of the Philistines (Genesis 21:34; Exodus 13:17).

● **Duplicate stories** The same story sometimes seems to have been recorded in two different versions. For example, Beersheba is given its name twice (Genesis 21:31; 26:33), as is Bethel – once when Jacob was running away to Haran (Genesis 28:19), and again when he was coming back (Genesis 35:15). Similarly, in the story of the covenant-making at Mt Sinai, Moses is said to have gone up the mountain three times, though there is no mention of him ever coming down (Exodus 24:9–18).

● **Inconsistencies** can be traced in certain stories. For example, in the story of creation, Genesis 1:26–31 suggests that people were created after all the animals, whereas in Genesis 2:7–20 a man is created first, and the animals are later created to be his companions. Or in the story of the great flood, the number of animals to be saved in the Ark is either one pair of each species (Genesis 6:19–20), or seven pairs (Genesis 7:2). Joseph appears to have been taken off to Egypt by both Ishmaelites (Genesis 37:25) and Midianites (Genesis 37:28) – and was it Reuben (Genesis 37:22) or Judah (Genesis 37:26) who was the good brother who tried to rescue him?

● **Legal differences** Scholars have also pointed out that the laws set out in Deuteronomy are sometimes different from the laws in other books of the Pentateuch. For example, in Exodus 20:24 sacrifices can be offered to God 'in every place that I set aside for you to worship me'; but in Deuteronomy 12:14, 'you must offer them only in the one place that the Lord will choose in the territory of one of your tribes'. Exodus 28:1 suggests that only Aaron's family had the priestly qualifications to offer sacrifices, while Deuteronomy 18:6–7 allows any Levite to do so. The actual methods to be adopted also vary: in Exodus 12:8–9 the Passover lamb must be roasted, while in Deuteronomy 16:7 it is to be boiled.

● **God's name** According to Exodus 6:2–3, Moses was the first person to know God's personal name, 'Yahweh'. But Genesis 4:26 states that from the very earliest times people had used this name in their worship. Alongside this, there are many other passages which call God by the name 'Elohim'. And it has also been argued that the different names indicate different ideas about God's character: in the stories that call him Yahweh, he can be thought of as a kind of superman, speaking and meeting with people in person; while in those that call him Elohim he appears more remotely through dreams and messengers.

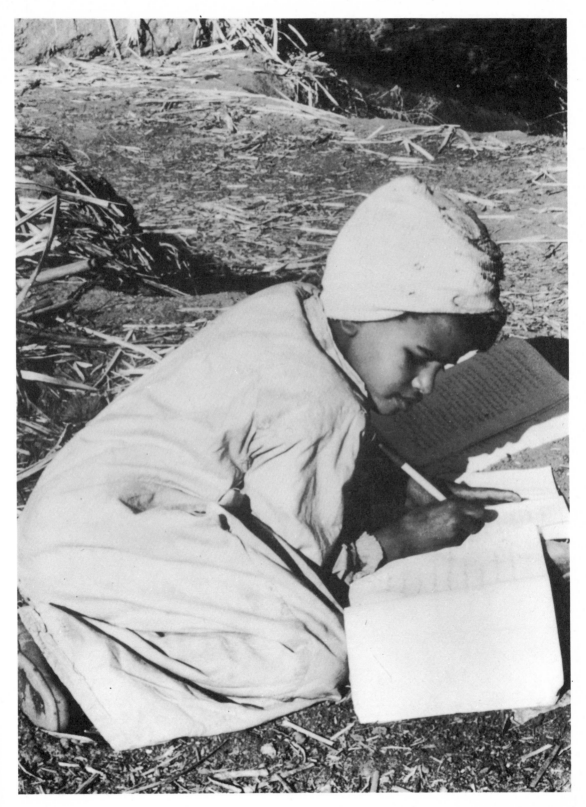

These five features are not all that important if we take them separately. But taken together, they have been regarded by scholars as a conclusive demonstration that the Pentateuch was not the product of just one author, either Moses or anyone else. According to the most widely accepted view, the Pentateuch as we know it today was compiled from four separate documentary sources: J (the source using the name Yahweh); E (the source using the name Elohim); D (Deuteronomy); and P (a priestly source, dealing mainly with sacrifice, etc.). This theory was most fully explained by the nineteenth-century German scholars, K.H. Graf and J. Wellhausen, and is often simply called the Graf-Wellhausen theory. Wellhausen also believed that these source documents reflect the whole course of Israel's national history, beginning with J (950–850 BC), followed by E (850–750 BC), D (621 BC), and P (about 450 BC).

In the early decades of the twentieth century, scholars set out with great enthusiasm to 'recover' and 'reconstruct' these four apparently lost documents. They concluded that J had originated among the southern tribes in the time of Solomon, and E among the northern tribes in the time of Elijah, and the two had been joined together some time after the fall of Samaria in 721 BC. D was generally identified with the law book discovered in the time of Josiah, though possibly of a northern origin. It was certainly quite a different kind of 'source' from the others, for whereas J and E could be traced more or less extensively throughout the Pentateuch, D appeared to be restricted to just the book of Deuteronomy. And P was regarded as an exclusively priestly collection, containing mainly the details of organized cultic religion, and anything connected with it – though also including certain other materials of a narrative type.

All this has been accepted in one form or another by most Old Testament scholars for the last 100 years. During that time, there have been those who pointed out the limitations of this or that detail in Wellhausen's analysis. But those who rejected it entirely were isolated individuals, usually regarded as eccentrics. The situation today, however, is quite different. The whole edifice of Wellhausen's theory is coming under increasingly heavy fire from all directions, and it is probably only a matter of time before the whole scholarly approach to these books will

have to undergo a thorough reappraisal. There are a number of reasons for this radical about-turn:

● Wellhausen's view was firmly based on a particular philosophical understanding of history and its development. Along with other thinkers of his day, he believed that human society had gradually evolved from primitive beginnings to the sophisticated thinking of his own day. Wellhausen therefore took it for granted that Israel's religious experience must have started off as a simple nature worship, which later evolved into the high moral standards of the Old Testament prophets. This evolutionary theory has since been totally discredited, and it is arguable that the literary analysis which Wellhausen built upon it has therefore been left with no rational foundation.

● Since Wellhausen's day our knowledge of the ancient world in general, and of Israel in particular, has changed almost beyond recognition. Wellhausen and his contemporaries were writing before the development of modern scientific archaeology. It was easy for them to look at the Old Testament as a kind of theological source book, rather than as a body of literature to be understood in its own true-life situation. Viewed in this way, it seemed plausible to think that Israel's religion could have evolved from a primitive animism to an elevated monotheism in the course of just a few hundred years. But the more we know about the Old Testament world, the less likely it has become that Israel's faith should be thought of in these terms. According to Wellhausen's theory, for example, almost all the details of Israel's ritual worship were the invention of the P writer, late in the Babylonian exile. But the discoveries at the site of ancient Ugarit have shown that even quite technical terms used in the Old Testament were in common use in Canaan long before the Israelite conquest, let alone the exile. Far from reflecting later stages in the development of religious thought, much of the Pentateuchal material reflects precisely the circumstances of the period of which it purports to tell. Of course, this does not prove that it was all written down at an earlier period – still less does it comment directly on its historical value – but it certainly demonstrates that the assumptions on which Wellhausen argued were simply mistaken.

● Criticisms of this sort have not prevented Old Testament scholars from continuing to refine and articulate more fully the theory that Wellhausen put forward. Even today some are still arguing about the dates of the various so-called source documents. But their conclusions vary widely, with even the J source being variously dated in periods as far apart as the ninth century and the post-exilic age! Others have suggested there was no such thing as an E source, while yet others argue that the four-source theory is inadequte, and the Pentateuch in fact contains many more sources than that. Some have further claimed to be able to trace J, E and P not only in the Pentateuch, but also in Joshua, Judges, Samuel, and even Kings. Much of this debate has been engendered by the surprising fact that the so-called sources are not actually consistent in their use of the different names for God, even though this was supposed to be their characteristic feature! Considering that scholars have been trying to define the nature and contents of these source documents for a century now, it is not unreasonable to expect them to have come to some sort of conclusion on the matter. The fact that they have so strikingly failed to do so raises serious questions about their very existence.

A number of scholars have noted the strength of this particular criticism, and have accordingly directed their energies elsewhere. Gerhard von Rad, for instance, argued that this section of the Old Testament (which for him extended into Joshua/Judges, the 'Hexateuch') was centred around two major themes. One was the exodus/entry into the land; the other was the covenant ceremony at Mt Sinai. Both of these were originally related to religious celebrations in the life of early Israel, and he suggested that the continuous narrative we now have grew out of the confessions and creeds that were so often repeated in worship. This process took place, he believes, in the time of Solomon. Martin Noth also proposed his own rather different thematic origin for the same materials. But all such attempts have still been firmly based on a Wellhausen-type source analysis, and they have not successfully avoided the general criticisms noted above.

● Recent discussion of this issue has emphasized the importance of treating the Pentateuch as real literature. Wellhausen and his followers worked with a very restricted view of how ancient literature was actually written. Their understanding has often been colourfully described as a 'scissors and paste' approach, which tended to

assume that the final editor of the books sat down with four documents in front of him, and chopped bits and pieces from here and there, which he then glued together (rather badly) to make a 'new' book. An idea like that can seem to make sense to a modern scholar sitting in his study. He could, after all, write a book like that himself. But this is not the way a national archive like the Old Testament comes into existence. Traditional ways of handing on ancient stories – sometimes by word of mouth – are not as methodical and clear-cut as this. What is more, the whole approach to literature espoused by Wellhausen is now widely questioned.

It has always been fashionable among Biblical scholars to suppose that the only way to understand a document is to explain where it came from. We can see this clearly enough in any of the multifarious introductions to both Old and New Testaments, which tend to be preoccupied with questions of origin, date and authorship, often to the exclusion of anything else. But the meaning of a book must surely begin with the text as it stands. No matter how much a work of literature may have been edited or rewritten, its ultimate meaning is to be found in the form it now has.

In the study of English literature, it is taken for granted that William Shakespeare often took the plots for his plays from other sources. But no one would dream of looking for the genius of their meaning in the sources, rather than in the mind of Shakespeare himself. And the Pentateuch is just the same. From a purely literary point of view, it is a connected story with its own message.

Indeed some scholars have argued on this basis that some of the features that led Wellhausen to his source theory could just as easily have been stylistic and literary devices. Take, for instance, the use of different names for God: is it wholly inconceivable that the term Yahweh might have been used when the writer was talking of Israel's own national God, while the term Elohim was reserved for contexts in which a more abstract, cosmic picture of God was in view? And even the existence of duplicate stories is not a necessary indication of badly assimilated source materials. For we find a very similar phenomenon in the texts from Ugarit, where frequent repetitions of the same passages have been indispensable to scholars in helping to restore gaps in broken texts.

During the exile, the Babylonian Empire went through a period of decline. Emperor Nabonidus, seen in this relief worshipping the sun-god, rejected the national religion and spent much of his time in retreat in the desert.

The upshot of all this is that there is today a re-examination of almost all the basic issues in Pentateuchal scholarship. This is motivated partly by dissatisfaction with the Graf-Wellhausen theory, but more especially by the realization that in the literary world at large there are other, more promising methods of analysis than source criticism.

What, then, may we conclude from all this? There are those who would like to think that the imminent collapse of the scholarly orthodoxy justifies a return to belief in a Mosaic authorship for the Pentateuch. But that does not necessarily follow at all. For one thing, the Bible itself gives us no reason to link his name with all these books. Only a few scattered references in the books themselves connect Moses with their writing, and they all relate to specific parts of the narrative, rather than to the Pentateuch as a whole (Exodus 24:4–8; Numbers 33:2; Deuteronomy 31:19–29). Writing was widely used in the earliest period of Israel's history, and many scholars today would confidently link Moses with significant features of the Pentateuch, such as the Ten Commandments. So there is no good reason why this leader of the ancient tribes should not have had some connection with the traditional stories and customs of his people. But later, even those things connected with Moses himself needed to be reinterpreted and applied to new situations. As new elements joined the population of Israel, their own stories handed on over many centuries would also be incorporated into Israel's national heritage. And the inauguration of the monarchy must have necessitated a considerable reinterpretation of Israel's traditional values and ideals, in order to suit the new circumstances.

But it now seems quite likely that, instead of passing through several written stages, all this took place in a more or less haphazard fashion until the Pentateuch itself was written in its present form. It certainly makes good sense to think that this epic story of Israel's earliest days was issued during the period of the early exile, as a means of explaining the failures of the past and of charting the course for the future. But the stories and laws were not newly created at that time. The new element was the perspective that the experience of the exile had given. With that hindsight the story of God and his people could become a source of renewal for Israel's national life, and the old stories could come alive in a new way.

A new beginning

The stories of Israel's past reminded the exiles of what God had done for their nation. Even at times of great despair, God's love had never failed them, and he would not abandon them now. It was not long before things began to stir in Babylonian politics that were regarded as the actions of God himself.

When Nebuchadnezzar died in 562 BC he was succeeded by a number of very weak and inept rulers. Only Nabonidus had a reign of any length (556-539 BC). But he was very unpopular: he was opposed to the national religion of Babylon – the worship of Marduk – and he took little interest in affairs in the capital, preferring instead to live at Teima in the Arabian desert. This was a very unsettled period in Babylonian history, and life for the exiles may well have become more difficult. There is a strong tradition in Jewish literature of how the exiles were subjected to harsh treatment, almost amounting to official persecution. In the Old

Daniel 1—6

Testament, the stories of the first section of the book of Daniel tell how Daniel and his friends were subjected to the most harrowing treatment by the Babylonian king Belshazzar (Nabonidus's son, and his official representative in Babylon). The same kind of picture is also painted in various additions to the books of Esther and Daniel which were contained in the Greek Old Testament, as well as in books like Judith and Tobit.

If this was a time of discomfort for the Jews in Babylon, it was short-lived. For by now, the power of the Babylonian Empire was spent, and when a little-known king from southern Persia emerged as a new leader, it was only a matter of time before he was able to take over the whole of the country. His name was Cyrus, and in 539 BC the people of Babylon actually welcomed him as their king, and he took control of the city without the use of force.

Cyrus set about the restoration of Babylonian society. The temples which Nabonidus had neglected were restored to their former glory, and Cyrus himself shared publicly in the worship of the god Marduk. But he did not become involved in sectarian arguments. Indeed, of all the ancient rulers with whom the Jews had to deal, Cyrus was the most liberal and humane. He did not see politics in terms of armed conflict between various national religions. Instead, he recognized the right of all nations to worship whatever gods they wished. Not only that, but he recognized that people should have the right to live wherever they chose. This was a massive reversal of the policies that had dominated Mesopotamian society for many centuries, but he was determined to make it work. He inherited a population with many people who had been uprooted from their own lands and settled in Babylon against their will. He decided to encourage these displaced people to go back home, and declared that he would give them financial aid to do so. The Cyrus Cylinder, now in the British Museum, contains details of all this. And the Jews were naturally included. The Old Testament book of Ezra preserves the text of an official document issued by Cyrus, dealing specifically with the plight of the Jewish exiles.

Ezra 6:3–5

The Cyrus Cylinder gives details of the reforms this Persian ruler undertook in Babylon after he had overthrown the Babylonians in a bloodless take-over. In Isaiah's prophecy, Cyrus is seen as the unwitting agent of the Lord in establishing the conditions for the exiles' return to Jerusalem.

Isaiah of Babylon

It is widely believed by modern scholars that the advance of Cyrus was seen by a Jewish prophet in Babylon, whose remarkable messages are to be found in Isaiah 40—55. As they stand, of course, these messages are a part of the book which reports the life and teaching of the prophet Isaiah, who lived in Jerusalem some 150 years earlier during the days of Ahaz and Hezekiah. A number of reasons are given for regarding these later sections of the book as originally separate:

● Isaiah 40—55 contains no mention at all of the prophet Isaiah. This is in strong contrast to Isaiah 1—39 which relate a number of stories about the prophet himself, especially his dealings with king and people in Jerusalem.

● The style and language of Isaiah 40—55 is also quite distinctive. These chapters use what is possibly the most sophisticated Hebrew in the entire Old

Testament. In addition, these messages do not have the form of the short, pointed sayings that were typical of most of the Old Testament prophets. They consist instead of sustained lyrical passages, celebrating God's sovereignty in creation and history. Because of their distinctive poetic structure, it has been thought that these messages may have originated in the context of worship. Perhaps they reflect the way that God's kingship was celebrated in the temple at Jerusalem during the heyday of the kingdom of Judah. But they are not just hymns, for they also contain many specific historical references, directly related to the message of the prophet himself.

● The fact that these specific references are based on the experiences of the Babylonian exile is one of the strongest reasons for assuming that they are the work of a prophet who lived at this time. The fall of Jerusalem is clearly stated to be a past event (51:17–23), and the fall of Babylon is imminent (43:14–15; 47:1–15). The people are encouraged to think they will soon be set free (48:20), and Cyrus himself is mentioned by name as the person who would bring this about (44:28—45:4). Other passages clearly envisage Cyrus's triumph, without actually naming him (41:2–4; 48:12–16). It is occasionally suggested that Isaiah of Jerusalem could have given such messages, and some believe he may have written them down during the reign of Hezekiah or Manasseh. But it is very difficult to see why he would have wished to do so. The Old Testament prophets were not star-gazers concerned with predicting a long-distant future, but political and social commentators wrestling with the spiritual significance of the affairs of their own day. In addition, we must face the fact that if Isaiah of Jerusalem was responsible for these messages about Cyrus, they must have been totally meaningless to the people of his own time, and also for several generations thereafter – and would anyone therefore have been likely to preserve them, especially through the turmoil of Judah's last days?

It makes much better sense to accept that the messages of Isaiah 40–55 were given to the exiles in Babylon at the time to which they relate, i.e. just before 539 BC. The prophet who delivered them had the same kind of outlook as his illustrious predecessor. Isaiah himself had gathered a group of disciples around him, so that the messages he gave could be safeguarded for later generations (Isaiah 8:16) – and these later messages may well have come from the same circle of disciples. What they were saying was a fresh application of old truths to new circumstances, and so they had no hesitation in including them all in the same book.

For convenience, we often call the prophet who delivered these later messages Isaiah of Babylon, or Deutero-Isaiah. But of course that would not be his real name. The fact that we do not apparently know his real name is the only compelling argument against his likely existence. If he was indeed one of the great prophetic figures of the Old Testament story, how is it that we have no explicit information about him? That question needs to be set against the fact that we actually know next to nothing about most of the other great prophets, apart from the messages that are recorded in their books. But the relative anonymity of this prophet in Babylon is consistent with his whole outlook. For he was concerned first and foremost with the might and power of God, rather than with himself. The change that he believed was about to take place would not be initiated by the exiles: it was to be the work of God himself, a 'new exodus' comparable with that under Moses, in which the escaping slaves (like the exiles) had been powerless, but were miraculously delivered by their all-powerful God (Isaiah 43:14–21).

A powerful God

Cyrus is seen as the instrument of this deliverance that was to come, but the people's trust should not be in Cyrus. The real power that would restore the Jewish people came from God himself. The glorious return to their homeland would be a world-wide movement, including those who had fled to Egypt (49:12). God's power would not be restricted by geography or national boundaries, as had sometimes been thought by Israel in the past. This prophet was convinced that his God was not one among many, but the only true God: 'The Lord is the everlasting God; he created all the world. He never grows tired or weary' (40:28). It was important for him to emphasize this, for some of the exiles had come to regard their plight as a direct result of the weakness of Israel's God when faced with the apparent 'power' of the gods of Babylon. Those who clung to the old covenant faith may even have been in the minority (Ezekiel 20:32; Daniel 1—6). But Isaiah of Babylon knew they were right.

Isaiah predicted that the Jews would return to their homeland with great joy. Both the journey itself and their new life in Jerusalem would see a restoration of their life as a community of God's people.

His contempt for the gods of Babylon was unbounded. In satirical vein, he points out how their own worshippers actually made them from the very same wood as they used to burn on the fire. To him, such an attitude was just blind ignorance: 'Such people are too stupid to know what they are doing. They close their eyes and their minds to the truth. The maker of idols hasn't the wit or the sense to say, "Some of the wood I burnt up. I baked some bread on the embers and I roasted meat and ate it. And the rest of the wood I made into an idol. Here I am bowing down to a block of wood!"' (44:18–19). That is not the kind of God who had revealed himself in Israel's history. He had been, and still was, a God of real power, the God of all creation: 'I am the Lord, the Creator of all things. I alone stretched out the heavens; when I made the earth, no one helped me' (44:24).

God's people and their land

With this emphasis on God's universal sovereignty, we might have expected his special relationship with Israel to have been forgotten, or at least pushed into the background. But it was not. The fact that God's power extended over the whole world meant that the exiles could go back to their homeland without worrying whether God would have the power to take care of them. Many of them probably needed this kind of encouragement. For even after Cyrus gave them permission to return, many preferred the safety and security of the life they knew to the hazards and unknown perils of a long journey and a strange land. But to those who would trust God, it was all a great spiritual adventure: 'From the distant east and the farthest west, I will bring your people home. I will tell the north to let them go and the south not to hold them back. Let my people return from distant lands, from every part of the world' (43:5–7). God had done it long centuries before in the exodus from Egypt, and he would do it again because of his great love for his people: 'Watch for the new thing I am going to do. It is happening already – you can see it now! I will make a road through the wilderness and give you streams of water there . . . (43:19). Jerusalem may be a ruined wasteland, but it would soon be restored to its former glory: 'I will show compassion to Jerusalem, to all who live in her ruins. Though her land is a desert, I will make it a garden, like the garden planted in Eden. Joy and gladness will be there, and songs of praise and thanks to me' (51:3).

God's servant and God's world

Despite this renewed emphasis on God's concern for his own people, this Babylonian prophet was convinced that God's love was not just for Israel alone.

Just as the whole world was the arena of God's activity, so all the people of the world would be the object of his love. This is the message of one of those passages that have been called 'the servant songs': 'The Lord said to me, "I have a greater task for you, my servant. Not only will you restore to greatness the people of Israel who have survived, but I will also make you a light to the nations – so that all the world may be saved"' (49:6).

There are four of these servant songs, and they seem to be separate and self-contained poems, though no doubt still the work of the prophet himself, and certainly an integral part of his message (42:1–4; 49:1–6; 50:4–9; 52:13—53:12). In these songs, the prophet talks of a specific individual, 'the servant', through whom God's plans for a great and glorious future age will come to fruition. But who was this servant? Elsewhere the prophet talks of the nation of Israel as the servant of God, and the person mentioned in the servant songs is often described in the same language as is used of Israel. Israel is 'my servant . . . the people that I have

The exile from Judah

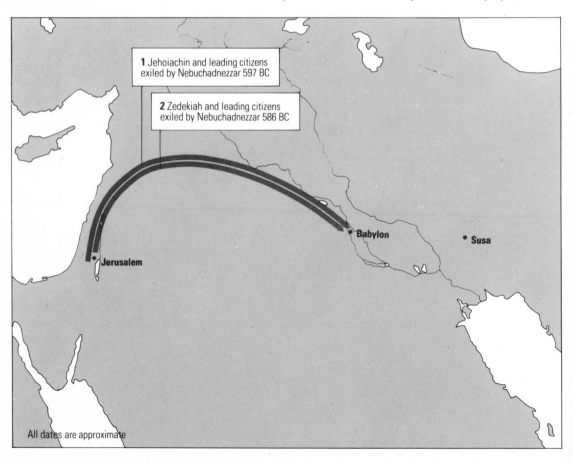

1 Jehoiachin and leading citizens exiled by Nebuchadnezzar 597 BC

2 Zedekiah and leading citizens exiled by Nebuchadnezzar 586 BC

Babylon

Susa

Jerusalem

All dates are approximate

chosen' (41:8), and so is the servant of the songs (42:1). Both of them were created by God himself (Israel, 43:1,7,15,21; 44:2,21,24; the servant, 49:5), and were endowed with God's own Spirit (Israel, 44:3; the servant, 42:1). This has led many scholars to conclude that when Isaiah talks of the suffering servant he is simply talking of God's people Israel in another way. But at the same time, things are said about the servant which are explicitly denied about Israel. The servant 'will not lose hope or courage' (42:4), nor has he 'rebelled or turned away' from God (50:5), as the nation so often did. In addition, he suffers patiently – not for his own wrongdoings like the nation, but for the wrongs of others (53:3–5). Most significant of all is the fact that while the nation needed restoration, the servant is sent to restore and renew Israel (49:5–6; 53:4–6). It is therefore difficult to see how the prophet could have identified this servant of God with the nation itself.

But who was he? Some people think the prophet had a particular living individual in mind, possibly Jehoiachin, or someone like Jeremiah, or conceivably even himself. But it is more likely that he was thinking of some future person in whose life the ideals of Israel's ancient faith would become a reality, and through whom God's intentions for his people and the world could be brought to pass. He is never actually called the Messiah in the Old Testament, nor did the Jewish people ever think to equate the two. But these passages exerted a powerful influence on the Christian understanding of Jesus as the Messiah of the Old Testament expectation. In particular, the account of the servant's suffering in the last song (52:13—53:12) has such amazing correspondences with the death of Jesus himself, that Professor G.W. Anderson has described it as 'one of the miracles of Old Testament literature'. As things turned out, both for Israel and the world, this is undoubtedly the greatest insight that we have from this prophet in Babylon: that the way to the world's salvation would be the way of suffering and service.

The return of the exiles

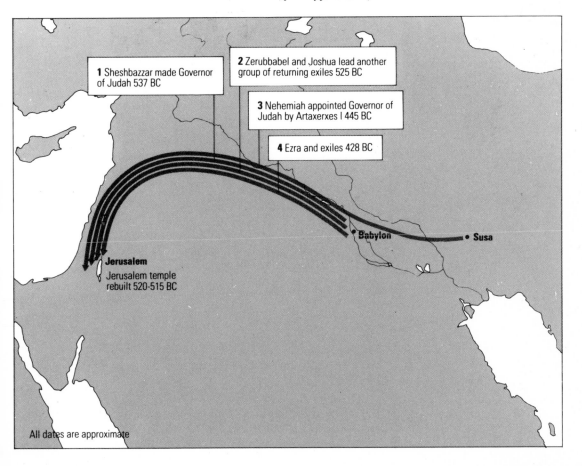

1 Sheshbazzar made Governor of Judah 537 BC

2 Zerubbabel and Joshua lead another group of returning exiles 525 BC

3 Nehemiah appointed Governor of Judah by Artaxerxes I 445 BC

4 Ezra and exiles 428 BC

Babylon

Susa

Jerusalem
Jerusalem temple
rebuilt 520-515 BC

All dates are approximate

Back to Jerusalem

Antiquities of the Jews XI.i.3

Ezra 5:16

Jeremiah 41:4–5

Cyrus had issued an edict allowing the temple in Jerusalem to be rebuilt at the beginning of his reign. But there was no great rush by the exiles in Babylon to return to Judah. Josephus reports that when they were given the chance to go back home, they did not want to leave the comfortable life they had established in exile. But it was important to the Persians that their repatriation policy should be set in motion. Though they undoubtedly had humanitarian reasons for introducing it, the benefits of having loyal and grateful subjects at strategic parts of their empire can hardly have escaped their notice. Since Palestine was near to the border with Egypt, it was important for them to re-establish a friendly state there.

So they appointed a man called Sheshbazzar as governor of Judah. His name was thoroughly Babylonian, though that does not mean he was not a Jew. We know very little about him, except that he made a start on rebuilding the foundations of the temple. We are better informed about a further group of exiles who returned a little later under the leadership of Zerubbabel and Joshua. Joshua was a priest, but Zerubbabel was the grandson of Jehoiachin, the last truly legitimate king of the royal family of David. He also held an official Persian appointment, and he could have been Sheshbazzar's successor as governor. The appointment of a member of the Jewish royal family may have been a conscious effort by the Persians to persuade more Jews to return. Zerubbabel certainly saw that, with Persian help, a new Jewish state could emerge from the ashes of the past. With the disappearance of most of the familiar features of the earlier kingdom, however, there was just one thing that united the new settlers with their ancestors. That was their faith in God. In exile, that faith had been centred on customs like circumcision and keeping the sabbath day, as well as prayer and the reading of the Torah. But now the temple could be rebuilt, and its repair and renovation was to be Zerubbabel's main task.

The temple ruins had probably continued to be a place of worship throughout the period since Nebuchadnezzar's destruction. Even in the aftermath of the invasion, the book of Jeremiah mentions worshippers making a pilgrimage to the site. They had come from the territory of the former northern kingdom of Israel, centred on Samaria. No doubt people from that quarter, as well as the Jewish population left behind in Judah itself had continued to worship there all along. So it was only natural for these people to offer their assistance to Zerubbabel. But he would have none of it. To him, these people were not real Jews. They may have thought they were worshipping the covenant God of Israel, but they had not shared in the experience of the exiles in Babylon – and they were the only true descendants of the ancient tribes. These other people were of uncertain (and partly non-Jewish) racial origins, and their worship of Yahweh was suspect.

The people of Samaria and their friends in Judah realized that the newcomers from Babylon were bent on forming their own Jewish state, in which the people who already lived in the land would have no place. And so, having had their offer of co-operation turned down, these people had no option but to oppose the plans of the returned exiles. They succeeded in delaying work on the temple for something like ten years or more, by persuading the Persian officials responsible for the western empire that something illegal was afoot. By this time, Darius I was the emperor, but Cyrus's original permission still stood, and the work was allowed to proceed. The new temple was much poorer than Solomon's had been. But its completion was a milestone in the life of this beleagured community.

Ezra 5
Ezra 3:12

Haggai and Zechariah

Zerubbabel and Joshua were encouraged in their work by the prophets Haggai and Zechariah. Their messages give us a vivid insight into the despair and apathy of the people at this time. The wave of euphoria that accompanied Cyrus's rise to power subsided soon after his death, for his son Cambyses (530–522 BC) did not share his father's ideals. He was more interested in military conquest, and during his campaign against Egypt in 525 BC it is likely that he plundered Judah for food supplies. This would have been bad enough in good times, but Haggai's messages show that conditions were far from that. The

returned exiles were living at poverty level, and their crops were blighted by drought and disease. This in itself made it hard to establish a stable society. But in addition, there was a military coup back in Persia while Cambyses was on his way home from Egypt. He committed suicide, and Darius, one of his generals, seized control of the army. He returned to Persia and became king there too, and in due course he emerged as one of the most powerful of all the Persian emperors. But at the time, the whole situation must have seemed very confused and uncertain to the Jewish community around Jerusalem. Was all this the beginning of the new age that they had spoken of back in Babylon? Or was it a sign of yet worse to come?

Haggai began speaking to the people in 520 BC, early in the reign of Darius. He urged them to make the rebuilding of the temple a real priority. They had built houses for themselves, so why should they neglect God? If he was not worshipped, they could hardly expect prosperity. But if they were prepared to put him first, then anything could happen. Zerubbabel was there as God's chosen spokesman, and the symbol of God's own presence – the temple – should also be reinstated as the centre of national life. When that happened, the scene would be set for the new age that the exiles had hoped for: 'On that day I will take you, Zerubbabel my servant, and I will appoint you to rule in my name. You are the one I have chosen' (Haggai 2:23).

Zechariah was a contemporary of Haggai, and his messages are essentially similar. He encouraged the completion of the rebuilt temple, and in a series of visions he depicted the new age that God would soon bring about. He too saw a special place for Zerubbabel in all this (4:6–10; 6:9–15), but he also emphasized that Zerubbabel's success depended not so much on the fact that he was descended from King David, but on the fact that God was with him in a

Emperor Darius I, from Media, continued Cyrus's policy of supporting the exiles' return. In his time the temple was rebuilt at Jerusalem.

special way: 'You will succeed, not by military might or by your own strength, but by my spirit. Obstacles as great as mountains will disappear before you. You will rebuild the Temple, and as you put the last stone in place, the people will shout, "Beautiful, Beautiful!"' (4:6–7).

The precise meaning of the statements made about Zerubbabel is unclear. The language used is undoubtedly what we could call 'messianic'. But at the same time, it can hardly have had a political implication, for Zerubbabel seems to have retained the confidence of the Persians. There are also hints that the high priest Joshua came to occupy an even more important place in the new community. In the days of the earlier kingdom of Judah, the temple had been under the personal direction of the king. But with the disappearance of the kingly office, some of his functions were now carried out by the priests. In preparation for his new responsibilities, Joshua was actually crowned in a kind of coronation ceremony (Zechariah 6:9–15). This was probably a significant development in Jewish thinking. Some 400 years later the Dead Sea Scrolls seem to expect the coming of a priest who would be the Messiah, and who was at least as important as the 'secular' Messiah who would be descended from David. The same idea is also found in the letter to the Hebrews in the New Testament. Unfortunately, we have so little definite knowledge of the time of Haggai and Zechariah that we cannot trace the possible connections of this idea in any greater detail.

Confusion and despair

The new temple was completed in about 515 BC. Now at last the people had a new hope. No doubt they went about their worship with joy and expectation, believing that the new age which they had been promised must surely be at hand. But the reality was to be quite different. We have no absolutely certain knowledge of life in Judah from 515 BC until 444 BC. But we have no reason to suppose that conditions improved, either religiously or economically. A number of prophetic messages seem to reflect life at this time. The book of Obadiah is a short poem deploring the advantage that the Edomites had gained out of Judah's national disaster – and also assuring the Jewish people that better times were on the way. The book of Joel also probably relates to this period. Its immediate occasion is a plague of locusts, which led to a great famine. But Joel assured his hearers that this was just a temporary setback, and would be the prelude to the new age that God would inaugurate. The same picture of despondency is found, according to some scholars, in the final section of the book of Isaiah. Some see this as the work of yet another prophet (Third or Trito-Isaiah). But it is more likely that these messages were the work of followers of Isaiah of Babylon. Their general outlook is simlar to his idealism, yet they seem to reflect the despair of this later age.

Isaiah 56—66

The only certain source of information from this period is the book of Malachi. This shows that, though the temple was indeed standing again, the spiritual realities that it should symbolize were still not being taken seriously. The priests themselves were neglecting their proper duties, and the true covenant religion of Yahweh had become mixed up with magical practices. Popular religion was just a form of practical atheism: '"You have said terrible things about me", says the Lord . . . "You have said, 'It's useless to serve God. What's the use of doing what he says or of trying to show the Lord Almighty that we are sorry for what we have done?'"' As in the past, this neglect of Israel's covenant faith was

Malachi 3:5

Malachi 3:13–14

leading to great social evils, and Malachi declared that God would step in to judge this rotten community: 'those who give false testimony, those who cheat employees out of their wages, and those *Malachi 3:5* who take advantage of widows, orphans and foreigners'. On top of that, the community of returned exiles was losing its true identity. The men were leaving their Jewish wives for more attractive younger women who belonged to the racially mixed population that had tried to stop the rebuilding of the temple. This was a serious matter, for it threatened the very existence of the fragile Jewish settlement. It would only be a matter of time before God would *Malachi 4* have to deal with these evils.

Renewing the covenant

It was not too long before moves were afoot to reform and re-establish the life of the Jewish community in Jerusalem. It began with the arrival of a man called Nehemiah. He was himself a Jew, and had risen to a position of some eminence in the Persian royal court. When he heard of the deprivation of his people in Judah and Jerusalem, he asked the Persian king, by now Artaxerxes I, to let him go there and help to rebuild the community. So he was *Nehemiah 1—2* appointed governor of Judah in 445 BC. There had probably been a succession of such governors ever since the days of Sheshbazzar about 100 years before. We know nothing of them or their work, but the brief report of their activities given in the book of Nehemiah suggests they had been more concerned with their own comfort *Nehemiah 5:15* than with the well-being of their people. The reaction of both upper-class Jews and the people of Samaria to Nehemiah's appointment certainly suggests that his predecessors did not share the commitment and religious idealism that were to be a hallmark of Nehemiah's work.

Building the walls

Nehemiah had a specific commission from the Persian emperor to rebuild the city of Jerusalem itself. But when he got there, he found that most of the Jews were satisfied with things as they were. From a social perspective, they had turned out to be model immigrants, for they had integrated almost entirely with the rest of Palestinian society. Their businessmen had established trading relations with the people of Samaria, to the mutual benefit of both groups, and this had led to co-operation over a wide range of other issues.

Of course, the people of Samaria were not total foreigners. For they too could trace their ancestry back to the original Israelite tribes. The only difference was that whereas the Jews from Babylon were of pure Israelite stock, these other people had married people of other races. Even so, they still worshipped the same God as the exiles from Babylon, and the two men from Samaria who turned out to be Nehemiah's most vociferous opponents – Sanballat and Tobiah – both felt that they had the same religious faith as their Jewish neighbours.

But Nehemiah could not accept all this. To him, integration between Jews and other people could only mean one thing: the loss of their distinctive Jewish identity. He believed that these people had abandoned the idealism that originally motivated their return from Babylon. The fact that he also saw the rich sections of the community exploiting the poor only made him the more determined to change things.

Nehemiah 5

He challenged the moral standards of the Jewish businessmen. But he could see that as long as there was easy access from Samaria to Jerusalem, the problems would persist. If there was ever to be a pure Jewish community then it would need to have its own political identity centred in the city of Jerusalem itself. Jerusalem must be properly fortified, with its own city walls. That would remind people like Sanballat and Tobiah that it did not belong to them, and it would also give the Jews a city to be proud of. Sanballat and Tobiah were deeply opposed to all this. Quite possibly they themselves had exercised some sort of jurisdiction over Jerusalem before Nehemiah came. They obviously had friendly relations with the Jewish leaders, and felt it was quite unjust for them to be cut off like this by an outsider. But Nehemiah managed to gather together a group of workmen from the area surrounding the city, and they set to work – half of them building, the other half guarding the unfinished wall. In the amazingly short time of fifty-two days, the

Nehemiah 6

wall was built. It was not as extensive as the wall that had surrounded the city before 586 BC, but its completion gave a great boost to the morale of its inhabitants. For the first time since Nebuchadnezzar had destroyed their city, Jerusalem and its people had their own self-contained society, and a new opportunity to establish their distinctive national and religious identity.

Nehemiah 13:6

Some twelve years after his arrival, Nehemiah returned to the Persian capital Susa to report back to Artaxerxes. He must have felt that he had made some progress. But when he came back, he discovered that things had not really changed. In his absence, things had returned to what they were before. Foreigners had come to live in Jerusalem, and the people were not observing the sabbath day. On top of that, the worship at the temple was not as strict as Nehemiah would have liked it to be. Some of the priests had been forced to leave their posts to go to work on the farms, just to make a living. At the same time, Eliashib the high priest had given a suite of rooms in the temple to Nehemiah's enemy Tobiah! But that was not the worst thing. For many Jewish people were again marrying foreigners – and even the high priest's own grandson had married

Nehemiah 13:4–31

the daughter of Sanballat!

Handing on the Law

Nehemiah was determined to change all this. But it was a Jewish priest by the name of Ezra who issued the most far-reaching challenge to the people of Jerusalem. He too was a Persian state official, who came to Jerusalem with royal authority to reorganize religious affairs. He was accompanied by a further group of returning exiles from Babylon, who brought with them a consi-

Ezra 7:1–26

derable financial endowment for the temple in Jerusalem. But they brought more than that, for Ezra was a 'scholar in the Law of the

Ezra 7:12

God of Heaven.' It was this Law that he set before the people, and

Part of the wall of Old Jerusalem is known as Nehemiah's wall. Nehemiah led the returned Jews in rebuilding the city walls, against fierce opposition from the tribes who had occupied the surrounding territory. His leadership helped to restore a sense of national religious identity to a people in danger of being demoralized by the difficult task of getting re-established in a long-neglected land.

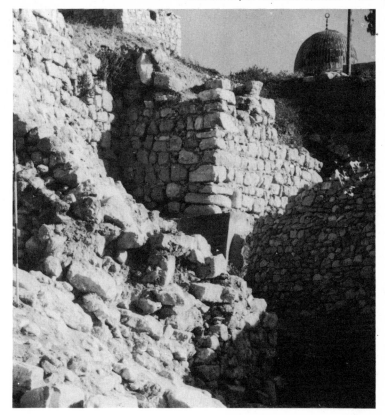

that was to have a profound and lasting influence on their whole way of life.

It is not absolutely clear from the Old Testament just what this Law was. But it is reasonable to suppose that it would be substantially identical with the Torah as we know it today. Among the exiles in Babylon, this had become of supreme importance. Away from Judah, and unable to continue the traditional worship in the temple, the exiles had laid great emphasis on those things that could still distinguish them from other nations – things like keeping the sabbath day, observing their own special food regulations, and circumcision. And all of this was found in their Law. The exiles clearly knew a good deal more about this than the people in Judah, for their reaction to it suggests that they were not at all familiar with its requirements. They were certainly unable to read it for themselves. Ezra read it aloud to them, but a group of priests (Levites) then 'gave an oral translation of God's Law and explained it so that the people could understand it.' This was necessary because the Law itself was written in Hebrew, whereas the people now spoke Aramaic, which was the official language of the Persian Empire. The rough translation made by the Levites was the forerunner of many such translations, know as Targums. At first, a Targum was only an oral translation, but as time went on its wording became more fixed, and the term Targum came to mean just the Aramaic version of the Old Testament.

Nehemiah 8:8

Nehemiah 8:9–18

When they heard the Law that Ezra read, the people were deeply moved, and decided they must celebrate the religious festivals which it mentioned. But Ezra was determined to tackle the other problems too, especially the question of Jews who were married to foreigners. He was more diplomatic than Nehemiah, but also more ruthless, and he forced the Jews to agree to divorce all such partners. From a modern perspective, Ezra can easily seem intolerant and bigoted. But his view was not unreasonable for his own day. In many of the marriage laws of ancient Greece and Rome, a man was not even allowed to marry a person outside his own class, let alone from a different race.

Whatever we may think of Ezra's attitudes, it is probably true that the community in Judah may not have survived as a distinctive entity without his efforts. But the people paid a high price for their survival. For this new emphasis on racial purity and a detailed observance of rules and regulations as the heart of the Jewish religion could so easily be misinterpreted to become that self-

Matthew 23:1–36

righteous legalism and hypocrisy that was roundly condemned by Jesus and which the Christian apostle Paul later felt to be so contrary to the original intention of the covenant relationship

Galatians

between God and his ancient people. Not all Jews were narrow-minded legalists, of course. But it was almost inevitable that many of them would be tempted to lay more emphasis on the mechanical performance of religious rules than on the dynamic relationship between God and his people that had up to this point formed the heart of the Old Testament story.

Two dissidents

Not everyone accepted this new emphasis on racial purity, the Law, and the temple. When Stephen, one of the leaders of the earliest Christian church, argued that the building of the temple was a mistake because 'The Most High God does not live in houses built by men' (Acts 7:48, quoting Isaiah 66:1–2), he had a long line of Jewish protest behind him. But at this earlier period, more criticism was focused on the policy of rigid separation from other races.

Many scholars believe that the Old Testament book of Ruth may have been published at this time, as a protest against Ezra's actions. The fact that the Jews placed it in the third section of the Old Testament – the Writings – certainly suggests that it may have been among the later Old Testament books. But in our English Bibles it is placed after Judges, because its story is set in that age. It tells how Elimelech, a native of Bethlehem, emigrated to Moab at a time of famine. He was accompanied by his wife, Naomi, and his two sons, both of whom married Moabite women. The father and the two sons all died in

Moab, and Naomi returned to Bethlehem along with her daughter-in-law Ruth. There, Ruth met Boaz, who was a relative of her husband's family, and they got married. As a result, Ruth, a Moabite woman, became the great-grandmother of King David.

Like other parts of the Old Testament, this story may have originated in earlier times. But the opening phrase of the book, 'Long ago, in the days before Israel had a king . . .', shows that it was only written down later. And though there is no positive evidence to prove it, it is plausible to think that it could have been written as a protest against the legislation of Ezra and Nehemiah: if a Moabite woman married to an Israelite could have been the ancestor of King David himself, then surely there was nothing wrong with mixed marriages!

The book of Jonah may also have originated in the same context. A prophet called Jonah is mentioned briefly in the time of Amos (2 Kings 14:25), but the book contains none of his messages. It tells the story of how

Jonah was sent by God to go to Nineveh, the capital city of the Assyrian Empire. Jonah, however, did not want to go, and boarded a ship going in the opposite direction. A great storm blew up, and the crew decided he must be the cause of it. At his own suggestion they threw him overboard, but he was swallowed by a fish which later deposited him on dry land. Again Jonah was sent to Nineveh, to announce the destruction of the city. But his preaching resulted in such a dramatic and thoroughgoing repentance that God withdrew the threat of destruction.

Jonah was disspirited at this, and went to sit alone outside the city. A plant grew up to give him much-needed shade from the sun, only to disappear as quickly – much to Jonah's annoyance. But his frustration then becomes the occasion for the book's message to be hammered home: 'The Lord said to him, "This plant grew up in one night and disappeared the next; you didn't do anything for it and you didn't make it grow – yet you feel sorry for it! How much more, then, should I have pity on Nineveh, that great city. After all, it has more than 120,000 innocent children in it, as well as many animals!"' (Jonah 4:10–11)

There are some indications that this book was written after the city of Nineveh had fallen (in 612 BC), and a few Aramaic expressions seem to date it in the Persian period. Its message would certainly be a corrective to the narrow exclusiveness of many Jews at that time. Like Jonah, they were often prepared to go to any lengths to avoid sharing their faith with others, preferring that non-Jews should be destroyed rather than repent.

The Chronicler and his history

The Old Testament books 1 and 2 Chronicles were written during this post-exilic period. In them, we have yet another view of the Old Testament story, a story which this time begins with Adam, the first man (1 Chronicles 1:1) and ends with Cyrus the Persian (2 Chronicles 36:22–23). The first nine chapters of 1 Chronicles consist entirely of various family and tribal lists and genealogies, and the story proper begins with the death of Saul, the first king of Israel (1 Chronicles 10). But he is mentioned only as a prelude to the story of David, and the main interest of the author of these books ('the Chronicler') centres on the history of Judah from the time of David onwards.

Inevitably, therefore, the stories of the books of Chronicles parallel those of the Deuteronomistic history books. Indeed, at many points the Chronicler shows that he has actually used the books of Samuel and Kings in the writing of his own story. This fact should make it easy for us to discover his own special reasons for telling the story yet again, simply by comparing his accounts of the same events described in the earlier books. Unfortunately, it seems likely that he was using a slightly different version of Samuel and Kings from the one that is now part of our Old Testament. We know of the existence of such a version from the Dead Sea Scrolls, a collection of scriptural and other writings preserved by a Jewish sect in the century immediately preceding the Christian era. But because of the doubt concerning the edition of Samuel and Kings used by the Chronicler, reconstructing his own historical method is not a straightforward business. Chronicles also contains other historical information not found in Samuel and Kings, much of which is of independent value in helping us to understand the events of Israel's earlier history.

On the whole, however, the Chronicler sets out not so much to record the facts about the past, as to comment on their meaning and significance. And though there may be doubt about some of the details, his main concerns are not difficult to discern. He looks back to the reigns of David and Solomon as a golden age in Judah's history. The kings who followed them were all disobedient to God's Law, and the northern kingdom of Israel is scarcely mentioned at all, for it was believed to be so corrupt right from its inception. The Deuteronomic picture of Solomon and David gives us a more realistic, balanced account of their reigns than we have in Chronicles. Not that the Chronicler necessarily invented his facts: he simply omitted significant elements from the story, and emphasized other aspects that to him were more important. So, for instance, there is no mention here of David's struggle for the kingdom against Ishbaal, Saul's son. Nor is there any mention of David's adultery with Bathsheba – or anything else that might cast David in a bad light. The same is true of the presentation of Solomon. The court intrigues that brought him to power are not mentioned, nor is his worship of false gods, or his involvement with foreign wives. Instead, both David and Solomon are praised because they built the temple. David's preparations for doing so, and Solomon's execution of his father's plans are described in far greater detail than in the earlier history books. Then, against this background, the later kings of Judah are all depicted as men who led their country to ruin because they neglected this all-important feature of Judah's national life.

The fact that Cyrus's edict is mentioned in the last paragraph of 2 Chronicles has led some to suggest that the two books may have been written to provide support for the work of Zerubbabel in rebuilding the temple after the exile. The fact that the issue of racial purity – so important later – does not feature in Chronicles may also support such a date. On the other hand, this may be too early, for the list of Jehoiachin's descendants in 1 Chronicles 3:17–24 goes well beyond the time of Zerubbabel, and possibly takes us to about 400 BC. In that case, the two books could have been written in support of Ezra's reforms. They certainly stress some of the same things – and in that context, the ignoring of the life of the northern kingdom of Israel could be seen as an encouragement to the people of Jerusalem to have nothing to do with their descendants who now lived in Samaria. On the other hand, some scholars have argued that we should not try to link Chronicles up to specific events and situations in this way, but simply see it as the product of a number of different political and theological currents in the post-exilic Jewish community.

Ezra and Nehemiah

The date of 1 and 2 Chronicles is closely bound up with their relationship to the books of Ezra and Nehemiah. Many scholars believe that all four of them together were originally written as a history of the Jews from creation itself up to the Chronicler's own day. If that is the case, then we would need to think of all four books as written about 400 BC, or possibly even later. The only substantial reason for seeing a connection between 1–2 Chronicles and Ezra/Nehemiah is the fact that the closing words of 2 Chronicles are identical with the opening paragraph of Ezra. But in other ways, their concerns are rather different. In particular, the deep interest of 1–2 Chronicles in David's family is not reflected in Ezra

and Nehemiah.

The style and general organization of material is also strikingly different. Whereas 1–2 Chronicles contain a coherent, well-organized account, Ezra and Nehemiah contain a very disjointed collection of stories and other materials. Temple records are quoted (Nehemiah 7:5; 12:23), as is the decree of Cyrus – in Hebrew (Ezra 1:1–4) and Aramaic (Ezra 6:3–5). Various other Aramaic letters are also included in Ezra (4:7–22; 5:6–17; 6:2–12; 7:12–26), while the actual story of Ezra's exploits is partly contained in the book of Ezra (7—10) and partly in Nehemiah (7:73–10:39) – and some of it has the appearance of being extracts from Ezra's own diary (Ezra 7:27—8:34; 9:1–15). Likewise, much of Nehemiah's story appears in the form of extracts from his own personal diary (Nehemiah 1:1—7:73, and sections of 11—13).

Then as the stories stand, there are complex issues involved in understanding the relationship between these two men. According to Ezra 7:7, Ezra went to Jerusalem in the seventh year of Artaxerxes' reign, and Nehemiah in his twentieth year (Nehemiah 1:1). That would place Ezra's arrival in 458 BC, and Nehemiah's in 444 BC. But this seems to imply that Ezra's reforms were a miserable failure, for when Nehemiah arrived he certainly found all the same abuses as Ezra fought so strenuously to overcome. There are other facts which further complicate matters. For instance, when Nehemiah arrived he set to work building a wall round Jerusalem, though Ezra 9:9 implies that there was already a wall there when Ezra arrived. There is also the fact that in Nehemiah's time, the high priest was Eliashib (Nehemiah 3:1), whereas in Ezra's time it appears to have been his grandson, Johanan (Ezra 10:6; Nehemiah 12:11,22).

Various attempts have been made to overcome this problem. Some suggest that Ezra perhaps came in the reign of Artaxerxes II, which would place his arrival in 398 BC – long after the time of Nehemiah. Others emphasize the fact that their careers do seem to have overlapped at some points (Nehemiah 8:9; 12:26,36). They have therefore suggested that the correct date for Ezra was the *twenty*-seventh year of Artaxerxes I, i.e. 428 BC. All three dates for Ezra – 458, 428, and 398 BC – have supporters today, and it is difficult to decide which is likely to be correct. In our account of the work of these two men, we have assumed that Nehemiah did precede Ezra, but probably not by a long period of time.

Perhaps the reason for this confusion can be found in the disjointed nature of the narratives of these two books. For as we read them carefully, they seem to be not so much a continuous story of Ezra and Nehemiah, as a kind of preliminary collection of information such as a historian might make before writing his polished account. The first six chapters of Ezra are more or less continuous, but between them and chapter seven there is a time gap of at least sixty years, and possibly more. The further fact that some parts of Ezra are written in Aramaic, while other parts are in Hebrew, also reinforces this impression of a collection of notes rather than a finished story.

If this is a correct understanding of the nature of Ezra and Nehemiah, it would then be possible that 1 and 2 Chronicles were written early during the period of the exile, and that these other materials were gathered together by some later author – perhaps a follower of the original Chronicler – as a means of bringing the story up to his own day. We have so little knowledge of this period that it is difficult to be certain. But this does not detract from the usefulness of these books, for all scholars are convinced that Nehemiah and Ezra contain important and valuable historical materials from the period which they describe.

This papyrus letter was written by Jews who were living in Elephantine, in southern Egypt near Aswan. It mentions Sanballat, governor of Samaria in the time of Nehemiah. Documents found at Elephantine show that Jews who lived there at that time continued to worship the Lord.

Jews in Egypt

The Jewish community in Jerusalem was not the only context in which the God of Israel was being worshipped at this time. We have already noticed that the inhabitants of Samaria felt themselves to be a part of the ancient covenant faith – and in a series of Aramaic documents discovered at the island of Elephantine, near Aswan on the River Nile, we are given a fascinating glimpse of life in another Jewish community at roughly the time of Nehemiah and Ezra.

The Jews who lived here were a military settlement. At the time of these documents, Egypt was a part of the Persian Empire, and they had perhaps been sent to guard the southern frontier of Egypt and the trading post of Syene, where traders from further south met the ships of Egyptian traders on the Nile. These Jews may well have been in this area long before Cambyses the Persian conquered Egypt in 525 BC, but they certainly had a military function rather than being (as some have supposed) the descendants either of a group of religious dissidents who left Jerusalem in protest at Josiah's reforms (621 BC), or of those Jews who took Jeremiah to Egypt after the fall of Jerusalem in 586 BC.

There are many different kinds of documents in this collection, including deeds for property, marriage contracts, and other legal transactions. But the most interesting ones to us are those that describe the religious practices of this group. For it soon emerges from them that the Judaism of this Egyptian garrison was very different indeed from the Judaism that was being taught at the same time in Jerusalem by Nehemiah and Ezra.

● In spite of the Deuteronomic law that sacrifices were to be offered only in Jerusalem, there was a Jewish temple in Elephantine at which sacrifices were offered. The priests who officiated here are not said to have belonged to the tribe of Levi, nor is there any evidence that they knew the Torah. After their temple had been destroyed in 410 BC, the governors of Judah and Samaria advised them to limit their sacrifices to meal offerings and incense. This could have been a gesture intended to show that the Elephantine temple was inferior in status to that in Jerusalem – but it could also have been because animal sacrifices were particularly offensive to the Egyptians.

Various explanations have been offered to account for the existence of this temple. Perhaps the Deuteronomic law of a single sanctuary applied only in Palestine. Or possibly the Jews of Elephantine had left Palestine already before the reforms of Hezekiah and Josiah had really taken a grip. We simply do not know, though some scholars have suggested that there may be a veiled reference to this Egyptian temple in Isaiah 19:19, which reads 'When that day comes, there will be an altar to the Lord in the land of Egypt and a stone pillar dedicated to him at the Egyptian border'. We know very little about this temple, except that it had pillars of stone, five gateways made of carved stone, and a roof of cedar wood. But there is not the slightest suggestion that the Jews of Elephantine thought there was anything wrong in having such a temple outside Jerusalem. Indeed, when it was destroyed they appealed for help in its rebuilding both to the Jewish leaders in Jerusalem, and to the people in Samaria who were so hostile to Nehemiah!

● Though this temple was definitely dedicated to Yahweh (or Yaho as he is called here), other gods and goddesses had some part in it. Some believe there were five deities worshipped here, represented by the five gates of the temple. Others believe there were only two or three, of whom Yaho was certainly one. Most of the other gods and goddesses mentioned in the texts are Canaanite. When we recall the habits of the people in Israel itself, we need not be surprised by this. The prophets were constantly complaining because the worship of Yahweh was mixed up with the worship of other gods and goddesses. And when Jeremiah met up with such people after his flight to Egypt, they justified their worship of 'the Queen of Heaven' by reminding him that this was 'just as we and our ancestors, our king and our leaders, used to do in the towns of Judah and in the streets of Jerusalem' (Jeremiah 44:17).

● One of the most interesting texts is the so-called 'Passover Papyrus'. This dates from 419 BC, and contains a decree said to have been issued by Darius, laying down regulations for the celebration of the festival of Passover. This suggests that the annual observance of Passover was not so regular in early times as it came to be in later Judaism. But the very existence of this text is itself unusual, though it is of the same type as other edicts contained in the books of Ezra and Nehemiah, which also give directions for the establishment of Jewish religious practices.

It is naturally tempting to try to find clear links between these documents and the Old Testament story. There is for example mention of people by the name of Hanani, as well as Johanan and Sanballat – all of whom figure in the stories of Nehemiah and Ezra. But there is no way of being certain that they indicate the same people. One of the things that is quite clear from these texts is that there were some people who believed it was possible to be a good Jew without necessarily following the rigid lines that had been drawn in Jerusalem. And in the next few centuries, this strand of Judaism was to be increasingly important in many parts of the Mediterranean world, not least in Egypt itself.

8 The challenge of a new age

Daniel

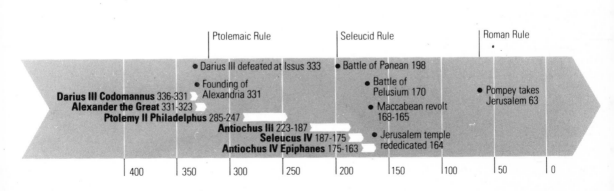

Ptolemaic Rule   Seleucid Rule   Roman Rule

● Darius III defeated at Issus 333

● Founding of Alexandria 331

● Battle of Panean 198

● Battle of Pelusium 170

● Maccabean revolt 168-165

● Pompey takes Jerusalem 63

Darius III Codomannus 336-331
Alexander the Great 331-323
Ptolemy II Philadelphus 285-247
Antiochus III 223-187
Seleucus IV 187-175
Antiochus IV Epiphanes 175-163

● Jerusalem temple rededicated 164

400   350   300   250   200   150   100   50   0

THE HISTORY books of the Old Testament tell us nothing about events after the times of Nehemiah and Ezra. But the Old Testament story does not end there. Life in Judah continued, and changing attitudes and experiences may well be reflected in some of the Old Testament books. We have very little specific knowledge of what life was really like in Judah in the seventy or eighty years following the work of Ezra. But the community which he founded on the twin principles of religious and racial exclusivism probably continued along the same lines. Judah was still a Persian province, but it was allowed to mint its own coins, and enjoyed other privileges that the community based on Samaria never had. During this period the differences between Jerusalem and Samaria eventually forced the two populations of Palestine to go their own separate ways.

A high priest, from the small community of Samaritans still living in Israel today. Their origins reach back at least to Sanballat and Tobiah in Nehemiah's time and possibly even to the racially mixed community who survived the fall of Samaria and the northern kingdom to the Assyrians. Though kept at a distance by mainline Judaism, the Samaritans have always looked on themselves as heirs to the Old Testament traditions.

Jews and Samaritans

The people of Samaria realized they would never again be allowed to worship God in Jerusalem. Yet they still felt themselves to be a legitimate part of the great national and spiritual movement that could be traced back to the Israelite tribes of the earliest days. As they read the ancient stories of Abraham, Isaac, Jacob, and Moses, they recognized them as their own story – and the God of whom they spoke was worshipped with as much fervour in Samaria as he was by the settlers in Jerusalem.

As they reassessed their own national life in the wake of Ezra's reforms, the people of Samaria gradually developed their own distinctive beliefs and culture, and emerged as the people whom we meet later in the pages of the New Testament as 'Samaritans'. Some think the Samaritans of New Testament times were a completely new sect that emerged in the days just before the beginning of the Christian era. They may, of course, have come under other influences then, but there seems no reason why they should not have been connected with the people led by Tobiah and Sanballat, and who were so fiercely opposed by Ezra and Nehemiah.

The Samaritans got their chance to establish their own national identity in 333 BC. This was the year when the Persian king Darius III Codomannus was defeated in battle at Issus in north-west Syria. The victor was a young, enthusiastic warrior from Macedonia (the northern part of modern Greece) – Alexander the Great. Having overcome the main Persian army, he moved south towards Egypt. The Samaritans seized this opportunity, and got permission to build a temple of their own on Mt Gerizim. At first they were more eager to co-operate with the Greeks than were the high priest and the ruling classes in Jerusalem. But for some unknown reason they soon revolted, and their city was made into a Greek military colony.

A new empire

The empire created by Alexander the Great's fourth-century conquests took in Judea. For the next centuries the dominant influence in the whole Eastern Mediterranean was 'Hellenism' - a culture based on Greek language and thinking.

Alexander's progress was spectacular. Egypt put up no resistance to him, and in 331 BC he was able to found a new city on the Nile delta. This was the city of Alexandria, and it was to have a considerable influence not only on Egypt, but on the Jewish people living in various parts of the Mediterranean world. It later became an important centre of early Christianity.

The establishment of new cities played an important part in Alexander's strategy. For he was not just out for political power: he also had an almost fanatical fervour about spreading Greek culture and the Greek language. He was remarkably successful in doing so, and although his empire did not last long as a united political entity, the cultural world that he created, based on all things Greek – 'Hellenism' – lasted for nearly 1,000 years.

Alexander himself died of a fever in 323 BC. By then his empire stretched from Greece in the west to Pakistan in the east. But it did not survive intact. After much feuding among Alexander's generals, Judah – or Judea as it was now to be called – came under the control of Ptolemy, who established himself and his successors as a new ruling dynasty in Egypt. From about 320 BC until 198 BC, the Jews came under the jurisdiction of these Greek rulers of Egypt. On the whole, they were tolerant of the religious scruples of the Jewish people. They forced many Jews to emigrate to the city of Alexandria, which was at the time under-populated. Many others also went voluntarily, and there was soon a thriving Jewish community in this new Egyptian city. The language of the city was Greek, of course, and it was there that the Old Testament was translated from its original language into Greek.

According to one ancient legend, the Jews of Egypt managed to persuade the Egyptian king, Ptolemy II Philadelphus to sponsor the project. He sent to Jerusalem for seventy men who knew both Hebrew and Greek, and locked them up in seventy cells while each one produced his translation. When the work was finished, to everyone's amazement the seventy men not only expressed the same ideas, but also used the very same Greek words to do so – whereupon Ptolemy was so impressed that he was immediately convinced of the divine origins of their work! In reality, the work of translating the Old Testament into Greek was more humdrum than that. The Greek Septuagint version (the LXX) probably just evolved over many generations. But it certainly seems to have had some connection with Alexandria, and it became increasingly important not only for the spread of Judaism in the Mediterranean world, but also for the earliest Christian believers, who adopted it as their own Bible.

The Septuagint and the Deutero-Canonical books

It is customary today to speak of 'the Septuagint' as if it were simply a Greek Old Testament. But the facts are not so simple. A modern translator begins with a complete Bible in Hebrew and Greek, and produces its equivalent in his own language. But what we now call the Septuagint was never a complete Bible until the early centuries of the Christian era. Before that, no one knew the techniques necessary to bind such a large volume of literature into one single volume. Writing materials were painstakingly made by hand, and individual sheets would then be glued or stitched together to make a strip long enough to contain a single book. This would then be rolled up for storage, and to possess a complete Old Testament required a large number of different rolls. In addition to this, different people were busy making their own translations of the Old Testament books into Greek – and when the Christians eventually produced a single-volume Greek Old Testament, they simply made a selection from the translations that were available to them. Even today, we have a great number of ancient translations of Hebrew Old Testament books into Greek, not to mention several revisions and new editions of the Septuagint itself, all of them made by early Christian authors.

This complex state of affairs has also led to considerable debate about the actual contents of the Old Testament. How many books should it contain? At first, this may seem an odd question to ask. But we only need to compare a selection of modern versions of the Old Testament to see that though they all contain the thirty-nine books of the Hebrew Bible, some also contain other books, called either 'The Apocrypha' or 'The Deutero-Canonical books'.

These writings are: 1—2 Esdras (also called 3—4 Ezra), Tobit, Judith, additions to Esther, Wisdom of Solomon, Ecclesiasticus, the Letter of Jeremiah, Baruch, Song of the Three Young Men, Susannah, Bel and the Dragon, Prayer of Manasseh, and 1—2 Maccabees. Like the thirty-nine Old Testament books, they represent many types of literature. Some are clearly history books (1—2 Maccabees), others are books of philosophy and religious poetry (Wisdom of Solomon, Ecclesiasticus), while others are moralistic novels (Tobit, Judith, Susannah, Bel and the Dragon), and yet others provide additional material for books in the main body of the Old Testament, or purport to give a ' clairvoyant view of the future (2 Esdras).

Almost all these books are known to us primarily from early Christian copies of the Greek Septuagint version of the Old Testament. But we know that not all of them came from the same sources. Fragments of some of them have been discovered written in Hebrew. Others were originally composed in Greek, while yet others were probably first written in Hebrew, but have only survived in their Greek versions.

If we knew more about the origins of the Septuagint itself, we might be able to say with certainty how the Egyptian Jews thought of these books. But there is no evidence at present that suggests they regarded them as a part of the Old Testament itself. That argument only became important when Christians had collected together the various Greek translations of Old Testament books into one volume. Once the Septuagint had become the Bible of the Christian church, a long debate began about the value of these 'extra books'. Roman Catholic Christians accept them as a true part of the Old Testament, though most others do not. Some, like the Episcopal churches, use them selectively, accepting the guidelines laid down in the *Articles of Religion* of the Church of England, that 'the Church doth read (them) for example of life and instruction of manners; but yet doth it not apply them to establish any doctrine.'

So are these books a part of the Bible or not? No doubt the final answer to that question will have to be a theological one. But as a historical question, their existence can be explained quite easily. For in the days before the Old Testament was literally one book, the various rolls in which its writings were contained needed to be stored safely, and were often kept in small boxes. These boxes were often used as a sort of classification system, and if there was room the owner would store similar kinds of writings in the same boxes. This was probably how the books we now call the Apocrypha came to be associated with the other Old Testament books. In content and style, they were not all that different from the books of the Hebrew Bible, and it was natural to keep them all together. In time, they came to be accepted as part and parcel of the books that collectively made up the Greek version of the Old Testament. So when the early Christians came to bind all these books into one volume, it was natural to include them – even though they had probably never been included in the Hebrew Old Testament used by most Jewish people.

Jews and Greeks

Ptolemy had not been the only one of Alexander's generals with designs on Judea. Seleucus, who ruled from Antioch in north Syria, was not too happy that Judea and Lebanon should belong to Egypt. Throughout the third century their respective successors were engaged in a kind of cold war, and actually became involved in a number of military encounters over this issue. The matter was

The Greek Empire

finally decided in 198 BC, when the Seleucid Antiochus III defeated Scopus, the general of Ptolemy V, at the battle of Paneon.

At first Antiochus adopted a tolerant policy towards the Jews. He reduced their taxes and made a generous grant towards their temple in Jerusalem. Unfortunately, he was soon forced to change his attitude. Having extended his power to the south, he tried to expand his empire in the west. But he had reckoned without the growing power of Rome, and in 190 BC he was defeated in a land and sea battle at Magnesia, near Ephesus. The peace treaty that he subsequently signed was a great humiliation, for he was forced to abandon his territory in Asia Minor. The loss of face was bad enough. But this territory had always been the wealthiest part of the Seleucid Empire, and the loss of its revenue led him to the brink of bankruptcy. He was soon desperate for money and just a year after signing the treaty with the Romans, Antiochus himself was killed in Elam while in the act of robbing a temple. He was succeeded by his son, Seleucus IV – who promptly despatched his chancellor, Heliodorus, to plunder the temple in Jerusalem.

2 Maccabees 3

Religion and politics

In the meantime, new tensions had emerged in Jewish society. Even before the Seleucids gained control of Judea, two of the leading families of Jerusalem – the Tobiads and the Oniads – had emerged as rivals, the one representing a rigid Jewish orthodoxy, and the other being more in sympathy with the new Hellenistic culture.

The climax of this power struggle within the Jewish hierarchy coincided with the murder of Seleucus IV and the accession of a new king, Antiochus IV Epiphanes. A member of the Oniad family called Jason bribed Antiochus to make him high priest in Jerusalem in place of his brother Onias. This suited Antiochus, for Jason was committed to the same policies of Hellenization as he was himself. With Jason's appointment, a thoroughgoing plan was set in motion to establish Jerusalem as a Greek city. Even the priests in the temple were soon hurrying through their work to have time to go off to the wrestling arena. The Greeks wore no clothes on such occasions, and to avoid possible embarrassment when they took part, the Jewish men even went so far as to try to disguise the fact that they had been circumcised. All this was too much for those who wanted to remain true to the traditions of their people, and it was not long before Jason was deposed and replaced by Menelaus, a member of the Tobiad family. Menelaus was appointed by Antiochus because he offered a higher bribe than Jason – but to the pious, he was no better than his predecessor.

2 Maccabees 4:13–15

1 Maccabees 1:10–15; 2 Maccabees 4:7–17

2 Maccabees 4:23–50

1 Maccabees 1:16–28

Meanwhile, Antiochus had set his sights on Egypt. The ruler of Egypt, Ptolemy VI, was only a boy, and Antiochus defeated his army without difficulty. As always, he was desperate for money, and on his way home he went to Jerusalem and robbed the temple.

He was not absent for long. In the spring of 168 BC he went back to Egypt. But this time, he found the Romans there, and they soon

In the days of Antiochus IV Epiphanes, there was a great struggle between the Jews and their Seleucid rulers over whether Jewish life and religion should continue its distinctive existence. The Seleucids wanted to make Jerusalem a purely Greek city, but the Jews fought strongly to retain the right to keep their Law.

sent him packing. In the meantime, a rumour had spread in Jerusalem that Antiochus was dead. Jason seized the opportunity to try to get rid of Menelaus. But Antiochus was in no mood for compromise. He had already been humiliated by the Romans, and he was determined to keep his grip on Judea. So he moved to Jerusalem again, and took what treasure was left in the temple, assisted this time by Menelaus himself.

2 Maccabees 5:1–20

Antiochus was determined to show who was in charge. His visit to Jerusalem was accompanied by great slaughter and destruction, and some of the people were taken off as slaves. But Antiochus knew that this was not just a political struggle: it was also a dispute among the Jews themselves about their own religion. This was something he neither understood nor cared for. But since it was causing trouble, he was determined that its power would have to be diminished. Circumcision, sabbath keeping, and reading the Law were all banned, and it was only a matter of time before Antiochus had arranged for the temple in Jerusalem to be given over to the worship of the Greek god Zeus. To add insult to injury, he opened the temple to the whole population of the land, including those who were not Jews. With this, Antiochus embarked on a thoroughgoing policy of enforced Hellenization. This had always been culturally desirable to the Seleucids, but now it was politically essential. Whether they liked it or not, the Jews would have to accept on equal terms the other racial groups with whom they lived – and the only practical way to achieve such integration was by everyone being united under the Greek religion and Greek ways of life.

2 Maccabees 5:11–14

1 Maccabees 1:41–50;
2 Maccabees 6:1–6

National pride and religious zeal

Antiochus had underestimated the strength of the Jewish resistance to all this. It was one thing to set up altars to the Greek gods – but it was to be another thing altogether to persuade the Jews to worship at them. Their resistance was fanatical, and was only strengthened by the fact that pigs (unclean animals to the Jews) were offered on

2 Maccabees 6:7–31

2 Maccabees 7

1 Maccabees 2:1–26

1 Maccabees 2:29–38

1 Maccabees 2:39–41

2 Maccabees 11:27–33

1 Maccabees 4:36–59;
2 Maccabees 10:5–8

these altars. Many pious individuals were prepared to die rather than take part in such ceremonies. Their resolution was matched only by the cruelty of Antiochus's soldiers, who on one occasion skinned and fried alive an entire family who refused to submit to this compulsory Hellenization.

Such passive resistance may have been morally praiseworthy – but it was hardly effective, and an armed resistance movement soon sprang to life. It began at the village of Modein, near Lydda. A priest by the name of Mattathias was ordered to offer a sacrifice at a pagan altar. When he refused, another Jew stepped forward in his place – whereupon Mattathias killed both him and the Seleucid officer who had given the order. That was the sign for one of the most remarkable resistance movements in Jewish history.

Mattathias and his five sons fled to the hills and began a guerilla war under the leadership of Judas. He was nicknamed 'The Hammer' *(Maccabi)* , and from that the whole movement came to be called 'the Maccabean revolt'. A particularly despicable act by the Seleucid soldiers soon brought support from other sources. Many Jews had no wish to become involved in an armed struggle, and among them was a large ultra-religious group (the Hasideans) who had tried to withdraw from the conflict by going into the Judean desert. The Seleucid army went after them, and challenged them to battle on the sabbath day. Naturally, they refused, for they would not work on the sabbath. But they were mercilessly butchered. It was obvious then that passive resistance was going to be useless – and equally obvious that if all Jews continued to uphold the Law like that, there would soon be none of them left! So the Maccabees decided that they would sometimes need to be prepared to break the Law, and fight even on the sabbath.

This realistic policy attracted new supporters, including the Hasideans themselves. Under the daring leadership of Judas, the rebels had an amazing success, and it was not long before the weary Antiochus was forced to reverse his policies. The Jewish Law could be reinstated as the foundation of Jewish society, and the temple itself was restored to its rightful purpose and rededicated on 14 December 164 BC – an occasion that is still celebrated by pious Jews today, in the annual feast of Hanukkah.

The Hasideans were happy. They had won the freedom to practise their own religion and keep their own laws. But Judas's family (the Hasmoneans) wanted more than that. This limited victory had given them the taste for power, and it was not long before they had more or less thrown off Seleucid rule and established themselves as a ruling dynasty in Judea. Under their leadership, Judea enjoyed a period of relative political independence until the Roman general Pompey took the city of Jerusalem in 63 BC. But the Hasmoneans did not always remember the religious struggle that had originally brought them to power, and as a result they soon lost the support of the Hasideans.

The Hasideans disappeared altogether as a united religious

group. Some of them found the corruption and Hellenism of the Hasmonean kings intolerable, and withdrew into the Judean desert, just as they had done in the days of Antiochus. It was probably a movement of this kind that led to the foundation of the Essene community at Qumran by the shores of the Dead Sea. Other Hasideans did not go that far, but regrouped as a protest movement within mainstream Jewish society. Many scholars believe that they were connected with the rise of the Pharisees in the centuries before the birth of Jesus. The Hasmoneans, for their part, often seem to have favoured the Sadducees – another religious grouping of the time of Jesus – though they themselves were perhaps the precursors of the intensely anti-Roman zealot movement that emerged in Palestine during the first century AD.

The ruins of Qumran, a Jewish monastic community on the shores of the Dead Sea. This Essene community formed a distinct tradition within Judaism, based on the idea of withdrawing into the desert to preserve a religiously pure way of life.

The book of Daniel and the Maccabean crisis

The story of these stirring and difficult times for the Jewish people is not contained in any of the history books of the Old Testament. But the book of Daniel seems to reflect and comment on them. It is an obscure and complex book. Indeed, it is more like two books. For the first section contains a number of stories about a young Jew named Daniel who, along with his friends, faced opposition to their religion and way of life during the exile in Babylon (Daniel 1—6). But then the character of the book suddenly changes, and instead of real people in plausible real-life situations, we read about a series of grotesque visions. They relate the exploits of various mythological animals, and contain complicated speculations about the chronology of other Old Testament passages as they relate to the reigns of various unspecified kings (Daniel 7—12). In addition to this division in the book's contents, Daniel also has a linguistic division. It is written in two languages, neither of which corresponds exactly to the two major sections of the book's message. Hebrew is used in 1:1—2:4 and 8:1—12:13, with Aramaic in 2:4—7:28. In addition to this, the vocabulary of Daniel is sprinkled with Persian, and even Greek loan-words.

What, then, does the book mean, and why was it written? The answers to these two questions are very closely connected, for our understanding of the book's message will determine when we think it was written. We must therefore examine the two aspects of this book in some detail.

Stories about Daniel and his friends

Many people will be familiar with this section of the book of Daniel. It tells of the adventures of a young Jew called Daniel. According to the story, he was taken off to exile in Babylon by

Facing page: The story in the first part of the book of Daniel concerns young Jews among the exiles in Babylon. They were given privileges within the Babylonian Court, but refused the temptation to compromise their Jewish religion and laws.

Nebuchadnezzar in the course of an otherwise unknown attack on Jerusalem in 605 BC (1:1), and he stayed there until at least after the triumph of Cyrus in 539 BC (6:28). Daniel and his friends were given the unexpected privilege of being educated in the king's own court. But this presented them with problems right from the start. For one thing, they were expected to eat food that pious Jews would never have eaten (1:3–17). They were also required to worship a great statue that Nebuchadnezzar set up. But they could not do that and still remain faithful to their own religion. As a punishment, Daniel's three friends – Shadrach, Meshach and Abednego – were thrown into a furnace to be roasted alive. But they were miraculously saved from destruction, and eventually even Nebuchadnezzar himself had to admit the great power of their God (3:1–30). Daniel found himself in a similar situation during the reign of King Darius. He was thrown into a den of lions because he insisted on worshipping his own God. But again, he was unexpectedly delivered and Darius was forced to accept the supremacy of the God of Israel (6:1–28).

Many other stories about Daniel are found in other Jewish literature. But we know nothing else about him. Some have suggested he may have been an ancient legendary figure, perhaps to be identified with the Danel mentioned in Ezekiel 14:14, whose exploits are also recorded in the texts from Ugarit. But whoever he was, his experiences were probably typical of some Jews during the

Babylonian exile. For many of the exiles, this was a time of great prosperity and new opportunities. But we have already seen that traces of a less comfortable existence can also be found in other parts of the Old Testament.

Visions of the future

The significance of these stories about Daniel and his friends begins to come out in the second part of the book. For the two sections are linked together by visions of four great empires. There is a story of how Nebuchadnezzar had a dream that he could not understand and, in the way of ancient oriental rulers, he sent for his advisers to explain it to him (2:1–13). When they failed, Daniel succeeded – and told Nebuchadnezzar that the dream was about four great empires, represented by a statue made of four different metals – gold, silver, bronze, and iron. Nebuchadnezzar's own empire was the first of them – the golden one – and the others were to be empires that would follow on in turn (2:24–45). The fourth one would be the most terrifying of all, for 'it will shatter and crush all the earlier empires'. But it will also have a weakness, for 'it will be a divided empire . . . part of the empire will be strong and part of it weak' (2:41–42).

The first of the visions in the second half of the book is very similar to that. This time, the four empires are pictured as four animals: a lion, a bear, a leopard, and a fourth animal modelled on a goat. Again the fourth one is to be even more terrifying than the others: not only did it have teeth of iron with which to crush its victims, it also had a number of horns, capable of much terror. Indeed, the horns contended among themselves, until finally ' a little horn' with 'human eyes and a mouth that was boasting proudly' sprang up and 'tore out three of the horns that were already there' (7:1–8).

The precise identity of these kingdoms has been one of the most hotly disputed issues in the whole of the Old Testament. But the book itself tells us clearly that the first empire was Nebuchadnezzar's (2:37–38), and if we start there the identity of the others becomes plain. The story of Belshazzar is probably meant to be a part of the first empire, for he is described as Nebuchadnezzar's son (5:2). But then comes a ruler of a different race, 'Darius the Mede' (5:31), and it therefore seems reasonable to suppose he was the representatitive of the second empire. We certainly know that the

A Persian and a Median nobleman depicted on a frieze among the ruins of Persepolis. The second and third of the four empires in the apocalyptic vision in Daniel 7 have been identified with the Medes and the Persians.

A wall painting found in the ruins of Pompeii shows Alexander the Great in battle with Darius at Issa. The fourth of Daniel's visionary empires is probably Alexander's.

power of the Medes was increasing in the years after Nebuchadnezzar's death, and they eventually joined with Cyrus the Persian in 550 BC, and thereafter were able to take over the Babylonian Empire. Cyrus's Persian Empire is the next one to feature in Daniel (6:28), and can therefore reasonably be identified with the third empire of the visions. The fourth one would then be the empire of the Greeks, set up by Alexander and later divided among his successors.

The symbolic language used of the fourth beast seems to allude clearly to the events following Alexander's death. One vision tells how ' . . . at the height of his power his horn was broken. In its place four prominent horns came up, each pointing in a different direction. Out of one of these four horns grew a little horn, whose power extended towards the south and the east and towards the Promised Land . . . It even defied the Prince of the heavenly army, stopped the daily sacrifices offered to him, and desecrated the Temple. People sinned there instead of offering the proper daily sacrifices, and true religion was thrown to the ground' (8:8–12). This is obviously a detailed description of how, at the zenith of Alexander's power, his empire was divided among four of his generals, and of how out of one of those kingdoms (the Seleucid) great persecution came upon the Jewish people, culminating in the defiling of the temple under Antiochus IV Epiphanes.

Later visions describe the precise events which led up to Antiochus's arrival in Jerusalem, including the story of his visits to Egypt, his humiliation at the hands of the Romans, and his erection of 'the Awful Horror' in the temple itself (11:21–31) – presumably the statue he set up there. The Maccabean revolt which followed is also implied here: ' . . . those who follow God will fight back . . . God's people will receive a little help, even though many who join them will do so for selfish reasons. Some of those wise leaders will be killed, but as a result of this the people will be purified' (11:32–35). The fact that the hope of purification is in the future may well indicate that the book itself was written while the war was still in progress. It is perhaps a litle odd to find the brave efforts of Judas and his band of guerillas described as only 'a little help', but some have concluded from this that the book of Daniel may have been the work of a Hasidean, who was still slightly uneasy with the Maccabean approach.

As we shall see, this identification of the kingdoms of the book of Daniel makes the best sense out of other aspects of its message. But some have argued otherwise. They point out that there never was a separate Median and Persian empire – and therefore the fourth empire would not be Alexander's Greek empire, but Rome. Others have wished to identify Alexander with the fourth empire, but used the same argument to suggest that Daniel's historical sense is inadequate, and that he simply got it wrong when he seemed to infer that the Medes and the Persians were two separate kingdoms. But neither of these inferences is necessary:

● The Medes did develop their power even before the end of the Babylonian Empire. Indeed, their position began to strengthen just after the death of Nebuchadnezzar in 562 BC. They subsequently united with the Persians under Cyrus in 550 BC – after which the two combined were able to achieve their imperial ambitions. They would probably not have been able to succeed separately – and in some places Daniel seems to reflect this quite clearly (5:28; 6:8; 8:20).

● We must also recognize that Daniel was using here a traditional literary scheme to describe these four kingdoms. It was quite common at the time to depict the activity of great nations by using the symbolism of the four metals gold, silver, bronze, and iron. This literary device in effect required Daniel to have four kingdoms rather than three – whatever the facts might actually be. So he accommodated them by giving the Medes a semi-autonomous position which, had he been writing in a more straightforward style, he would probably not have done.

The book and its message

Modern interpreters of the book of Daniel are virtually unanimous in regarding it as a message of encouragement to those people who were suffering for their faith under the oppression of Antiochus IV Epiphanes. The visions of the second part of the book assure their readers that, though things might seem to be out of control, their future – indeed, the whole of history – is in the control of a loving and all-powerful God. For the final terrifying beast is not overcome by their own efforts, but by the direct activity of God himself (8:25; 12:1–13), just as the great statue mentioned earlier in the book was destroyed by a stone without any human intervention (2:31–35). That stone did not disappear, but 'grew to be a mountain that covered the whole earth' (2:35). And, after these great empires had done their worst, God himself 'will establish a kingdom that will never end. It will never be conquered, but will completely destroy all those empires, and then last for ever' (2:44).

This assurance that the world was not out of control must have meant a great deal to the beleaguered Jews in the early second century BC. But the book contains even more specific encouragement than that. For the earlier stories about Daniel himself have also obviously been selected with an eye to the circumstances that faithful Jews now had to contend with. Indeed, the prominence of Nebuchadnezzar in these stories may be intended as a conscious reference to Antiochus himself:

● The form of Nebuchadnezzar's name here is not the same as that found elsewhere in the Old Testament. But the word used in Daniel may have been intended to symbolize Antiochus. In Hebrew, as in many other ancient languages, names and words often had a numerical value, for each letter of the alphabet was also a number. And it is unlikely to be a coincidence that when the numbers represented by 'Nebuchadnezzar' are added up they come to exactly the same figure (423) as the numbers of the name 'Antiochus Epiphanes'.

● The issue of food which features so largely in the opening story of Daniel (1:3–17) was one of the crucial points at issue in the whole argument about Hellenism. Much of the opposition that sparked off the Maccabean revolt was concerned with the unwillingness of pious Jews to eat pork and other unclean foods.

● The worship of the great statue set up by Nebuchadnezzar (3:1–18) also involved the same principles as Antiochus's action in setting up an image of Zeus in the temple at Jerusalem. Indeed, in both cases it may be implied that the images were actually statues of the kings themselves. Even the story of Nebuchadnezzar's subsequent madness (4:19–33) may have been intended to be reminiscent of the commonly held belief that Antiochus himself was mad, because he thought of himself as an incarnation ('Epiphanes') of Zeus.

● Other details of the stories in the early chapters of Daniel are also similar to the conditions prevailing in the early Hellenistic age. Belshazzar, for example, falls from power because he defiled the sacred objects taken from the temple in Jerusalem (5:1–4) – just as Antiochus repeatedly robbed the temple. The people of a later age would also recognize the Jews who collaborated with the pagan Seleucids in the duplicitous figures of the spies and informers who plotted against Daniel and ensured that he was shut up in the den of lions (6:1–14).

The book in its context

The book of Daniel is unique in the Old Testament. Its detailed descriptions of visionary experiences are found nowhere else in such a concentration. But books like this were to become increasingly popular in the two centuries before the birth of Jesus, and in the New Testament the book of Revelation is of a similar type. These books have come to be known collectively as 'apocalypses', from a Greek word which means 'a revealing of secret things'. A number of special features make them readily recognizable:

● They are essentially literary works. In this respect they are quite different from the work of the earlier Old Testament prophets, who always used plain language that could be readily understood by anyone. The prophets also frequently used pithy poetic sayings that people could remember. But the apocalyptic books are complex prose compositions. They have long connected discourses, with many quotations and obscure allusions. Everyday events are usually described in a symbolic way, often with many references to real or imaginary animals and monsters.

● They also often portray God as a transcendent, remote figure. Indeed their whole emphasis is on the life of heaven rather than the everyday world of human experience. Events in this world are mentioned, but usually they are important only insofar as they are thought to reveal something about events taking place in another, spiritual world. Because of this, the apocalyptic writings often emphasize dreams, visions and communications given to people by angels. God's plan for the nations is fixed and unchanging. The Old Testament prophets often give the impression that the future course of history in some way depends on how people respond to the prophet's message. But for the apocalyptic writers, nothing can ever change the predetermined course of history as it moves to a final climax.

● This final climax is also to be revealed in a distinctive way. The new age is never thought of as part of the ongoing life of this world. Instead, it is either something that exists only in a different, heavenly world – or something that breaks into this world from outside by the direct intervention of God himself. This too is significantly different from the future hopes of most of the Old Testament prophets. For they generally expected a new age to dawn as a result of God's actions in the course of ordinary history – and it would be inaugurated by a human prince of the royal family of David, rather than by the kind of supernatural figures who appear in some apocalyptic books.

The apparent differences between apocalyptic and what seems to be the mainstream of Old Testament thinking have led many people today to think of all this as a rather eccentric and unprofitable sideline of Jewish religious thought. It has often been dismissed as the result of foreign (and therefore pagan) influences being incorporated into the Jewish faith as a result of the exile. But there is more to it than that:

● For a start, we need to remember that some of the most distinctive Christian beliefs seem to have originated among people who thought like this. It is unlikely that Jesus himself had too much sympathy for the apocalyptists of his day, but there can be no denying that the Christian understanding of life as a struggle against evil forces, together with the hope of future resurrection – not to mention the belief that history is moving towards a definite and meaningful goal – are clear developments of ideas that we first find in the writings of Jewish apocalyptists.

● We must also set the growth of apocalyptic in its own historical context. It is easy for us to criticize it from the relative comfort of our own perspective. But the hard realities for the people of Palestine at this time were quite different. The Old Testament prophets had suggested clearly enough that obedience to God would lead to prosperity, and disobedience would lead to hard times. The course of Israel's history up to the time of the Babylonian exile seemed to confirm that. But in the days following the collapse of the Persian Empire, things were quite different. With the arrival of a rampant Hellenism, new questions began to present themselves. As time went on, the way to prosperity seemed to lie more in collaboration with people like Antiochus than in continued faithfulness to the old values of the Jewish religion. Those who tried to keep the Old Testament faith alive found themselves more and more in a minority, and those who prospered often did so by neglecting their fathers' faith, or even abandoning it altogether. There were urgent questions to be answered: why did faithfulness not lead to prosperity? Why were the righteous suffering? Why did God not put an end to the power of evil forces? And to add more point to such questions, there seemed little sign of God's activity on the political and military front. He may well have raised up Cyrus in a previous generation, but in the period between Alexander the Great and Antiochus IV Epiphanes, Jerusalem had been captured at least ten times, while scores of major battles had been fought all over the country – and God seemed to be absent from the scene. In facing up to facts like these, the apocalyptists asserted that all the present difficulties were only relative. They needed to be set in the broader context of God's overall control of the world and its destiny – and in that time scale, the righteous would eventually triumph and the oppressive domination of evil would soon be relaxed.

● There is an increasing body of opinion today that would regard apocalyptic not as an alien intrusion into the religion of the Old Testament, but as a legitimate – indeed, inevitable – development of the work of the great prophets themselves. Even in the earliest of the prophets – Amos – we find the expectation of a great day of crisis, 'the Day of the Lord', when God would step into history and inaugurate a new age of justice for his people (Amos 5:18–20). The same idea was developed by others, and passages in both Isaiah (e.g. 2:1–4; 9:1–7; 11:1–9) and Micah (e.g. 4:1–5) are couched in such idealistic terms that they almost demand the apocalyptic perspective to give them some meaning. With the passage of time, these themes took on a greater importance, and when viewed from the perspective of Jewish experience during the exile and after, it is not difficult to see how these earlier expectations were transformed into an altogether grander vision. Some scholars have tried to link apocalyptic with the wisdom books of the Old Testament, through their common use of encyclopedic lists, and interest in astronomy and chronology. If this could be sustained, it would again anchor it firmly in the centre of Old Testament thinking. But it is unlikely that its roots lie there. It is more significant that the messages of Daniel are presented as in some sense a reinterpretation and new application of the messages of the earlier prophets (Daniel 9:1–2).

The end of the story

From the time of the Maccabees through to the New Testament period, Jewish history was dominated by the issues that emerged in the course of the early struggles with Hellenism. The twin issues of politics and religion were to become inextricably interwoven. The Jewish people tried to reconcile their aspirations for a society in which God would be all-important with the plain fact that their world was dominated by unbelieving pagan rulers. Within Jewish society itself, one political intrigue followed hard on the heels of another, until eventually the Romans stepped in and destroyed the temple at Jerusalem in AD 70, and by the early part of the second century AD, Jerusalem itself had become a pagan city.

In the midst of this constant turmoil many ordinary people no doubt wondered what had happened to the ideals of the Old Testament story. At the beginning of that story stood their ancestor Abraham, a man in whose life God was a living reality – a person who could be known as a friend to be loved, as well as a God to be worshipped. The same themes of God's love and his people's response had been contained in the work of the great prophets. But now, by common consent, the time of direct communication between God and his people seemed to have ended. In the closing decades of the first century BC, many groups in Jewish society were desperately searching for the word from God that would speak to them in their own situation. Some sought for meaning in the solitary silence of the desert. Others looked in vain to the lurid speculations of the apocalyptists. And yet others concluded that

At one level the Old Testament closes with the Jewish world in ruins. But it was not a world without hope. God's promises to Israel still held and many still believed them. They were a gateway to a better future.

their ancestral faith had lost its relevance, and looked for fulfilment in political opportunism.

At the end of the Old Testament story we have an unforgettable picture of God's people in turmoil. But we also have an unfading reminder of God's continuing love even for people like this. Out of their failure of nerve the author of the book of Daniel fashioned a picture of a kingdom in which God alone would be the supreme sovereign.

No doubt many Jewish people thought of this as a kingdom in which they themselves would occupy the centre of the stage. But as Christians have read the Old Testament story, they have always believed that its real climax was to be found not in the speculations of such discredited optimists, but in the one person in whose life God was truly king: Jesus of Nazareth. As the earliest groups of his disciples faced up to the implications of his person and his message, they began to assert that the whole Old Testament story was encapsulated in him. They saw him as the ideal son of David – the Messiah – of whom the prophets had dimly spoken. They identified him with 'the Son of Man' to whom the authority of God's kingdom had been given in the visions of Daniel. But they saw him also as the true descendant of Abraham himself. The Old Testament story began with God's promise to Abraham, that 'through you I will bless all the nations'. And for Christians, the story ended with Jesus, in whose life, death and resurrection God did precisely that. For they see in him a person in whom God demonstrated his loving care not only for those who stand at the centre of the Old Testament story, but for the whole world and its many races.

Other books on the Old Testament

The books listed here are restricted to those which the general reader could comfortably cope with, though one or two are for more advanced study (these are marked with an asterisk*). This list includes only books directly relevant to the subjects dealt with in this book – i.e. historical and literary questions. Old Testament religion and theology are dealt with in the companion book to this one, *The Old Testament Faith*.

General

B.W. Anderson, *The Living World of the Old Testament,* third edition, Longmans, 1978, published in USA as *Understanding the Old Testament,* Prentice-Hall, 1975.

W. Beyerlin (ed.), *Near Eastern Religious Texts Relating to the Old Testament,* SCM Press/Westminster Press, 1978.

John Bright, *A History of Israel,* third edition, SCM Press/Westminster Press, 1981. The standard conservative treatment of its subject.

F.F. Bruce, *Israel and the Nations,* Paternoster Press/Eerdmans, 1963. A particularly useful treatment of the end of the Old Testament period.

O. Eissfeldt, *The Old Testament. An Introduction,* Blackwell/Harper & Row, 1965. A detailed literary study of the Old Testament books.

J.H. Hayes & J.M. Miller, *Israelite & Judaean History,* SCM Press/Westminster Press, 1977. An invaluable survey of the present state of scholarly research and opinion on historical issues.

E.W. Heaton, *Everyday Life in Old Testament Times,* Batsford, 1956/Scribners, 1977.

S. Herrmann, *A History of Israel in Old Testament Times,* SCM Press/Fortress, 1975.

M. Noth, *The History of Israel,* A. & C. Black/Harper & Row, second edition, 1960. A more radical treatment of its subject than either Bright or Herrmann.

M. Noth, *The Old Testament World,* A. & C. Black/Fortress, 1966.

D.F. Payne, *Kingdoms of the Lord,* Paternoster Press/Eerdmans, 1981. From Saul to the fall of Jerusalem.

J.B. Pritchard, *Ancient Near Eastern Texts Relating to the Old Testament,* third edition, Princeton University Press, 1969. The standard collection of comparative texts from other cultures and nations.

J.A. Soggin, *Introduction to the Old Testament,* SCM Press/Westminster Press, 1976. Deals with the Old Testament book by book.

R. de Vaux, *Ancient Israel: its Life and Institutions,* Darton, Longman & Todd/McGraw-Hill, 1961. An invaluable insight into everyday life in ancient Israel.

D. Winton Thomas (ed.), *Documents from Old Testament Times,* Nelson, 1958/Harper & Row, 1961. A handy smaller collection of historical and religious texts relating the Old Testament to its wider background.

Chapter One. Introducing the Old Testament

G.W. Anderson (ed.), *Tradition and Interpretation,* OUP, 1979. Essays by leading Old Testament scholars summarizing the present opinions on various aspects of the Old Testament literature.

R. Davidson & A.R.C. Leaney, *Biblical Criticism,* Penguin Books, 1970. An excellent short account of the nature of modern study of the Bible (New Testament as well as Old Testament).

H.T. Frank, *An Archaeological Companion to the Bible,* Abingdon Press, 1971/SCM Press, 1972.

J. Goldingay, *Approaches to Old Testament Interpretation,* IVP, 1981. A critical account of various ways to read and interpret the Old Testament.

H.F. Hahn, *The Old Testament in Modern Research,* second edition, Fortress, 1966. A readable account of the work of scholars up to 1966. Needs to be supplemented by *Tradition and Interpretation* (previously listed).

J.H. Hayes, *An Introduction to Old Testament Study,* Abingdon Press, 1979. Covers the same material as *Tradition & Interpretation,* though in a slightly more readable form.

K.M. Kenyon, *The Bible and Recent Archaeology,* British Museum/John Knox Press, 1978.

Chapter Two. The founding of the nation

J.J. Bimson, *Redating the Exodus and Conquest,* Almond Press/Eisenbrauns, 1981, second edition. Argues for a fifteenth-century date of the exodus.

D.J. McCarthy, *Old Testament Covenant,* Blackwell/John Knox Press, 1972. A survey of opinions on the covenant idea in the Old Testament.

A.R. Millard & D.J. Wiseman (eds.), *Essays on the Patriarchal Narratives,* Inter-Varsity Press, 1980. A series of conservative essays arguing for the essential historicity of the patriarchal narratives, and trying to answer some recent criticisms.

* J. Van Seters, *Abraham in History and Tradition,* Yale University Press, 1975.

A more radical reappraisal of history in the patriarchal narratives.

* T.L. Thompson, *The Historicity of the Patriarchal Narratives,* de Gruyter, 1974. Independently reaches similar conclusions to Van Seters.

R. de Vaux, *The Early History of Israel,* volume 1, Darton, Longman & Todd/Westminster Press, 1978.

Chapter Three. A land flowing with milk and honey

P.C. Craigie, *Ugarit and the Bible*, Eerdmans, 1982. A readable and reliable account of the discoveries from Ras Shamra, and a balanced appraisal of their relevance for Old Testament study.

J. Garstang, *The Story of Jericho*, Hodder & Stoughton, 1940. The classic story of the early excavations at Jericho.

J.C.L. Gibson, *Canaanite Myths and Legends*, T. & T. Clark/Attic Press, 1978, second edition. The standard translation of the texts from ancient Ugarit.

N.K. Gottwald, *The Tribes of Yahweh*, Orbis Books, 1979/SCM Press 1980. The most thorough presentation of the idea that the 'conquest' was a form of cultural revolution.

J.L. McKenzie, *The World of the Judges*, Geoffrey Chapman/Prentice-Hall, 1966.

* A.D.H. Mayes, *Israel in the Period of the Judges*, SCM Press/Allenson-Breckinridge, 1974.

Chapter Four. A king like the other nations

W. Brueggemann, *In Man we Trust*, John Knox Press, 1972. A helpful expositon of the wisdom movement in Israel.

J.L Crenshaw, *Old Testament Wisdom*, John Knox Press, 1981/SCM Press, 1982.

R. Gordis, *The Book of God and Man*, University of Chicago Press, 1965. An exposition of the book of Job.

J. Gray, *The Biblical Doctrine of the Reign of God*, T. & T. Clark/Attic Press, 1979. Deals extensively with the theme of God's kingship, mostly following the arguments of Mowinckel.

H. Gunkel, *The Psalms*, Fortress, 1967. The only work by Gunkel to have been translated into English.

* D.M. Gunn, *The Story of King David*, JSOT Press/Eisenbrauns, 1978. A new approach to the Succession Narrative.

J.H. Hayes, *Understanding the Psalms*, Judson Press, 1976. A readable introduction to the book of Psalms.

E.W. Heaton, *Solomon's New Men*, Thames & Hudson, 1974/Universe Press, 1975. An assessment of the social changes that came about after Solomon's time.

* A.R. Johnson, *Sacral Kingship in Ancient Israel*, University of Wales Press, 1967.

* A.R. Johnson, *The Cultic Prophet and Israel's Psalmody*, University of Wales Press, 1976.

D.F. Morgan, *Wisdom in the Old Testament Traditions*, John

Knox/Blackwell, 1981. A helpful assessment of the contribution of the wisdom movement to the concerns of the Old Testament as a whole.

S. Mowinckel, *The Psalms in Israel's Worship*, Blackwell/Abingdon Press, 1962.

G. von Rad, *Wisdom in Israel*, SCM Press, 1972.

N.H. Snaith, *The Jewish New Year Festival*, SPCK, 1947. Strongly critical of the arguments of Mowinckel, Gray, and others.

R.N. Whybray, *The Succession Narrative*, SCM Press/Allenson-Breckinridge, 1968. An account of the interpretation of the Succession Narrative, together with a reassessment of its significance.

Chapters Five and Six. The two kingdoms/Judah and Jerusalem

B.W. Anderson, *The Eighth Century Prophets*, Fortress, 1978/SPCK, 1979.

* R.E. Clements, *Isaiah and the Deliverance of Jerusalem*, JSOT Press/Eisenbrauns, 1980.

E.W. Heaton, *The Old Testament Prophets*, second edition, Darton, Longman and Todd/John Knox Press, 1977.

* J. Lindblom, *Prophecy in Ancient Israel*, Blackwell/Fortress, 1962.

J. McKay, *Religion in Judah under the Assyrians*, SCM Press/Allenson-Breckinridge, 1973.

J. Maxwell Miller, *The Old Testament & the Historian*, Fortress/SPCK, 1976. Explores various areas of difficulty, including the problems of dating the Old Testament story.

H. Mowvley, *Guide to Old Testament Prophecy*, Lutterworth, 1979, also published as *Reading the Old Testament Prophets Today*, John Knox Press, 1979. One of the most useful recent books on the prophets.

G. von Rad, *The Message of the Prophets*, SCM Press, 1968/Harper & Row.

B. Vawter, *The Conscience of Israel;* Sheed & Ward, 1961. An introduction to the Old Testament prophets.

R.R. Wilson, *Prophecy & Society in Ancient Israel*, Fortress, 1980. Assesses the social role of the Old Testament prophets.

Chapter Seven. Dashed hopes and new horizons

P.R. Ackroyd, *Exile and Restoration*, SCM Press/Westminster, 1968. An excellent study of the exile and its immediate aftermath.

P.R. Ackroyd, *Israel under Babylon and Persia*, OUP, 1970.

D.J.A. Clines, *The Theme of the Pentateuch*, JSOT Press/Eisenbrauns, 1978. An effort to understand the Pentateuch as coherent literature, rather than as a collection of separate sources.

* M. Noth, *The Deuteronomistic History*, JSOT Press/Eisenbrauns, 1981.

* G. von Rad, *The Problem of the Hexateuch & Other Essays*, Oliver & Boyd/McGraw-Hill, 1966.

J. Wellhausen, *Prolegomena to the History of Israel*, A. & C. Black, 1885.

* H.G.M. Williamson, *Israel in the books of Chronicles*, CUP, 1977.

Chapter Eight. The challenge of a new age

F.F. Bruce, *The Books & the Parchments*, Pickering & Inglis/Revell 1971, fourth edition. Deals with the text of the Old Testament, including the question of the Septuagint, Apocrypha, etc.

R.J. Coggins, *Samaritans and Jews*, Blackwell/John Knox Press, 1975. An interesting reappraisal of relations between the two groups.

D.E. Gowan, *Bridge between the Testaments*, Pickwick Press, 1976. A helpful account of the historical and literary developments in the inter-testamental period of Israel's history.

M. Hengel, *Jews, Greeks & Barbarians*, SCM Press/Fortress, 1980. A readable account of the Maccabean period by a noted scholar (to a certain extent, this parallels his more detailed work, *Judaism and Hellenism*, SCM Press, 1974/Fortress 1981.

R.W. Klein, *Textual Criticism of the Old Testament*, Fortress, 1974. A general introduction to its subject.

D.S. Russell, *Daniel*, St. Andrew Press/Westminster Press, 1981. One of the best recent commentaries on this difficult book.

Commentaries

As well as the books listed above, there are many commentaries covering the Old Testament writings. The volumes in the following series will be found most useful. They are listed in order of increasing difficulty:

The Cambridge Bible Commentary CUP

The Tyndale Old Testament Commentaries IVP/Eerdmans

The New International Commentary on the Old Testament Eerdmans

The New Century Bible Oliphants/Eerdmans

The Anchor Bible Doubleday

The Old Testament Library SCM Press/Westminster. Not all the volumes in this series are commentaries, but the majority are.

Hermeneia Fortress

Index